Accession no.
36196724

DESIRE & DISASTER IN NEW ORLEANS

D1615197

DESIRE & DISASTER IN NEW ORLEANS

Tourism, Race, and Historical Memory   Lynnell L. Thomas

LIS LIBRARY

Date	Fund
18/5/15	bs-Che

Order No

2601047

University of Chester

DUKE UNIVERSITY PRESS • DURHAM AND LONDON • 2014

© 2014 Duke University Press

All rights reserved

Printed in the United States of America on acid-free paper ∞

Designed by Courtney Leigh Baker

Typeset in Arno Pro by Copperline Book Services, Inc.

Library of Congress Cataloging-in-Publication Data

Thomas, Lynnell L., 1971–

Desire and disaster in New Orleans : tourism, race, and

historical memory / Lynnell L. Thomas.

pages cm

Includes bibliographical references and index.

ISBN 978-0-8223-5714-8 (cloth : alk. paper)

ISBN 978-0-8223-5728-5 (pbk. : alk. paper)

1. New Orleans (La.)—Description and travel.

2. Tourism—Louisiana—New Orleans.

3. African Americans—Louisiana—New Orleans. I. Title.

F379.N54T46 2014

917.63'3504—dc23 2014005680

Cover art: Tyrone Turner/National Geographic Creative

In loving memory of my most steadfast mentor,
JAMES E. McLEOD, *who encouraged me to "do it now"*
and gave me the tools to persevere later.

Contents

Acknowledgments

Like the road to Katrina that I document in these pages, my road to this book has been long and circuitous. I am indebted to the fellow travelers who guided me past roadblocks; provided clear, useful directions; or offered me a safe place to rest and recharge along the way.

I am grateful to my professors and advisers at Tulane University for laying the foundation for this project. Rebecca Mark's graduate English seminars, independent study, and advising provided the first opportunities for me to critically examine my experiences growing up black in post–civil rights era New Orleans, as part of the first generation since Reconstruction to attend desegregated schools (and the first, since *Plessy v. Ferguson*, to witness their gradual resegregation). She encouraged my interest in material culture, literary analysis, ethnography, and oral history and, though I didn't appreciate it at the time, took me on my first plantation tour. Joseph Roach made incisive suggestions and posed important, challenging questions about my work that continue to inform my research and writing.

I am also indebted to the many faculty and staff members in or affiliated with the Graduate Institute of the Liberal Arts at Emory University who offered guidance and support as I expanded the interdisciplinary scope of the project. In the Department of English, Frances Smith-Foster taught me how to interrogate nontraditional sources, trace the scholarly debates animating the discipline of African American studies, and rethink the relationship between theory and practice. James Roark and Dan Carter in the Department of History introduced me to a diverse body of scholarship and source material on the old and new Souths and challenged me to appreciate the horrors of slavery and racial oppression without losing sight of the humanity and agency of the enslaved and oppressed. I am especially grateful to Mark Sanders (African American Studies) and Dana White (Graduate Institute of the Liberal Arts) who offered me insightful comments and patient guidance in the early stages of conceptualization, research, and writing. Cindy

Patton, the consummate adviser, continued to provide useful feedback, encouragement, and mentorship long after our tenures at Emory University had ended. Much of my ethnographic research on pre-Katrina New Orleans was made possible by an Emory-Mellon Graduate Teaching Fellowship that permitted me to teach at Dillard University, a historically black institution in New Orleans, while I conducted research. I am thankful for the experience of working alongside Dillard University faculty and staff members and students who graciously welcomed me back home and powerfully refuted the racial distortions of the city's tourist representations.

Just as I prepared to begin revising my project into a book manuscript in 2005, Hurricane Katrina hit, ravaging countless lives, scholarly and cultural repositories, and the city's tourism industry. In between the daily frustrations and humiliations of navigating the Road Home—Louisiana's scandal-ridden federally funded rebuilding program—I was compelled to reframe my project in light of the storm and post-Katrina developments in the tourism industry. During this difficult period of reassessment, rebuilding, and recovery, my new colleagues, students, and friends at the University of Massachusetts, Boston, supported and sustained me and my work. Thanks to all of you—too many to list here—who showed concern and compassion. I must single out my colleagues in other departments who modeled the best of interdisciplinary collegiality and fellowship. Doreen Drury, Brian Halley, and Tim Sieber read and commented on early drafts and revisions and supported me in countless ways; Barbara Lewis and Rita Nethersole collaborated with me on a Katrina anniversary symposium that helped me reflect on the historical antecedents and national implications of post-Katrina New Orleans; Jim Green and Rajini Srikanth gave scholarly advice; Ping-Ann Addo, Elora Chowdhury, David Hunt, Ellie Kutz, Denise Patmon, Aminah Pilgrim, and Shirley Tang offered personal sanctuary. Each of my colleagues in the Department of American Studies has been generous and supportive. I am particularly grateful to Aaron Lecklider, who patiently and insightfully responded to each of my panicked phone calls, emails, and text messages—and there were embarrassingly many—throughout the revision and production stages; Lois Rudnick and Judith Smith, who read drafts of the work at various stages, offered substantive suggestions for revision, and guided me through the academic publishing process; Marisol Negrón, who has been a faithful "writing date," the book's talented unofficial photographer, and an unwavering supporter; Rachel Rubin, who graciously offered a forum to translate my work to a broader audience; and Shauna Manning and Kelly MacDonald Weeks, one of my former graduate students, who helped to ease my transition to the university, the city of Boston, and New England winters. In addition to these human resources, the institutional support I received from the University of Massachusetts, Boston, proved invaluable for conducting research on post-Katrina New Orleans. Financial assistance came in the form of research grants from the College of Liberal Arts's Dean's Fund for Faculty Development, a Joseph P. Healey Research Grant, an Endowed Faculty Career Development Award, and the Roy J. Zuckerberg Research Fellowship.

This project has also been enriched by mentors, colleagues, and role models outside of these institutions who offered suggestions, encouragement, and inspiration: Connie Atkinson, Gerald Early, Lewis Gordon, Miriam Greenberg, Leslie Harris and the New Orleans Research Collaborative, Arnold Hirsch, Ann Holder, Amy Lesen, Alecia Long, Catherine Michna, Lawrence Powell, Kerry Ann Rockquemore and the National Center for Faculty Development and Diversity, Jim Smethurst, J. Mark Souther, Anthony Stanonis, and especially the late Clyde Woods and the late Jim McLeod. The book could not have been written without the cooperation of the men and women who agreed to be interviewed or accommodated me on their tours. Thank you to Bill Coble, Dan Brown, Phala Mire, Paul Nevski, Gregory Osborn, Gwen Reidus, Toni Rice, and the anonymous or pseudonymous staff members, tour guides, and tourists I interviewed and interacted with from Cajun Encounters Tours, Celebration Tours, Dixie Tours, Eclectic Tours, Friends of the Cabildo French Quarter Walking Tours, Gray Line Tours, Le Monde Créole French Quarter Courtyards Tour, Louisiana Swamp Tours, Tennessee Williams Festival's African American Legacy Heritage Tour, and Tours by Isabelle.

I owe special thanks to those who facilitated the archival research for the manuscript, in particular Daniel Hammer of the Williams Research Center at the Historic New Orleans Collection; Florence Jumonville, of the Louisiana and Special Collections Department at the Earl K. Long Library of the University of New Orleans; Andrew Salinas, of the Amistad Research Center at Tulane University; David Stoughton of the New Orleans Jazz National Historical Park; and the librarians and staff members of the Greater New Orleans Multicultural Tourism Network, the Midlo Center for New Orleans Studies at the University of New Orleans, and the New Orleans Public Library. The editorial staff at Duke University Press has been incredibly patient and helpful throughout the publication process. Thanks to Courtney

Berger, Christine Choi, Danielle Szulczewski, Erin Hanas, and Jeanne Ferris for your accessibility and your professionalism.

As I reflect on my journey down this road, I must thank the members of my large extended family, who paved the way. My grandparents, Georgiaetta C. Duplechain, the late Leroy Duplechain Sr., Cornelia Bell Thomas, and Leonard Thomas Sr., taught me dignity, resilience, and civic engagement in the face of injustice. My parents, Sargiena Thomas and Leonard Thomas Jr., worked hard to provide a life for their children in New Orleans that was open to opportunities and possibilities that they could have never imagined for themselves. My sisters, Lori Gray and Leah Valdez, kept me grounded and attuned to what really matters. My in-laws, especially my mother-in-law, Bernadine Pettway, housed me and humored me as I worked on this project throughout the years. My aunts, uncles, cousins, nieces, nephews, close friends, and neighbors in New Orleans, Atlanta, Boston, and beyond buoyed me with their love and support. Most important, I want to acknowledge Phillip Andrews, the person who lifted me up and carried me down this road, who has been a devoted husband—and an even better "wife"—and who, along with our son, Nyle, has made my work and life more meaningful.

AN EARLIER VERSION of chapters 1 and 2 originally appeared as "'The City I Used to . . . Visit': Tourist New Orleans and the Racialized Response to Hurricane Katrina," in *Seeking Higher Ground: The Hurricane Katrina Crisis, Race, and Public Policy Reader*, edited by Manning Marable and Kristen Clarke (New York: Palgrave Macmillan, 2007). An earlier version of chapter 5 originally appeared as "'Roots Run Deep Here': The Construction of Black New Orleans in Post-Katrina Tourism Narratives," *American Quarterly* 61, no. 3 (2009). An earlier version of the section "Tourist Sites and Sounds in Treme" in the epilogue was published as "'People Want to See What Happened': Treme, Televisual Tourism, and the Racial Remapping of Post-Katrina New Orleans," *Television and New Media* 13, no. 3 (2012).

One. "The City I Used to Come to Visit"

HERITAGE TOURISM AND RACIALIZED

DISASTER IN NEW ORLEANS

New Orleans Tourism on the Road to Katrina

In late August 2005, like so many other people around the world, I sat glued to news coverage of Hurricane Katrina and the now infamous images of African Americans stranded on rooftops, wading through flooded streets, and trapped in unsanitary and unsuitable "shelters of last resort." Their hypervisibility symbolized a corporeal indictment of American politics and policies. Not only was I appalled by what I was witnessing, but I was also desperate for information about my husband and other family members who had remained in our New Orleans home during the storm. That information was filtered through an image of the city that had been cultivated by writers and tourism boosters whose racial mythologizing left a lasting imprint on the national popular imagination. In those critical days of anxiety and outrage, I recognized in a new and painful way how the city's tourist image and its attendant racial representations continued to shape Americans' view of New Orleans by defining and delimiting black citizenship. The tourism narrative was manifest, during Katrina and in its immediate aftermath, in representations of the city that prioritized the French Quarter and the city's European identity, labeled historically and predominantly black areas of the city as dangerous, and obscured or distorted the African presence and participation in the development and sustenance of the city.

During those early days of reportage on Katrina and the damage it caused, I observed in disbelief three critical ways that the city's racialized tourism narratives recirculated to seal the fates of the city's most vulnerable populations.[1] First, news reporters who were firmly anchored in the

French Quarter—the icon of tourist New Orleans—repeatedly and falsely reported that the city had escaped major damage as floodwaters engulfed nontourist areas of the city, where most African American residents lived. Second, even as levees remained breached, rescue efforts were suspended because of alleged violence by black New Orleanians (later revealed to be largely exaggerated), leaving tens of thousands of people stranded and unprotected from the rising floodwaters. The failure by so many to corroborate these allegations reinforced the city's tourist geography, which steered tourists and consumers to heavily policed tourist zones and restricted or discouraged access to nontourist black neighborhoods that were automatically presumed to be risky, unsafe, or violent. Finally, local, state, and national public officials and media collaborated in the tourist promotion of debauchery and degradation as the most predominant and enduring features of black New Orleans.[2] In each of these examples, media spectators were reacquainted with spectacles of blackness already made available for consumption by the city's tourism industry.

Hurricane Katrina exposed the devastating human cost of New Orleans's racialized tourism narratives on black New Orleanians and our prospects for rescue and rebuilding. Those who were most responsible for representing the city and its citizens in the aftermath of Katrina did so from a limited perspective that conformed to a narrative perpetuated in tourist representations of the city. Catering to outside visitors whose histories were intertwined with New Orleans as a site of desire and disaster, these representations lacked adequate terms and conventions to represent New Orleans's rich black experience as diverse, varied, and sometimes conflicted. Media coverage of the storm and subsequent policy debates about storm survivors grotesquely mimicked the distortions of the tourism narratives, placing a premium on safeguarding the French Quarter and other tourism spaces to the exclusion of black neighborhoods. The reckless spread of rumors about black lawlessness and inhumanity that brought rescue efforts to a halt and the inadequate, and often reluctant, dispersal of resources to the most vulnerable communities both relied on static, stereotypical constructions of the city's black population. This problematic tourism narrative had paved the road to the damage inflicted by Hurricane Katrina.

Representations of Katrina point to the historic invisibility of New Orleans's black residential population that was facilitated through the city's promotion of and dependence on its tourism industry. The limited categories in the public imagination for representing this population and conventions available for identifying its members even after the storm's victims demanded recognition reveal the costs of the distortion that tourism narratives impose on black people's lives. Tourist shorthand is not without consequence: competing representations of race in contemporary New Orleans tourism offer important insights into the processes of racialization in the post–civil rights era that might help us better understand the ways that race, as a socially constructed category, is simultaneously being erased and employed to erode the gains of the civil rights movement. Although the legal end of segregation and its attendant social and cultural transformations seemed to significantly democratize U.S. political and popular culture, New Orleans has found itself among a growing number of tourist destinations faced with the difficult challenge of reconciling traditional tourism narratives with more inclusive stories that incorporate and validate racial minorities and other marginalized groups. Yet often in these cases, as the Colonial Williamsburg historian Anders Greenspan reminds us, "the old message was grafted uncomfortably on the new."[3] The responses to Katrina reflected this tension by eerily emulating the popular representations of the city that have become the hallmark of its traditional tourism narrative.

Given the contemporary fact that tourism is New Orleans's most lucrative industry and the historical reality that most outsiders'—and a good number of insiders'—perceptions of the city have been filtered through travel accounts, literature, film, and other popular depictions, it should have come as little surprise that even in the midst of unprecedented crisis, the portrayal of New Orleans during Hurricane Katrina continued to be dominated by the troubling images and ideas of the city's tourist iconography.[4]

Place Identity: A Brief History

New Orleans tourism capitalizes on its unique place identity. The resulting narrative represents a long historical trajectory that brings into alignment local residents' sense of place and personal attachment to their city; marketing professionals' use of mass media to promote a particular image of New Orleans; and the city's civic reputation, or how New Orleans is perceived by outsiders.[5] In his introduction to *Inventing New Orleans: Writings of Lafcadio Hearn*, the historian S. Frederick Starr encapsulates the relationship between the city's deep-seated popular image and the tourism industry, noting that the popular images of "fading grandeur, cultural hybridization, noble simplicity, eroticism, authenticity of expression (and a hint of danger)" promulgated in fictional accounts of New Orleans have been accepted as faithful representations of the city and have been promoted as such through the tourism industry.[6] New Orleans's place identity shapes and is shaped by a tourist-oriented narrative that, although not uncontested, has certainly become ubiquitous, forged through the conflict and conciliation of visitors, local residents, and business elites whose visions of the city have reflected the changing technological and cultural landscape over the past century or more.

Beginning in the French colonial period during the eighteenth century, the bustling, lawless port city attracted a multilingual, multiracial population of slaves, slave owners, members of the military, merchants, and travelers. Early nineteenth-century visitors to New Orleans were already part of a proto-tourism industry that catered to elite travelers for whom New Orleans winters offered a milder climate and a more animated social season than they found in their permanent residences. In the late nineteenth century, several developments provided more coherence and structure to the city's amorphous tourist appeal: New Orleans's antebellum reputation as a "great Southern Babylon" of vice, hedonistic unrestraint, and socially sanctioned racial and sexual transgression was concretized with the designation of Storyville, a sanctioned prostitution district; literary representations of the city that provided spatial and imaginative maps for travelers hoping to experience the exotic New Orleans they had encountered in novels, newspaper articles, and guidebooks; and the restructuring of Carnival with the formation of elite white krewes, or social clubs, and racially hierarchical rituals that offered an easily marketable product for potential white tourists.[7]

By the early twentieth century, the emergence of a shared national commercial culture—facilitated by widespread railroad travel, hotel development, popular amusements, and local boosterism—had helped New Orleans to join the ranks of other tourist destinations that each projected what the historian Jim Weeks refers to as "an image created by the marketplace." New Orleans, like Gettysburg and other cities profiting from sanitized portrayals of the historical past, was "a product of the market that hummed by masking its unpleasant inner workings," particularly the complicated racial histories and meanings that undergirded the city's popular image.[8] New Orleans tourism expanded in the years between the two world wars, as interstate automobile travel, mass consumerism, population shifts to urban areas, changing gender roles, and the dramatic decline of industries that had long been economic strongholds converged to beget the modern tourism industry. This modern industry helped popularize racial stereotypes and perpetuate white supremacy, serving as a reflection of the Jim Crow society in which it emerged.[9]

Like other southern cities propelled by U.S. affluence after World War II, more affordable options for lodging, the establishment of tourism bureaus, the sanitizing of the past, and the acquisition of professional sports teams, New Orleans increasingly marketed its premodern mystique to white middle-class travelers. Unlike these other cities, however, New Orleans cultivated tourism at the expense of other economic and commercial development.[10] In the latter half of the twentieth century, the city was transformed by "a touristic culture," in which New Orleans's economic, political, cultural, and social institutions and practices became dependent on and defined by the tourism industry.[11] Though there were certainly antecedents in the previous eras, French Quarter preservation, cultural and heritage tourism, tourism-driven repackaging of black cultural productions as emblems of a vanishing past, and the internationalization and corporatization of New Orleans as a place and an idea were firmly entrenched and formalized by the time Hurricane Katrina hit. However, what was new in the second half of the twentieth century was the dilemma that middle-class African Americans—enfranchised and emboldened by civil rights legislation—posed for tourism promoters. In the post–civil rights era, tourism promoters recognized black tourists as both a new niche market and a potential threat to the city's racially exclusive tourist image. In important ways, New Orleans's touristic culture resulted from, responded to, or reacted against the effects of the civil rights movement, which publicly gave voice to ongoing struggles over memory, history, identity, and citizenship that the city's predominant tourism narrative had for so long attempted to efface.[12]

Post–Civil Rights Public Sphere

By the late twentieth century, the New Orleans tourism industry was operating within a post–civil rights public sphere, marked by the widespread institutionalization and global circulation of black cultural production, conspicuously spearheaded by a contingent of influential African American artists, activists, and intellectuals. Their contributions to commercial public culture, such as sports, film, music, television, and politics, fundamentally reconfigured U.S. popular culture and facilitated African American recognition and inclusion in the body politic. Yet they also revealed the inadequacy of a politics of representation as an enduring and effective challenge to structural racism and inequality. In the decades following the enactment of the Civil Rights and Voting Rights Acts, black representation and cultural production have been co-opted by conservatives and liberals alike to manipulate the political process through the use of racially coded images and language that helped exacerbate racial and class inequalities. Ironically, at the same time that the political process was becoming more racialized, race was being evacuated from the political discourse, which increasingly promulgated tropes of color blindness, multiculturalism, and, more recently, postracialism to help nullify policies and practices designed to ameliorate historical inequities.[13]

Many scholars have attributed these contradictory uses and understandings of race to the development of the modern liberal state and its failure to address—as well as its complicity in maintaining—the social, structural, and institutional nature of race and racism. "Even the history of the Civil Rights movement," the historian Carol Horton reminds us, "has been largely rewritten to support the conservative crusade for color-blindness and against affirmative action."[14] This national memory of a watered-down civil rights movement illustrates the ways that race, as a category, has become simultaneously pervasive and irrelevant, except insofar as it applies to individual, private experience. In this context, the proliferation of black representation and even black popular cultural production often displaces and distorts the political and moral project of the civil rights movement.[15] The black culture industry abets the post–civil rights public sphere of "racism without racists" that constrains political activism and trivializes the needs and demands of African Americans.[16] Through its veneration of New Orleans black culture, promotion of selected black heritage sites and historical actors, and commitment to attracting and sustaining a new niche market of African American travelers and consumers, New Orleans's tourism industry paradoxically has made concessions to the post–civil rights public sphere even as those concessions have masked—if not exacerbated—the gross racial and class divisions exposed by Hurricane Katrina.

Desire and Disaster

The tourism narrative that developed in the decades preceding Katrina clearly exploited the tension between Jim Crow legacies of racially motivated violence, disfranchisement, and exclusion, on the one hand, and civil rights claims to full citizenship, access, and inclusion, on the other hand. Most notably, New Orleans's tourism narrative represented black culture through two distinct but intersecting frames: desire and disaster. Tourists were encouraged to think that they were experiencing and celebrating black culture by eating Creole cuisine, dancing to local music, participating in the traditional "second line" street parade, attending jazz funerals, and listening to anecdotes of quadroon balls and secret voodoo rites. At the same time, however, tourists were directed to adopt the white supremacist memory of slavery and black culture that views the old South with a sense of loss and nostalgia by touring plantations, lodging and dining in repurposed slave dwellings, purchasing slavery memorabilia, and being pampered by black service workers. In effect, the city's promotion of black cultural consumption produced a desire for blackness at the same time that this blackness was used to signify the disaster of black emancipation and desegregation and the perceived social ills of poverty, crime, immorality, educational inadequacy, and political corruption of the postbellum and post–civil rights eras. New Orleans's tourism narrative, then, was part of the historically paradoxical construction of blackness that acknowledges and celebrates black cultural contributions while simultaneously insisting on black social and cultural inferiority. In the end, these competing impulses of desire and disaster facilitated the symbolic continuance of slavery as the appropriation of black labor and denial of black history and agency even as they highlighted the city's black cultural contributions and appealed to black residents and visitors.

One way that the tourism narrative achieved this duality was by limiting its historical focus to the colonial and antebellum periods and focusing almost exclusively on the purportedly exceptional race relations that distinguished New Orleans from the rest of the slaveholding South. The emphasis on selected features of these eras — such as European cultural influences, the relative freedom of New Orleans's black population, the city's laissez faire attitudes regarding race, the social sanctioning of interracial unions, and a large population of free blacks — lent itself to the construction of New Orleans as benefiting from the most liberal and refined elements of southern culture while avoiding its most brutal, inhumane, and inegalitarian features. As a result, New Orleans was often erroneously portrayed by tourism promoters, artists, and even historians as a racially exceptional city that was not sullied by the racial tension and conflict affecting other southern cities. The dearth of mainstream tours that depicted the history of the Reconstruction or civil rights eras and their bitter struggles for racial justice means that the prevailing romantic, idyllic narrative of racial harmony and equality has gone largely unchallenged. These racial fictions have been exemplified by the modernizing of slave quarters into trendy restaurants, hotels, and tourist sites; the proliferation of racially stereotypical images and merchandise on display in tourist shops (figures 1.1–1.3); and the omnipresence of African Americans in the service industry whose performance of happy servitude is mandated by the conventions of the local tourist economy.[17] In each case, tourists are encouraged to consume or gaze on black culture without the uncomfortable acknowledgment of an exploitative slave system or its persistent legacy of racial and class inequality. New Orleans tourists, then, become acquainted with a representation of blackness that leaves the actual black New Orleans invisible.

This disjuncture shaped my own childhood in post–civil rights New Orleans, where I was continually confronted by a tourist landscape of black docility, subservience, and stereotypical distortion. Like other African American New Orleanians, I was faced with the challenge of reconciling the omnipresence of these representations with the reality of black agency, autonomy, and community that shaped my lived experience. In part, this book is an attempt to affirm that lived experience and to present a counternarrative to the tourist-oriented construction of New Orleans. It is also an attempt to interrogate that construction of the city during the ascendance of black heritage and multicultural tourism, which affords a unique opportunity to examine the complex and often contradictory ideas about race that have reshaped national discourse. During the past thirty years, the New Orleans tourism industry has attempted to respond to public and scholarly demands for a more inclusive representation of history, and both mainstream and black heritage tours have incorporated the language and symbols of diversity, multiculturalism, and black history.

Indeed, one might have expected to find such a counternarrative in the recent development of multicultural tourism that attempts to represent African American culture and history. However, these tours just as often offered their perspective through the persistent lens of New Orleans's racial exceptionalism. Following the lead of the city's dominant tourism narrative, multicultural tours also dissociated the city and its history from national and regional patterns of racial discrimination, violence, and black struggles for liberation. New Orleans's construction as a multicultural city reinforces the idea that racism in the city is either nonexistent or aberrant.

FIGURE 1.1 • Pickaninny dolls for sale in a French Quarter tourist shop.
Photograph by author.

FIGURE 1.2 • Racially stereotypical merchandise, including Mammy and Sambo
figurines, on display in a French Quarter tourist shop. Photograph by author.

FIGURE 1.3 · Contemptible collectible postcards displayed in a French Quarter tourist shop. Photograph by author.

A noteworthy example is the portrayal of the city's colonial and antebellum Creoles of color, whose economic, civic, artistic, and educational accomplishments are used as evidence of New Orleans's fluid racial boundaries and progressive race relations. In the popular imagination, and even in historiography, this population has been simplistically cast as a distinct racial group of tragic mulattoes who unwaveringly upheld elite, white interests through slave ownership; endogamy; and an insistence on a cultural, political, and social divide between themselves and enslaved blacks. Despite recent scholarly challenges to this history, New Orleans's tourism industry continues to construct blackness based on this clichéd racial image.[18]

Given the fact that the inclusion of free people of color in New Orleans's tourism narrative marked a rare occasion when black culture was discussed at all, its problematic portrayal had far-reaching implications, not only for the popular imagination but also for the political and economic realities of people's lived experiences. If we accept the proposition that free people of color were equally, if not more, white than whites were in their appearance, cultivation, education, and contempt for and castigation of black people, then we fail to recognize how the presence of this group challenged the legitimacy of racial categories, the premise of racial separation, and the inviolability of the color line. We also deny the labor, contributions, and agency of other black New Orleanians, who—we are left to assume—did not contribute anything worthwhile to the city and are consequently unworthy of historical, political, or popular attention. The salience of these ideas was unmistakable in the pre-Katrina tourism narrative and would have dramatic implications for post-Katrina policies. Ultimately, the tourism narrative's assertions of French and Spanish leniency during the colonial period; depictions of a romantic, paternal slave system during the antebellum period; and an oversimplified insistence on a constantly self-sustaining, vibrant class of free people of color who were allegedly more aligned with the interests of whites than those of other blacks all obscured the fact that free people of color, as well as enslaved and free blacks, found a range of ways to navigate and circumvent the black-white binary that undergirded Anglo-slave society.[19] Throughout New Orleans history, Afro-Creoles and African Americans fought in myriad ways to obtain or expand their freedom, assert their rights, and demand equitable treatment.

New Orleans's black heritage tourism seemed to take on the task of presenting that history to the city's visitors. In the 1960s New Orleans African Americans—through local and national political and civic organizations—

organized at the grassroots level, litigated for desegregation, forged coalitions, engaged in direct action protests, agitated for economic opportunities, and slowly wielded their hard-won bargaining power to wrest concessions from the previously whites-only tourism industry. The crux of this bargaining power stemmed from the activists' recognition of their ability to hurt New Orleans's tourist image and disrupt the tourism trade. As the historian Adam Fairclough asserts, African Americans' strategy of "bluff and brinkmanship" relied on the understanding that "the city's dependence on tourism made white businessmen in New Orleans peculiarly sensitive to the threat of disruption."[20] African American activists had learned to appropriate the rhetorical conventions of the local tourism industry to fight for civil rights and would eventually employ this same rhetoric to gain entry into the tourism industry itself.[21]

By the mid-1980s, increasing numbers of New Orleans tour owners, guides, and promoters began responding to post–civil rights movement demands by black New Orleanians for a stake in the burgeoning tourism industry and for the presentation to tourists of stories that reflected the complexity and contributions of New Orleans's black culture. At the same time that the city turned almost exclusively to tourism to alleviate the economic crisis that followed the late-1980s oil bust and the worsening of urban blight, there was an exponential rise in black heritage tourism and the increased marketing of African Americans' historical past by mainstream institutions.[22] In New Orleans, the creation of the Louisiana Black Culture Commission in 1984, the Greater New Orleans Black Tourism Center in 1986, the Greater New Orleans Black Tourism Network in 1990 (whose name was changed to the New Orleans Multicultural Tourism Network in 1999), the Essence Music Festival in 1995, the multicultural branch of the Louisiana Office of Tourism in 1996, and even mainstream tours celebrating racial and cultural diversity, responded to demands for a more inclusive, authentic representation of the city's African American past and attempted to provide opportunities for an economically viable future.

However, the inclusion of African Americans in the tourism industry came at a cost. The new attention to black New Orleans further entrenched the predominant tourism narrative for three primary reasons. First, African American inclusion was often confined to the politics of representation that promoted visibility at the expense of political, economic, and social equity. As had been the case throughout the twentieth century, New Orleans's tourism industry often referenced and even staged black history and cultural productions, such as traditional jazz performances, second line parades, and voodoo ceremonies. Tourism promoters did so primarily by exploiting and commodifying black culture to suit the expectations of mostly white visitors. Just as in other southern cities, such as Charleston, which were concurrently developing into tourist destinations, in New Orleans the production of black culture (and that of other marginalized groups) was often transformed into what the historian Stephanie Yuhl describes as a "therapeutic performative commodity that whites around the country eagerly consumed."[23] Wrenched from their cultural and community contexts, these static performances of black culture were physically and symbolically removed from local neighborhoods and living traditions characterized by resistance, survival, and innovation.[24]

Second, because predominantly poor and working-class African Americans had few employment options beyond the low-paying service industry, they were compelled by economic necessity to conform to these tourist performances that distorted and trivialized black history and culture. Many African American performers, tour guides, and service industry employees found themselves in the position of seeking the economic rewards of the local tourism industry, while simultaneously leveling incisive, if not sweeping, critiques of hegemonic discourses.[25] For instance, some African Americans developed their own black heritage tours or subtly revised mainstream tours to craft counternarratives to the city's racialized mythology. In these tours, they incorporated histories of slave uprisings; black entrepreneurship; civil rights milestones; and African American educational, political, and cultural institutions. Yet they faced systemic and institutional obstacles to financing and marketing their own black heritage tours in a tourism industry that exalted the city's European heritage over its African one.

The final reason, then, why these critiques did not supplant the predominant tourism narrative is that they could not successfully compete against the mainstream tourism industry. An imbalance of resources, marketing, and industry support relegated most black heritage sites and tours to the periphery of the city's tourism industry.[26] Hence, on the eve of Hurricane Katrina, the predominant historical and thematic tourism narrative about New Orleans had so effaced the lived experiences of the city's black community that this community was effectively rendered invisible to the rest of the nation. It took the catastrophic destruction of Katrina to lay bare the city's long history of racial and class disparities.

The failure of even the city's multicultural and black heritage tourism narratives to present a viable counternarrrative to the myth of New Orleans's racial exceptionalism points to the difficulty of overcoming a deeply entrenched narrative that provides economic benefit to the city and psychological rewards to many of its locals and visitors. After all, to fully revise this narrative would necessitate not simply an inclusion of black characters or a commitment to more accurate or authentic cultural representations but a revision of the idea of New Orleans itself. Such a revision is a costly one, for the idea of New Orleans—a city of uncontested contradictions that include its simultaneous claim of uniqueness from the rest of the South and its old South romance; its celebration of racial exoticism and mixture and its insistence on racial boundaries and exclusiveness; its allure of decadence and danger and its continual demarcation of safe spaces—is one that appeals to and validates a broad spectrum of locals and visitors.

For many whites, this idea of New Orleans provides a safe, sanctioned space to indulge in black culture and unite with black bodies, if only vicariously. As the historian Alecia Long demonstrated in her study of Storyville, the early twentieth-century vice district, New Orleans has long operated as "a geographic and metaphoric safety valve" that provides a simultaneous respite from and entrenchment of "the racial, religious, and behavioral strictures" found in other U.S. cities.[27] In the context of New Orleans tourism, racialized consumption is afforded without censure and with the added benefit of absolving whites of guilt and culpability for a racist past or present. In the post–civil rights era, white tourists' consumption of black culture substitutes for the much more difficult and abnegating task of sustained antiracist work to create economic, educational, and environmental parity for the black residents of the city. The idea of New Orleans has also provided psychological and economic benefit for blacks in the city, who are not only able to subsist on tourism dollars but for whom a glorified past of beneficent slavery, wealthy and independent free people of color, and racial harmony counters a far less redeeming or dignified history of dehumanizing slavery, chronic poverty, and racism.[28]

Just as the city's tourism narrative neglected or misrepresented New Orleans's black history and clearly delimited the proper, safe New Orleans as nonblack, representations of the city in the aftermath of Hurricane Katrina ignored the complexity and diversity of New Orleans's black experience and continued to entrench the boundaries around the French Quarter, abandoning the rest of the city as too dangerous and menacing to rescue or rebuild. In an article describing the widespread exaggeration and false reporting in the aftermath of Katrina, two local journalists observed: "The picture that emerged was one of the impoverished, masses of flood victims resorting to utter depravity, randomly attacking each other, as well as the police trying to protect them and the rescue workers trying to save them. [New Orleans Mayor Ray] Nagin told [Oprah] Winfrey the crowd has descended to an 'almost animalistic state.'"[29]

More frequently, Hurricane Katrina survivors, such as my husband, forged a community for mutual support and protection in the days following the storm, instead of waiting for the uncoordinated and ineffective national response to materialize. Residents pooled resources by sharing necessary supplies, including food, water, generators, and working cell phones; they coordinated and staffed makeshift shelters in abandoned homes, schools, and churches; they patrolled neighborhoods to search for elderly and infirm relatives and neighbors; they held continuous vigils to discourage looters; and they saved lives using their own fishing boats, rafts, and whatever else would float.[30] This type of community effort reflects black New Orleans's history of grassroots organizing, strong kinship ties, and multigenerational cooperation, a perspective largely absent in the media coverage and other public portrayals of the city in the immediate aftermath of Katrina.

The city's racialized tourism narrative anticipated a man-made disaster of media misrepresentation and governmental neglect. The vilification of black New Orleans as an incorrigible drain on financial and civic resources shaped the debate about whether to proceed with rebuilding efforts and illustrates the limited terms and conventions available to policy makers and the news media as they tried to understand who New Orleans residents were and what they might need. We witnessed the public policy impact of the city's tourism narrative in the insufficiency of federal relief; redlining of black neighborhoods; lack of a coordinated rebuilding effort; disregard of the interests of renters and public housing tenants, most of whom were black; silence around the decimation of the black middle class; and exclusion of minority contractors and community leaders, as well as black residents, from the rebuilding efforts.[31]

That is why it is not surprising that during a brief visit to New Orleans less than five months after the storm, President George W. Bush bypassed the worst-hit, predominantly black areas of the city and instead went to the Lower Garden District, which had not been flooded during Katrina. His comments to Mayor Nagin and a group of business owners and community leaders reflected the degree to which New Orleans's tourism image continues to obfuscate the realities of black agency and racial inequality in the city. Bush announced to the group: "I will tell you, the contrast between when I was last here and today . . . is pretty dramatic. It may be hard for you to see, but from when I first came here to today, New Orleans is reminding me of the city I used to come to visit. It's a heck of a place to bring your family. It's a great place to find some of the greatest food in the world and some wonderful fun. And I'm glad you got your infrastructure back on its feet. I know you're beginning to welcome citizens from all around the country here to New Orleans. And for folks around the country who are looking for a great place to have a convention, or a great place to visit, I'd suggest coming here to the great—New Orleans."[32]

The fact that the president returned to the familiar image of the "city [he] used to come to visit"—one of frivolity and flavorful food—in the midst of a national catastrophe speaks volumes about the impact and enduring legacy of New Orleans's problematic racialized narratives. Even in the midst of heart-wrenching devastation and potentially new understandings of race and poverty in the city and the nation, the president circulated a construction of New Orleans that relied on the romance of black labor (to prepare the great food and provide the wonderful fun) while ignoring the needs of the predominantly black citizenry. Instead, the president encouraged "citizens from all around the country"—tourists—to return to New Orleans, not the mostly black New Orleans residents who were anxiously awaiting the opportunity to return and rebuild their communities that had been devastated by the flood.

Even as I write this chapter, nearly eight years after Hurricane Katrina, parts of the city look just as they did when the rest of the world was first introduced to them immediately following the storm. Interspersed with new construction are demolished homes, deserted neighborhoods, and broken-up streets. Yet, while many New Orleans residents remain mired in bureaucratic processes and battles with politicians and power brokers over affordable housing, quality education, and accessible health care, New Orleans tourism has rebounded, and the tourist sites of the pre-Katrina era—largely undamaged by the storm—have been revived.[33] Their revival has been augmented by the rise of post-Katrina tourism, featuring new sites, tours, and geographies of the city that incorporate African American neighborhoods, *lieux de mémoire*, and narratives of survival and resilience. These more recent tours are, nevertheless, troublingly dependent on the racial tropes that characterized pre-Katrina tourism.

New Orleans's tourist landscape is inextricably linked to the city's physical and racial geographies. The city's precarious location, its scarcity of habitable land, and its vulnerability to floods and disease compelled a heterogeneous populace to cohabit and work in close proximity to one another through the early twentieth century. The absence of geographic racial segregation, however, did not translate into social integration, as the systems of slavery and Jim Crow segregation entrenched racial and class inequalities. Throughout the twentieth century, new technologies that facilitated the drainage of former back swamps, marshes, and other environmentally vulnerable lands, white flight, gentrification, programs of urban renewal, economic downturns, and the displacement of the poor and working class from tourist and commercial districts resulted in a residential pattern that more closely mirrored and perpetuated the city's racial and class divides.[34]

From the late 1960s to the end of the twentieth century—correlating with the post–civil rights era—the interrelated processes of suburban sprawl and racial segregation mimicked the shift in racial demographics that the city experienced during Reconstruction with the influx of poor, recently freed slaves. As the city's mostly white middle-class population left for surrounding parishes and affluent all-white enclaves—often in the most structurally and environmentally stable neighborhoods—the city's African American population grew and spread primarily into more affordable, lower lying, and less environmentally sustainable areas of the city, such as the Lower Ninth Ward, parts of Gentilly, and New Orleans East. Not surprisingly, the majority of black neighborhoods—geographically and ideologically isolated from the historic and tourist core of the city—were wracked by debilitating poverty, unemployment, and failing schools.[35] In his geography of New Orleans, originally published in 1976, Peirce Lewis uses evidence of the growing racial divide to challenge persistent claims of New Orleans exceptionalism: "In New Orleans, as elsewhere, blacks are relatively poor and ill-housed, and their neighborhoods are poorly attended by municipal services. Educational levels are low, crime rates high. Meanwhile, whites flee and the proportion of blacks continues to increase, as do the isolation and alienation of a population that sees itself as abandoned and abused."[36]

Although African Americans became the largest racial group in the city's population in 1974, their increased electoral presence and growing political influence failed to reverse these trends. Even when black voters

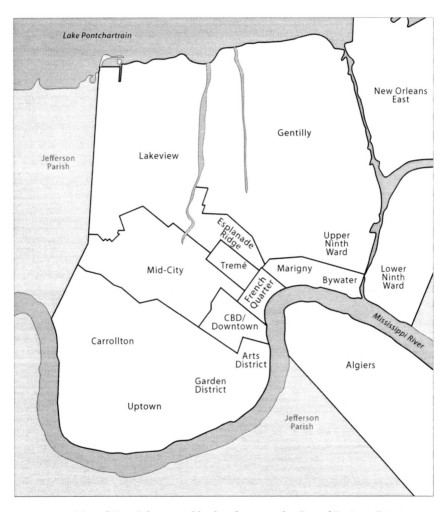

MAP 1.1 • Map of New Orleans neighborhoods. CBD is the Central Business District.

rejected the traditional model of white patronage and historical and cultural black-Creole divisions to elect the city's first black mayor—Ernest "Dutch" Morial—in 1977, New Orleans's new leadership was forced to confront daunting challenges with limited resources and few economic prospects. In fact, although Morial's reformist approach to local government was a promising departure from traditional city politics, his uncompromising efforts to disband the city's political, social, and economic oligarchy and provide equal access to city government to all New Orleans citizens ultimately alienated him from whites and deepened the electoral racial divide.[37]

Conditions only deteriorated further with the oil bust in 1986 and the attendant departure of jobs and the middle-class tax base that had supported essential municipal services. Morial's two-term successor, Sidney Barthelemy, the city's second African American mayor, turned exclusively to tourism to redress the problems facing the city and ushered in an era of a tourism-dominated economy. By 2000 New Orleans had one of the highest rates of poverty in the country. Hardest hit were black New Orleanians, already among the city's poorest and least educated. In the final decades of the twentieth century, disproportionate rates of poverty and unemployment for black New Orleanians, whites' desertion of the public school system, and a new pattern of residential segregation that concentrated poor African Americans in public housing projects and other isolated ghettos made New Orleans more geographically, economically, educationally, and politically segregated than at any other time in its history. As a result, the city's racial cartography was referred to descriptively as a "white teapot," the shape appearing on maps that depicted the concentration of whites in the highest elevations of the city. This racial geography was produced by historical patterns of environmental racism, educational and economic disparities, and residential segregation.[38] Ironically, in spite of—or perhaps in response to—the gains of the civil rights movement, New Orleans had become a separate and unequal city.

The tourist landscape clearly reflected and exacerbated these inequalities as it helped shape a range of social and economic patterns, including gentrification and unequal property values and distribution of resources. By the beginning of the twenty-first century, New Orleans's tourist geography had extended beyond the French Quarter but was still limited to distinct tourism areas that included the Warehouse District, the Garden District, and the Central Business District. The addition of new streetcar lines and an Audubon Institute riverboat ferry gave tourists more convenient (and more easily contained) ways of getting from the French Quarter and downtown hotels to attractions on the riverfront, uptown, and in City Park. The viability of these tourism districts directly correlated to the deterioration of many of the city's nontourist neighborhoods. The resources that the city poured into the tourist districts for continuous police protection, debris removal, beautification, and infrastructure maintenance reduced the services available for other areas of the city. The lack of community-engaged policing, eroding streets and blighted housing, and irregular trash collection and landscaping in these nontourist areas displayed a literal and symbolic disregard primarily for the city's poor, black residents. In the decades before Katrina, the systematic neglect of these nontourist sections of the city foreshadowed the devastation they incurred during the hurricane.[39]

African American neighborhoods suffered the most from the combination of these economic, social, environmental, and political factors. Although the Lower Ninth Ward was not among the poorest or lowest-lying New Orleans neighborhoods, it was decimated by Katrina because of a long history of local and federal policies that had isolated the neighborhood and facilitated its environmental degradation. Long the site of the city's most distasteful and dangerous industries and operations because of its location downriver from the heart of the city, the Lower Ninth Ward was dramatically affected by the expansion of the city's port industry. Beginning in the early twentieth century, a succession of navigation canals were carved through the Ninth Ward, physically separating the neighborhood from the city proper and leaving it inadequately protected against the bodies of water that surrounded it on three sides. Black and poor Lower Nine residents, who had already been relegated to the lower-lying area, referred to as back of town, were further alienated by racial discrimination, white flight, and class inequities in the decades before Katrina.[40] Yet, the condition of the Lower Ninth Ward and its residents could no longer be ignored following the hurricane, and tourism became a vital, albeit problematic, way that Americans and the rest of the world attempted to see, understand, and—in the case of "voluntourism"—ameliorate these conditions.

Despite their shorter histories and different geographies, parts of the Gentilly and New Orleans East neighborhoods shared the Lower Ninth Ward's pre- and post-Katrina fate. Until the twentieth century, the marshlands on the outskirts of the city were sporadically and unevenly developed because of the inhospitable terrain, limited access, inadequate transportation, and poor drainage. In both Gentilly and New Orleans East, the dredging of canals, the construction of levees and highways, and the implementation of advanced drainage technologies facilitated the development of previously uninhabitable neighborhoods and eventuated in soil erosion that left most of the area below sea level and susceptible to hurricanes and storm surges. Racial integration of Gentilly's once-segregated subdivisions, white flight, and the devastation of historically black communities with the construction of an interstate highway enticed middle-class African American homeowners to previously all-white inner suburbs. New Orleans East likewise experienced a demographic shift in the second half of the twentieth century. The eastern edge of the city drew developers who were willing to ignore or gloss over environmental risks, such as soil subsidence and the impending threats of hurricanes and storm surges, to capitalize on increasing land values. Though New Orleans East was initially marketed to whites as a suburb within the city limits, development companies ultimately failed to lure significant numbers of affluent whites to the area. Throughout the 1970s and 1980s, however, the newly drained wetlands did attract middle-class and affluent African Americans who, in the post–civil rights era, were finally able to stake a claim to the suburban American Dream. The East also became home to displaced poor and working-class African Americans who took advantage of affordable housing and government-subsidized rents following the oil bust, demolitions of public housing, and the gentrification of historic neighborhoods. The exodus of middle-class whites from Gentilly and New Orleans East and the accompanying loss in tax base coincided with the city's economic depression and surge in crime, further cementing the citywide patterns of racial and economic polarization.[41]

The historic Afro-Creole Faubourg Tremé, a nineteenth-century suburb adjacent to the French Quarter, escaped many of the environmental and geographic hazards of other low-lying African American neighborhoods. As both the site of Congo Square, where slaves and their descendants gathered to meld and pass down expressive culture traditions, and home to Homer Plessy, whose iconic failed challenge to racial segregation was part of a much longer history of radical Afro-Creole activism, the Tremé commands a place at the epicenter of the city's—and even the nation's—early black cultural, spiritual, social, civic, and political life. Following the exodus of whites in the early twentieth century, the poor and working-class African Americans who remained in the neighborhood sustained existing black institutions and cultural practices and created new ones, as evidenced in the cultural and built environment of dance and jazz clubs, second line

parades, funeral homes and insurance companies, mutual aid and benevolent societies, and other neighborhood organizations. Despite its historic
importance—or, more accurately, because of it—the district became
a contested space as African American residents competed with the city
of New Orleans and gentrifiers over its meanings and uses. The city's urban
renewal plans have included the leveling of significant historic structures,
the razing of entire neighborhoods, and the dislocation of residents to erect
a highway overpass, civic and cultural centers, and a park in honor of Louis
Armstrong.[42] Critics have questioned the prudence of memorializing the
city's "most famous son by destroying a portion of the old neighborhood
in which jazz evolved and replacing it with unseemly berms and bridged la-
goons."[43] In instances such as this, the tourist packaging of Tremé's cultural
contributions to the city has taken precedence over the cultural contribu-
tors themselves, who are left to contend with a seriously diminished physical and cultural landscape. At the same time, the prevalence of nineteenth-
century architecture, the proximity to the French Quarter and the Central
Business District, and economic incentives to renovate deteriorating properties have made some parts of the neighborhood appealing to affluent
blacks and whites whose ideas about aesthetics and propriety are often
at odds with long-standing black traditions and practices. These tensions
have taken a toll on the neighborhood, which suffered the same problems
of crime and urban decay as other predominantly black areas of the city.[44]

Because of these historical patterns of racism, poverty, economic exploitation, environmental hazards, and geographic isolation and alienation,
these African American neighborhoods were especially vulnerable to Katrina and the glaringly inefficient bureaucratic response that ensued. When
the hurricane hit, more than two-thirds of the city's black residents lived
in areas prone to flooding. In disproportionate numbers, African American and poor residents were trapped in the city by the flood waters and a
fatally botched rescue operation. Flooding from the hurricane and storm
surges caused the evacuation, dispersal, and, in some cases, demise of entire
black communities throughout the Lower Ninth Ward, New Orleans East,
Gentilly, and Tremé. In addition to the devastating losses that they suffered
as a direct result of the storm and uncoordinated rescue efforts, African
American and poor residents—as well as the black professional class whose
businesses and practices were sustained by them—have faced daunting
challenges to rebuilding and recovery in the storm's aftermath. Disproportionately affected by flooding and housing damage, the absence or delayed

return of municipal services, the demolition and ongoing dearth of public housing, and the racially inequitable disbursement of federal funds for rebuilding, African Americans have returned to New Orleans more slowly and at lower rates than all other racial and ethnic groups. Data from the 2010 census suggest that just 60 percent of the city's population is now black, down from 67 percent before Katrina—a decline of more than 100,000 people. The displacement of so many black New Orleanians has already significantly altered the city's cultural, economic, and political landscape, precipitating an influx of more affluent white residents; the election of the first white mayor in over thirty years; a 5–2 majority-white city council; the loss of a congressional seat; and the consolidation of some majority-black legislative districts.[45] These immediate developments may foretell more sweeping changes to New Orleans's racial geography, compounding the problematic relationship between race and tourist space that paved the road to Katrina.

New Orleans Tourism as Racial Project

Desire and Disaster explores New Orleans's tourism industry, and the modern urban tourism industry more generally, as a racial project that explicitly integrates racial structures and representations.[46] As a racialized social structure, New Orleans tourism redistributes resources to tourism zones and initiatives; maintains a racially, educationally, and economically stratified workforce; and designates certain segments of society and communities as dangerous or as disaster zones, resulting in the type of isolation and systematic neglect that make these communities even more susceptible to natural and man-made disasters. As a form of racial representation, urban tourism superficially trumpets the value of racial difference and diversity through the commodification and consumption of customs, foodways, and cultural traditions associated with certain racial and ethnic groups. Embedded within the racial ideologies of multiculturalism, racial exceptionalism, color blindness, and postracialism, contemporary urban tourism responds to the desire of consumers in the post–civil rights era for racial diversity to the detriment of racial equality. Using race as a lens to study New Orleans tourism offers a way to explore the often constrained, but determined, efforts of black heritage tours to resist and critique the structural and representational manifestations of the mainstream tourism industry. Overall, analyzing New Orleans's tourism narratives and practices illuminates the

ways that public policy and popular culture in the post–civil rights era respond to racialized subjects simultaneously as objects of desire who invite
imitation and as sites of disaster in need of remediation.[47]

In theorizing desire and disaster, I set out to show how New Orleans
tourism in the post–civil rights era serves as a critical site where national
understandings, popular memories, and public policy decisions about African Americans are debated and deployed. As I demonstrate in the following chapters, New Orleans's tourism narrative in the late twentieth century
hinged on a partial and incomplete historical, political, and social understanding of the city's black population. This fictitious narrative nonetheless
advanced a powerful and persuasive argument about African American citizenship that contributed to and exacerbated Hurricane Katrina's disproportionate impact on black residents. By highlighting the relationship between
racial desire and manmade disaster, this study responds to Lewis's call for "a
new generation of Muckrakers" willing to expose and work collaboratively
to address "the worst problems—such as threats from hurricanes and racial
divisions" that beset New Orleans long before Katrina struck.[48]

Desire and Disaster focuses on New Orleans's quotidian mainstream tourism package, including year-round, regularly produced or operating tours;
promotional materials; and landmarks, as opposed to more spectacular and
renowned seasonal attractions such as Mardi Gras and the Jazz Fest. This
study offers the first focused history of African American tourism in New
Orleans and one of the first histories of African American tourism in the
United States due to its rather recent development and a scarcity of source
material. By focusing on everyday tourist practices and how multicultural
and black heritage tourism re-create and resist those practices, and following Michel de Certeau, I seek "to make explicit the systems of operational
combination (*les combinatoires d'operations*) which also compose a 'culture,'
and to bring to light the models of action characteristic of users whose status as the dominated element in society (a status that does not mean that
they are either passive or docile) is concealed by the euphemistic term
'consumers.' Everyday life invents itself by poaching in countless ways on
the property of others."[49] The distinct processes of racialization articulated
and newly emerging in response to the popularization of multiculturalism,
the rise of black heritage tourism, and the debates surrounding Hurricane
Katrina have elicited new tactics by black New Orleanians eager to take
advantage of the city's tourism industry. Ultimately, by reading the national
response to Katrina through New Orleans's tourism narrative, this book

implicitly argues for a more truthful and thoughtful historical assessment, interpretation, and reimagining of New Orleans on the part of cultural institutions, the tourism industry, and public officials. What is at stake is not only a guide for remembering the past but a blueprint for reenvisioning New Orleans's future.

In the decades preceding Katrina, the creation of more and better-funded destination marketing organizations, the acquisition of professional sports teams, the efforts to integrate and democratize Mardi Gras, and the targeting—through new media such as the Internet—of new niche markets offered evidence of a more economically, politically, and culturally empowered class of African American visitors and local residents.[50] However, I argue that these developments also masked and, in some cases, exacerbated a growing racial and class divide and in the process made the city's African American community more vulnerable to the natural and man-made disasters set into motion by Katrina. Post-Katrina New Orleans demonstrates the political, social, and economic implications of an exclusionary historical memory. Henceforth, we can ignore tourism and other popular narratives only at our own peril. The limitations of the responses to Katrina uncovered the ways that racial representations in popular culture profoundly affect the ways that we live and die.

DESIRE AND DISASTER unfolds in five chapters. In this introductory chapter, I have attempted to show how the city's dominant tourism narrative helped frame the response to the city, and specifically its black residents, following Hurricane Katrina. Focusing specifically on the construction of blackness in New Orleans tourism in the post–civil rights era, chapter 2 suggests how the city's promotion of black cultural consumption in the form of entertainment, service, and symbolic representations and re-creations of slavery produced a desire for representations of blackness that denied black agency or racial equality. Chapter 3 examines the multicultural framing of New Orleans's tourism narrative through a case study of Le Monde Créole French Quarter Courtyards Tour. Despite its attention to black historical figures and events, Le Monde Créole demonstrates the recalcitrance of the dominant racial narrative, notwithstanding its rhetorical and substantive allusions to pluralism and social justice.

Though much of this book focuses on the official tourism narratives, chapter 4 shifts focus to document strategies of resistance among black tour guides who used their own black heritage tours or subtle revisions of main-stream tours to craft counternarratives to the city's racialized mythology. The chapter highlights their struggle to operate in a tourism industry that frequently distorts or denies black culture, history, and agency. Chapter 5 concludes *Desire and Disaster in New Orleans* by exploring the evolution of a new, post-Katrina tourism narrative. This final chapter suggests implications for the reconstruction of both New Orleans and its tourism industry.

Taken together, these chapters open a window onto the current historical moment in which the prevalence of multiculturalist discourse, the ubiquity of black cultural production, and the ancillary postulation of a postracial society have supplanted public policy initiatives to ameliorate persistent racial and economic inequality. Despite the rhetorical and symbolic shifts attending post–civil rights racial discourse and neoliberal practices, mythologies of racial exceptionalism and black inferiority remain intact, with blackness coded as simultaneously desirous and disastrous.

Two. "Life the Way It Used to Be in the Old South"

THE CONSTRUCTION OF BLACK DESIRE IN NEW ORLEANS'S
POST–CIVIL RIGHTS TOURISM NARRATIVE

CLEO, MARKET LADY: Traditionally this lady held an honored position in the Southern household. Her duties were to keep the house running smoothly by overseeing the house servants and attending to errands, especially marketing. Because of her high station she was respected by the other servants and loved by the family she served.

EMMA, CIRCA 1850: Harvest time, from the earliest days of settlement to the mid-1900's, brought family and friends together and the whole community would work side by side to bring in their crops. Cotton was ready for the mills in the summer, and the children would help, too. Many festivals and country fairs evolved from this type of community effort. In the cotton fields, everyone would grab a sack and sing and carry on lively conversations as they walked through the rows of cotton filling their sacks. Emma represents a woman of this era and wears a typical country dress and carries a sack of cotton by her side.

—*Hang tags on African American dolls produced by C. V. Gambina Inc. in New Orleans*

The collectible Gambina dolls sold (and now auctioned) all over the world represent the convergence of two predominant themes in New Orleans's pre-Katrina tourism narrative: history and diversity. Their meticulous period clothing and accessories, from Cleo's gold bracelet to Emma's bag of real cotton, as well as the accompanying historical narratives of both figures' traditional roles and legacies, evoke a romantic southern past. Likewise, their smooth brown skin, highlighted with make-up and colorful head wraps, perfectly positioned to reveal luxurious black hair, all pay homage to 1960s-era black cultural nationalism, illustrating that even in slavery "black is beautiful" (see figures 2.1–2.2).[1] A range of black Gambina dolls—from Odelia, the praline lady, to Scarlett, the southern belle (dressed in the obligatory full skirt and wearing a hang tag with the ironic explanatory description that "ladies' [sic] were not allowed to have suntanned complexions")—take their places as equals alongside white Gambina dolls and together market a fictional, incongruous history of class- and color-blind citizenship and slavery.[2] The fascination with this "history" is exemplified in one journalist's assessment that "New Orleans has always been an irresistible magnet for those who wanted to experience 20th century 'good times' in a 19th century atmosphere."[3] Gambina's "servant" dolls offer such an experience by both glamorizing the history of slavery and celebrating the contributions and dignity of African Americans whose labor and cultural innovations are credited with shaping a distinctive New Orleans mythos. In so doing, the dolls reference and recast two separate disasters in white southern historical memory—the Civil War and the civil rights movement—two upheavals that fundamentally altered the city's racial hierarchy and social, economic, and political structures. Gambina servant dolls symbolically mitigate these disasters through reconciliationist popular memories of the Lost Cause and desegregation that entirely avoid the central motivation of racial justice.[4]

The dolls represent a modern contribution to the city's tourist iconography. Since its origins in the nineteenth century, this iconography has been racialized, and early associations of the city with voodoo, jazz, Creole culture, decadence, sexual permissiveness, and exoticism—which marked the city as other, dangerous, and lascivious—were inextricably linked to racial mythologies about the city's black population. Ironically, however, the titillation with blackness that would be used to market the city to visitors operated alongside the distortion and often denial of black history and agency. Throughout the twentieth century—in response to national trends in the emergence of modern tourism and local economic imperatives—these stories of New Orleans were concretized into a predominant tourism narrative, one that exalts the city's European heritage at the expense of its African one, that sentimentalizes slavery, and that ultimately sustains and propagates a racialized image of the city that diminishes and distorts African American history and culture.[5]

These dual representations of black desire and disaster sustained the stereotypes of black servility and inferiority and, in the process, ignored the historical and contemporary realities of the city's African Americans. One reason for this distortion was a dearth of tours and sites that referenced the city's deeply rooted African culture. For decades before Hurricane Katrina struck, many potential sites and areas of the city that would have been ideal

FIGURE 2.1 • "Cleo, Market Lady," a "servant" doll and FIGURE 2.2 • "Emma, circa 1850," another "servant" doll sold by C. V. Gambina, Inc. Photographs by Marisol Negrón.

black heritage sites were either destroyed, neglected, or undeveloped by the city of New Orleans. A relevant example was the city's neglect of its jazz architectural history. The creation of jazz in New Orleans by classically trained and self-taught black musicians influenced by African musical traditions is widely viewed as both exemplary of a distinctive African American culture and a singularly American contribution. Yet these early jazz musicians, including the much-touted Louis Armstrong, were shamefully underrepresented by historical monuments. In fact, in her article on New Orleans's jazz tourism, one reporter notes that the former homes and hangouts of the city's early black jazz musicians were "now abandoned buildings, dilapidated Creole cottages, and in some cases, parking lots."[6] Perhaps the most egregious examples were the urban renewal projects implemented in the Tremé district throughout the twentieth century, resulting in the construction of several insufficiently funded, underused, and questionably designed structures, as well as an elevated expressway that cut through the heart of the community. In an effort to compete with other tourist cities and appease white elites, city planners displaced thousands of poor African American residents, leveled entire neighborhoods and historic structures, and disrupted community activism and traditions. Decades-long efforts to memorialize Louis Armstrong and to commemorate New Orleans jazz as "a rare and valuable natural resource" have been hampered by political wrangling; community distrust; poor planning; inadequate funding; and disputes over the design, access, management, and maintenance of jazz sites.[7] New Orleans's physical landscape—with the deteriorating and demolished cultural structures that existed long before the destruction caused by Hurricane Katrina—was suggestive of its tourist landscape, which abandoned local black communities and their social memories in obeisance to tourism-oriented dictates.

Another reason for the omission of potential black heritage sites and spaces from the official tourist landscape was their designation as unsafe. Throughout New Orleans's history, conflations of jazz, voodoo, quadroon balls, and other tourist preoccupations with danger, disruption, and racial contamination prompted tourism promoters to "whiten" or sanitize black cultural productions to make them more palatable to whites and less threatening to white supremacist notions. By the late twentieth century, these purportedly black experiences had been limited to the safe tourist space of the heavily policed French Quarter, where they could be more effectively controlled and contained.[8] This trend is exemplified in an unsettling description in a Greater New Orleans Tourist and Convention Commission (GNOTCC) tourism brochure that identifies the Orleans Hotel ballroom as the site of "the naughty-nice quadroon balls, where mothers would offer their virginal, golden-skinned daughters to the aristocratic young white men of the city, so that a man might choose one whom he would make his concubine, setting her up, often for life, in a little house in a special section of the city a few blocks from the ballroom."[9] Outside the boundaries of the French Quarter, however, the city's real-life majority African American population was portrayed as physically and socially threatening. Dramatic spikes in violent crime during this period exacerbated these portrayals and brought the city a spate of negative international publicity, further cementing its reputation as black and lawless. Throughout the 1980s and 1990s, city and tourism industry leaders responded to the notoriety with a series of initiatives intended to salvage New Orleans's tourist image. They allocated additional resources and dispatched police patrols primarily to the French Quarter and Central Business District, which attracted the largest numbers of tourists. Consequently, tourist brochures, websites, and safety notices began reassuring visitors about their safety in these areas, while tacitly or overtly discouraging ventures into other areas of the city. Many of these other areas were either predominantly or historically black neighborhoods, which were almost always excluded from the accepted demarcation of tourist New Orleans. In fact, despite the recent trend to encourage visitors to explore beyond the city's French Quarter, the sanctioned spaces for these excursions rarely included black neighborhoods or black heritage sites.[10]

By the time Hurricane Katrina hit New Orleans, the racial iconography of the city's cultural tourism, virtually unchanged since the nineteenth century, had both exoticized and erased black New Orleans.[11] African Americans, who had become players in the tourism industry in the late twentieth century, were used by the industry to attract visitors seeking more unconventional tourist experiences and, in turn, used the industry to gain an economic and political foothold in the city. Analyses of websites, promotional literature, tourist magazines, and images from the late twentieth and twenty-first centuries illustrate that New Orleans's predominant tourism narrative alternated between constructions of Old World and old South memories and identities at the expense of the city's African and African American history and legacy. An almost exclusive emphasis on New Orleans's colonial European heritage and its antebellum charm obscured the brutality of slavery, the agency and group solidarity of Africans and African Americans, and the civil rights battles that continued to wage in the years preceding Hurricane Katrina. These late twentieth-century images and other representations perpetuated long-standing stereotypes even as the tourist literature adopted the rhetoric and tone of multiculturalism and diversity. This more palatable picture of New Orleans as a city steeped in a racially unthreatening past belied the more uneasy reality of a New Orleans that was racially and economically unequal.

The 1986 creation of the Greater New Orleans Black Tourism Center reflected both New Orleans's nascent status as an unabashedly tourist city and its concessions to the demands of the post–civil rights era. The city's public servants, law enforcement personnel, administrators, and ordinary citizens had grown accustomed to the presence of tourists and dependent on their dollars, which accounted for the bulk of New Orleans's industry, particularly following the decimation of the city's oil and gas industries in the 1980s.[12] As the daily local news broadcasts indicated, the number of tourists visiting the city and the amount of money they spent was a constant concern for New Orleanians. In an effort to maintain this viable industry, the city had become expert at marketing itself to visitors using a variety of formats. In the late twentieth and early twenty-first centuries, the most frequently used of these formats were the Internet and tourist brochures and pamphlets.

A search of the Internet using the keyword *New Orleans* leads to numerous websites that target potential visitors, while the glossy, coupon-filled tourist literature in the city's airport, visitor's centers, and hotel lobbies entice visitors who have already arrived in the city. Despite the more modern formats and varied sponsors and points of view, print and online tourist literature in the late twentieth and early twenty-first centuries persists in presenting New Orleans as a place that is unique in the United States, if not in the world.[13] Chuck Taggart's website, GumboPages.com, makes a typical claim: "New Orleans is a world apart, in many ways its own little city-state, part of the United States but at the same time so different from every other place in that country."[14] Although most cities' tourism marketing includes claims to uniqueness, New Orleans's tourism rhetoric suggests not only a distinction from other cities but also a cultural, historical, and ideological distinction from the United States, and occasionally the rest of the world.

This notion of New Orleans's uniqueness pervaded the tourism industry's descriptions of every aspect of the city, from its topography and climate to its history and architecture. In fact, the print and online literature described a city whose very attitude had been shaped by its unique historical and environmental distinctions. The 2000 *New Orleans Official Visitors Guide*, published by the New Orleans Metropolitan Convention and Visitors Bureau (NOMCVB), encapsulates this idea: "From the crowds who celebrate around the clock on Bourbon Street to the Cajun fais-do-do, where dancing, eating and talking with friends rules the evening, joie de vivre oozes out of every pore of New Orleans. The tropical climate that seems to cultivate both plant-life and human appetites; a deep and intricate history, and a prominent position on the Mississippi River have provided the Crescent City with a complex blend of cultures, social mores and delights."[15] The tourist literature concurred with the prevailing scholarship that New Orleans's origins and subsequent development differed substantially from those of the rest of the United States. Its geographic isolation, French and Spanish colonial history, predominant Catholicism, use of the French language, and influx of cultures and nationalities distinguished New Orleans from the British colonies of North America and ultimately set the stage for the city's most famous or infamous attractions for visitors—jazz, Mardi Gras, aboveground cemeteries, voodoo, Creole cuisine, and historic architecture.[16]

Ultimately, these different descriptions make the case that New Orleans's geographic, climatic, historical, and culinary distinctions have resulted in a unique New Orleans way of life, one that was often accompanied in the tourist literature by terms such as "joie de vivre," "laissez les bons temps rouler," and "enjoying life." On the NOMCVB website, Paul Greenberg's history of New Orleans distinguishes it from other cities with this claim: "While other cities count megabytes, old New Orleans still loves to party till dawn, have stiff coffee by the meandering riverbank and wile [sic] away the hours in a city that legislators, royalty and armies alike have all tried vainly to tame."[17] Echoing the sentiments of city boosters and visitors since the nineteenth century, pre-Katrina tourist literature rendered New Orleans as a timeless, insulated space of exoticism, decadence, mystery, and magic, as shown in the city's many designations: "the City that Care Forgot," the city "built where God never intended a city to be built," "the Big Easy," "Paris of the Americas," and "the Crescent City." Strikingly, the image of New Orleans in the twenty-first century differed very little from the mythologized South that had attracted northern tourists in the decades following the Civil War. Pre-Katrina white tourists, like their postbellum predecessors, sought in New Orleans an escape from class uncertainties and racial problems and the promise of established tradition, romantic history, and social stability seemingly lacking from their own lives.[18]

As has been the trend in recent historiography, which seeks to revise prior dominant narratives by incorporating the voices and histories of the city's black population, in explicating New Orleans's uniqueness, websites and tourist brochures invariably alluded to the city's racial heritage, particularly the city's complicated colonial and antebellum racial and caste systems.[19] Yet these allusions were fraught with the racial ambivalence and anxiety that have characterized the historical, political, and economic development of New Orleans since its founding.

The tourist literature focused on the racial distinctions that defined New Orleans as a world apart, to the exclusion of the characteristics that bound the city to the rest of the United States, particularly the South. The city's portrayal as racially unique was supported by the notion that the racism and racial conflict that continued to haunt other U.S. cities was largely lacking or lessened in New Orleans because of its unique historical and cultural legacy. As a result of this prevailing notion, two primary racial representations of the city persisted in the tourist literature: New Orleans as a historic city—with an emphasis on its European colonial history and its southern American antebellum history—and New Orleans as a melting pot or multicultural city, both of which were often invoked in the same publications and even the same descriptions.

On the surface, these representations of New Orleans as cosmopolitan, as well as ethnically, racially, and culturally diverse, marked a conscious departure from previous tendencies to focus exclusively on white, elite grand narratives in tourism portrayals. This shift in perspective resulted in a more inclusive selection of subjects and, purportedly, a more authentic portrayal of them.[20] However, as the sociologist Kevin Gotham observes in *Authentic New Orleans*, "specific racial meanings and manifestations of discrimination were institutionalized within the tourism industry during the twentieth century."[21] The resulting battles over the competing images and realities of New Orleans illustrate the persistent exclusions and divisions that characterized the city's tourism narrative. The tourist representation of New Orleans history is one such site of contention.

Historic New Orleans

It seems somewhat ironic that pre-Katrina New Orleans, a city long associated with the transitory concepts of immediate gratification and living for the moment, was equally concerned with the more momentous and enduring domain of history. In tourist literature, the city's more frivolous attractions vied with its historic ones, and websites and brochures enumerated important dates, figures, and battles with surprising regularity. Tourist literature described New Orleans as a city that is at once modern and ancient. *The Soul of New Orleans*, the official visitor's guide of the Greater New Orleans Multicultural Tourism Network, explains: "With a history older than that of the United States, New Orleans is a contemporary city steeped heavily in its past."[22] On his "New Orleans History" web page, Edward Branley says: "New Orleans is a city rich in history. We have claims to many 'oldest this' and 'oldest thats.'"[23] Indeed, numerous websites and brochures allocated a significant amount of space for the identification of historical sites and events. Yet New Orleans seemed almost exclusively preoccupied with two historical periods—the colonial period under French and Spanish rule and the antebellum period following the Louisiana Purchase.[24] The emphasis on these periods (to the exclusion of more recent history) and the depiction of these periods together created a troubling, incomplete racial image of the city.

In the pre-Katrina tourist literature, New Orleans's colonial history was almost always equated with a white European identity, stemming from the city's French and Spanish colonial periods in the seventeenth and eighteenth centuries. In "Uncommon Character," on the website of the New Orleans Metropolitan Convention and Visitors Bureau, Jonathan Fricker, former director of the Louisiana Division of Historic Preservation, reiterates a predominant theme in New Orleans tourism literature: "New Orleans, with its richly mottled old buildings, its sly, sophisticated—sometimes almost disreputable—air, and its Hispanic-Gallic traditions, has more the flavor of an old European capital than an American city."[25] One of the bureau's web pages points to New Orleans's "French and Spanish patrimony and cultural influences," and an article on French Quarter architecture in *Visitor Magazine* refers to New Orleans as "the most European American city," although the historian Gwendolyn Hall's designation of New Orleans as "the most African city in the United States" is far more accurate.[26]

New Orleans Online's "Historical Facts about New Orleans" epitomizes the "New Orleans as European city" tourism construction: "First-time visitors are often struck by the European flavor of New Orleans, and little wonder. It's everywhere! Visitors see it in our architecture, taste it in our food, hear it in the music that abounds, and experience it in the hospitality and characteristic accent of our locals."[27] The 1991 brochure "New Orleans," published by the GNOTCC, stereotypically alludes to "scarifying voodoo secrets," a "natural instinct for soul-stirring music," and "truly exotic" cuisine to hint at New Orleans's African-inspired culture, meanwhile attributing the city's "architectural splendors," "creole origins," and title as "the European Queen of the Mississippi" to its French and Spanish colonial heritage.[28] The GNOTCC's brochures borrowed heavily from the article "New Orleans: America's European Masterpiece," commissioned by the organization's public relations department.[29] The colonial construction of New Orleans credited the city's white, European heritage for most of what makes the city unique—from its architecture to its zydeco.

Not surprisingly, the French Quarter, the city's most renowned tourist destination, was also portrayed as its most European.[30] DiscoverNewOrleans .com's "French Quarter Guide" argues that the French Quarter, "the heart and soul of New Orleans," offers "a quintessentially European experience that has lost little of its old-world character and appeal despite the ravages of time and the influx of visitors that descend upon it."[31] The NOMCVB visitor's guide adds that despite more modern attractions, "it is still the city's old world charm that fascinates most visitors, particularly the very European 'Vieux Carre,' or French Quarter."[32] One GNOTCC executive said in an interview that the "trend among whites in the tourism industry . . . to see and promote New Orleans as 'Old World European'" was intended to ameliorate the damage caused by the tourism industry's history of racist marketing. Yet, as her African American interviewer observed, this trend has resulted in "the absence of *any* Black representation" (emphasis in original).[33]

Just as the French Quarter garnered more attention than the rest of New Orleans's tourist attractions, the city's French heritage was emphasized over its colonial African culture. The tourist literature evoked the city's French colonial period repeatedly to distinguish New Orleans's development from that of other U.S. cities. As Gateway New Orleans points out, the French have even influenced New Orleans's laws: "As part of Louisiana's French legacy counties are called 'parishes' and the Napoleonic Code (rather than Common Law) holds sway in the state's courtrooms."[34] DiscoverNewOrleans .com's "French Quarter Guide" erroneously contrasts the early French settlement with British colonies whose population was often composed of dissidents. The guide states: "The original citizens of New Orleans proudly embraced and celebrated their French heritage, often sending their children to school on the continent."[35] Phil Johnson, a local journalist, also celebrated New Orleans's French heritage. In a 1967 essay excerpted on Gumbo-Pages.com, he exclaims: "But the French, ah the French! They came here full blown with life and love, not refugees. God-centered and narrow; but adventurers, gamblers, fat with a culture that made living a love affair of the senses, and secure in the knowledge that while sin was the work of the devil, its nearest occasions were the particular art of the French."[36] These expressions of reverence and gratitude to the French privileged a particular episode in New Orleans history and a particular racial and cultural group. New Orleans's tourist literature exalted European and particularly French culture as the most predominant and influential culture in New Orleans's history, despite the tremendous presence and influence of Africans and Native Americans throughout the colonial period.[37]

The tourism industry's homage to the French and Spanish extended to those nations' purported benevolence toward enslaved Africans, illustrated by the widespread claim that in New Orleans "the Creole attitude to slavery was somewhat more humane than that of the Americans."[38] In the rare instances when they addressed slavery at all, tour guides and tourism marketing literature focused almost exclusively on it during the colonial period, emphasizing a supposed unique and favored position of New Orleans slaves who were protected by the Code Noir, were given Sundays off to congregate in Congo Square, and were allowed to purchase their own freedom. One website's assessment is typical: "There were . . . important differences between Louisiana and other slave-driven Southern states. Here slavery was more in the West Indian mould [sic] than the Anglo-American. The Black Code of Louisiana, established by the French, upheld by the Spanish and then effectively broken by the Americans, gave slaves rights unparalleled elsewhere, including permission to marry, meet socially and take Sundays off. The black population of New Orleans in particular was renowned as [being] exceptionally literate and cosmopolitan."[39] Although neither website condones slavery, they both clearly distinguish, and to some extent privilege, Louisiana slavery in the colonial period as an act of European beneficence, an idea refuted in recent historiography. The historian Thomas Ingersoll argues: "The principal intent of the Black Code of 1724 . . . was evident in the many measures aimed at ensuring the subjugation of all blacks and separating the races so as to limit the numbers of mixed-race and free black people."[40] Even Ingersoll's detractors, who argue for distinctions between the British and French or Spanish systems of slavery, generally attribute gains made by Africans and their descendants primarily to their own agency, aptitude, and creativity, not to their enslavers' compassion or generosity.[41] Despite historical evidence to the contrary, colonial New Orleans emerges in the pre-Katrina tourism narrative as a city whose attitudes about race and treatment of its residents of African descent—in both historical and contemporary representations—were exceptionally benign.

And if New Orleans's tourism narrative diminished the brutality and degradation of slavery under the French and Spanish, it completely erased the more rigid system of slavery that evolved in the nineteenth century, marked by a more tenuous position for the city's free people of color and the near impossibility for bondsmen and -women to purchase their own freedom.[42] Although the emphasis on New Orleans's European or French heritage highlighted the city's distinctiveness, an emphasis on the antebellum period in the tourist literature blurred those distinctions by situating New Orleans in the clichéd and romantic version of the antebellum South. The old South was invoked countless times in descriptions of contemporary New Orleans. For instance, an NOMCVB web page entices "history buffs" to visit Victorian mansions and museums to "[catch] a glimpse of life the way it used to be in the Old South and other locales of yesteryear."[43] The tourism narrative that emerged from this literature invited tourists to experience firsthand the old South, although this experience rarely incorporated the experiences of those bondsmen, -women, and children who supported the mansions and sustained, through great sacrifice and hardship, the fabled "locales of yesteryear."

Most websites and tourist brochures advertised or featured nearby plantations and plantation tours and represented them as authentic re-creations of New Orleans's antebellum past.[44] With few exceptions, however, this authenticity was reserved solely for decorative and architectural artifacts of the antebellum South that "are beautifully maintained today."[45] Advertisements and descriptions of the plantations and tours incorporated language that almost literally reconstructs an antebellum mythology. "Grand winding staircase, original slave cabins, magnificent oaks," "tours by guides in [a]ntebellum dress," "Belter & Mallard furnishings, five hand-painted ceilings, faux marbling and wood graining," and "elaborate wrought iron trimmed galleries, ornate friezes and medallions" conjure up hackneyed notions of "romance, history, and beauty" associated with the "grandeur and elegance of 19th century southern living" (see figure 2.3).[46] Although River Road and many of its plantations are listed in the National Register of Historic Places, very few of the plantation tours interrogated the history that the sites represent—namely, the slavery that enabled the wealth and accompanying lifestyles that the plantation tours celebrate. Viator's Thingstodo-NewOrleans.com concurs:

> The stories of plantation slave society get short shrift. Instead, the emphasis is on the glory of days past, when black men and women of bondage labored at the behest of white masters. Save for the ascendant, but struggling, African American Museum at the Tezcuco Plantation and the Laura Plantation tours, you will get a feel for what life was like for the master and missus, but rarely will you catch a glimpse

of life out the back of the big house, where slaves made the bricks, raised the roofs, tended the fires and worked the fields. Instead, expect costumed guides leading interior tours of 45 to 60 minutes, which focus on the lovely architecture, ornate gardens and genteel lifestyle of antebellum Louisiana.[47]

Even when slave dwellings remained on these properties, they formed part of the backdrop to the romanticized southern mystique, thereby enhancing, not countering, the mythology of a glorious southern past.[48] Many of these plantation houses and their outbuildings, including the slave cabins, had been renovated into bed-and-breakfasts, exploiting the performative possibilities of a white antebellum southern mythology. Examples include Oak Alley Plantation Restaurant and Inn and Nottoway Plantation Restaurant and Inn, which advertised its site as a place to "enjoy elegant accommodations overlooking the Mississippi River or the charming surroundings of the overseer's cottage."[49] Similarly, the 1990 GNOTCC document "What Makes New Orleans Special?" invited tourists to "experience the grace and elegance of another time, the wealth of white-pillared society, the glory of the Old South in antebellum days, by touring or even staying in some of Louisiana's plantation homes."[50] The southern past was reduced to a checklist of objects and images—period furnishings, oak and fruit trees, Greek Revival or Italianate architecture, slave quarters—that provided ideal settings for filmic and literary portrayals of the antebellum South.[51] Implicit in the invitation for visitors to "feel the gentle breeze of southern hospitality on a tour that takes you back to a time of mint juleps, gracious living and the glory of the Old South" is either the erasure of the South's slave past or an appropriation of that history to suit a more romantic, idyllic narrative of slavery.[52] In their study of plantation museums, Jennifer Eichstedt and Stephen Small refer to this distillation of images and ideas as "strategic rhetorics [that] are part of a racialized regime of representation that valorizes the white elite of the preemancipation South while generally erasing or minimizing the experiences of enslaved African Americans."[53] What resulted from this racialized regime of representation was a rewriting of the historical narrative that negated the violence, exploitation, and deprivation of slavery and the accompanying culpability of whites. Such a history both validated the myth of a benevolent, paternal slave system promoted in nineteenth-century proslavery ideology and reproduced racial inequities in the contemporary moment.[54]

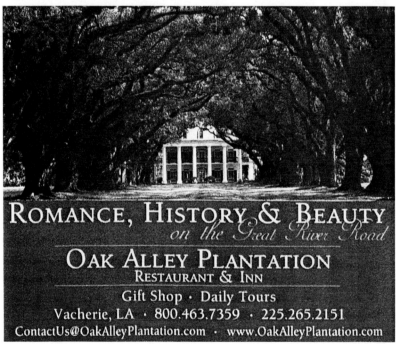

FIGURE 2.3 · Advertisements for River Road plantations in
New Orleans Official Visitors Guide (2002–3).

This rewriting of slavery was not limited to outlying plantation tours. New Orleans Online included a web page on historic homes within the city limits of New Orleans. By visiting selected "architectural treasures"—mansions and "palatial antebellum residences"—the page invites visitors to "step into the past" and "learn about the culture and history of the city's colorful and hospitable past."[55] Although descriptions of these historic homes did not allude to the city's slave history (yet another erasure of that history), the romanticization of slavery for local and tourist consumption abounded in the city. Tour guides, hotels, realtors, and restaurants marketed former slave quarters as chic, quaint, and picturesque, illustrating how the history of slavery was removed from its historical context in New Orleans's tourism industry in the post–civil rights era. Consequently, these venues offered potential visitors and buyers the "sheer romance," and the opportunity to "go native" that coincided with being entertained, fed, or housed in "quite attractive" or "liberated, languorous cottages" that once housed the city's enslaved black population.[56] In these topsy-turvy appropriations of slavery, the remnants of New Orleans's slave system were beautified and decontextualized, so much so that one travel writer tersely invokes a luxury hotel's slave history with her comment, "Tennessee Williams, a slave to cottage Number 9, stayed here often."[57] These descriptions imaginatively wrested slavery away from its historical and ideological contexts and repackaged it for tourist consumption; visitors to the city—for a price—were able to reap the material and psychological rewards of others' labor. Beyond these imaginative reenactments of slavery, several French Quarter restaurants and hotels literally bore the mark of the city's slave past (see figure 2.4).[58] The façade of the upscale Omni Royal Orleans Hotel still carries the ironic inscription "change," the remaining letters from the word "exchange" that denoted its use as an auction house for the sale of property, including slaves (see figure 2.5).[59]

Along with the promotion of former slave quarters, the sale, display, and dispersal of an array of images of slavery and reproductions of artifacts created a disturbing tourist landscape, as the New Orleans writer and future Louisiana poet laureate Brenda Marie Osbey wrote in 1987 in a scathing critique: "In an effort to sell New Orleans as a Southern paradise, scenes of plantation life in which Blacks are depicted as happy slaves, as well as miniature porcelains and life-sized stuffed dolls of nigger mammies and grinning sambos, depictions of Black children and mindless pickaninnies, and post cards, prints and posters representing Black men and women as shiftless and happy-go-lucky, can still be found in windows along Canal or

FIGURE 2.4 • Plaque
on the outside wall
of the Original Pierre
Maspero's Restaurant
in the French Quarter.
Photograph by author.

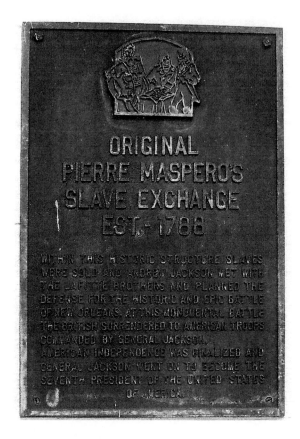

ORIGINAL
PIERRE MASPERO'S
SLAVE EXCHANGE
EST. - 1788

WITHIN THIS HISTORIC STRUCTURE SLAVES
WERE SOLD AND ANDREW JACKSON MET WITH
THE LAFITTE BROTHERS AND PLANNED THE
DEFENSE FOR THE HISTORIC AND EPIC BATTLE
OF NEW ORLEANS. AT THIS MONUMENTAL BATTLE
THE BRITISH SURRENDERED TO AMERICAN TROOPS
COMMANDED BY GENERAL JACKSON.
AMERICAN INDEPENDENCE WAS FINALIZED AND
GENERAL JACKSON WENT ON TO BECOME THE
SEVENTH PRESIDENT OF THE UNITED STATES
OF AMERICA.

Royal Streets today."[60] The racist iconography that Osbey describes had its roots in late nineteenth-century mass consumer culture, when the circulation of derogatory racial images in advertising, souvenirs, and other mass-produced consumer goods helped to reduce postbellum sectional differences, naturalize and nationalize white supremacist ideologies, and quell southern whites' anxieties about African American challenges to the racial hierarchy. This "symbolic slavery" was employed to avert the perceived social and political disaster posed by black emancipation and economic independence even as it relied on northern and southern whites' desire for the life of leisure proffered by the mythology of the old South.[61] The proliferation of slavery memorabilia in late twentieth-century tourist New Orleans reflected a renewed discomfort with African Americans whose numerical majority, political influence, and perceived criminality threatened the city's elite white power structure. Tracing the resurgence of racial branding

FIGURE 2.5 · Façade of Omni Royal Orleans Hotel, previously known as the City Exchange and St. Louis Hotel, a popular site of slave auctions in the nineteenth century. Photograph by author.

among national fast food chains, the historian Anthony Stanonis concludes: "Such a longing for a return to happy darkies reflected a white society weary of the social changes brought by the civil rights movement."[62] On the eve of Katrina and in the years after the hurricane, these images continued to appear on everything from store signs to souvenirs, perpetuating an idea of the antebellum South that caricatured and trivialized black contributions to and contests over southern history.

Despite the omnipresence of these markers of slavery, the tourism narrative generally failed to include a discussion of those who were enslaved. Even when antebellum slavery was discussed, tourism narratives focused primarily on New Orleans's wealth and prosperity during the nineteenth century, not on the human cost of this wealth.[63] Usually, however, antebellum slavery was not discussed, despite the wealth of firsthand accounts of the slave system in nineteenth-century New Orleans. The city was, after all, the leading North American slave-trading city by the 1850s, with numerous slave auction houses and regular auctions.[64] During their tour of North America, Alexis de Tocqueville and his compatriot, Gustave de Beaumont, observed that slavery in Louisiana was "as ruthless in the remnants of French Louisiana as in the Anglo-American South," and numerous nineteenth-century slave narratives record the harrowing experiences that bondsmen and -women faced in New Orleans's slave market.[65] The tourism narrative's exclusion of these accounts to promote New Orleans's racial exceptionalism further perpetuated an idea of a city that was devoid of any real black presence or significance.

This omission was compounded by the fact that the tourism narrative did not pay any sustained attention to the historical period following the Civil War and continuing through the post–civil rights era, the period when most African Americans obtained their freedom and made more concerted efforts to demand and exercise their civil rights.[66] The dismissal of this history shaped tourism accounts of New Orleans's more recent past. On the rare occasions when recent history was presented to tourists, it was a history that did little to challenge the mythology of New Orleans's racial, cultural, and social harmony. For instance, NewOrleans.com explains that New Orleans's 1960 school desegregation "was not marked by the racial strife found in other Southern cities."[67] Of course, this rather innocuous account ignores the years of struggle preceding and following six-year-old Ruby Bridges's heartrending walk through menacing white protestors to desegregate New Orleans's public schools.[68] Because so much effort went into sustaining New Orleans's image as a historic city—including reverence toward the city's colonial past, careful preservation efforts, and attention to genealogies and historical figures—the history of New Orleans presented in tours and tourist literature gained an air of credibility and comprehensiveness that it did not always deserve, particularly as it related to the city's multiracial and multicultural heritage.

Multicultural New Orleans

Ironically, even as tourism promoters continued to distort New Orleans's black history, a confluence of economic factors and societal trends effected important changes in the city's tourist image. By the late 1980s, the waning economic impact of the port and the dispersion of the oil and gas industries prompted a more systematic, comprehensive plan to market the city to discretionary travelers and capitalize on the growth of cultural tourism.[69] The city's adoption of cultural tourism was epitomized by the 1988 symposium "Selling the City . . . without Selling Out: The Challenge of Tourism Management," sponsored by Tulane University, the University of New Orleans, the Preservation Resource Center, the Bureau of Governmental Research, and the GNOTCC. Richard Roddewig's keynote address, "What *Is* Cultural Tourism?," defined the new trend of cultural or heritage tourism as "experiencing a way of life" through distinctive locales and historic sites. Roddewig encouraged city and state officials to cultivate relationships among tourism, historic preservation, and the arts to create a product "so unique and inviting that it will attract visitors on its own."[70] Two immediate responses were a public television production that aired on WLAE in 1988 to discuss ways the city's image could be promoted without jeopardizing the authenticity of its culture and heritage and the creation of the New Orleans Joint Center for Tourism in 1989, to develop cultural tourism. By 1992 mayor Marc Morial—son of the city's first African American mayor, Ernest "Dutch" Morial—had commissioned a study to explore a partnership between the Arts Council of New Orleans and the New Orleans Tourism Marketing Corporation that culminated in the formation of the Arts Tourism Partnership in 1995.[71] Over the long term, these initial efforts to attract visitors seeking authentic experiences in regional history and architecture would be reflected in the mainstream tourist image, as tourism promoters came to recognize that "cultural diversity and heritage are the city's tourism equity."[72] In many instances, this new recognition changed the appearance and rhetoric of New Orleans's tourist image. A "blended" television commercial incorporated African Americans because, as one tourism promoter affirmed, "it truly represents our city's cultural and racial gumbo."[73] Likewise, brochures, websites, and other promotional materials reflected African Americans' insistent demands for inclusion, the changing expectations of tourists, and the burgeoning cultural and heritage tourism industries.[74]

With the rise of multicultural tours, the city's tourism industry provided competing narratives that acknowledged New Orleans's multiracial heritage and the contributions of black people to the city. By the 1990s, New Orleans's predominant tourism narrative increasingly reflected the changing racial discourse of the post–civil rights era, which coincided with the burgeoning of cultural or heritage tourism. New Orleans tourism promoters responded to the emerging trends by adopting new ways of romanticizing a racially innocent past with allusions to the diversity and harmony that allegedly distinguished New Orleans culture. Despite the seeming embrace of different cultural, linguistic, and social influences, this updated narrative

LIBRARY, UNIVERSITY OF CHESTER

generally reinforced the racial ambivalence and anxiety of the mainstream narrative or remained ephemeral or marginal to the city's tourist image. The city's multicultural tourism narrative was cloaked in the conventions of a problematic cultural assimilationism that ultimately promoted a clichéd, trivialized understanding of race. In other words, the language may have changed, but the mythologies of black desire and disaster remained the same. In many ways the message of multicultural New Orleans was often as conservative and regressive as the more racially exclusive representations of the city.[75]

The New Orleans melting pot—or, more accurately, "gumbo" pot— motif demonstrates the limitations of the multicultural narrative. The success of New Orleans's culinary assimilation of foods from around the world was used to symbolize an equally successful and satisfying racial and cultural assimilation in the city. In the past two decades, this trope proliferated in the tourism literature. New Orleans Online refers to the city's ethnic communities as a "melting pot, filled with many different cultures"; another website describes a "'gumbo' of ethnic cultures" eliciting "an admiration for all that is truly exotic"; the New Orleans Official Visitors Guide characterizes the people of New Orleans "as diverse and unique as the ingredients in gumbo"; and the website of the New Orleans Multicultural Tourism Network (NOMTN) describes New Orleans as "a gumbo of cultures that blend together, yet maintain their own unique flavor."[76] In fairness, it is likely that the gumbo pot rhetoric originated as a direct challenge to previously dominant tourism narratives that ignored or distorted the contributions of non-Europeans. NOMTN has been explicit in making this challenge. The "Welcome" in The Soul of New Orleans, explains to visitors: "To simply say that we are America's most European city does not begin to explain the vast and ever-present influences of so many cultures, so many people. More than a European city, we are a world city. Here, more than anywhere, we are a delicious gumbo of cultures blended together, with each ingredient retaining its own identity. Come taste our flavor."[77] Most mainstream tourism promoters were not nearly as explicit in their rebuke of the traditional tourism narrative. Their use of terms such as melting pot, diversity, and multicultural rarely correlated with progressive agendas of social change. Instead, these terms often intimated an image of social transformation, particularly in reference to racial equality, that was not substantiated by the realities of New Orleans's historical and contemporary experiences. What resulted was yet another mythology of New Orleans's racial history, perhaps more palatable than the one portrayed by the plantation and slave cabin stories, but equally as inaccurate. In this construction of the city, New Orleans is (and has always been) a place of racial harmony.

Notably, having benefited from the post–civil rights racial and political climate, the city's African American leadership joined white tourism promoters in advancing this notion of unity that transcends racial, class, religious, and other divisions. One example is former mayor Marc Morial's introduction to the 2000 *New Orleans Official Visitors Guide*. Morial boasts: "Proud of our heritage, we have combined the influences of our European, African, Caribbean and, of course, American forefathers into how we live, what we eat and how we celebrate."[78] His African American successor as mayor, Ray Nagin, took this idea even further in his welcome letter for the official multicultural visitor guide, *The Soul of New Orleans*. He invokes the customary "cultural gumbo" and proffers the city's diversity as a commodity "within easy reach of visitors and locals alike." Most tellingly, Nagin attributes the origin of jazz to the "waves of immigration from Africa, Europe, the Caribbean, Latin America and Asia." In an effort to portray present-day New Orleanians as equal participants in the city's culture, his assessment muddles the history of jazz, whose creation is generally attributed to the united efforts of classically trained and formerly enslaved Afro-Creoles and African Americans, and obscures the history of slavery, which evidently was New Orleans's main source of "immigration from Africa."[79] Like the new multicultural history that was being developed contemporaneously at Colonial Williamsburg, New Orleans multicultural tourism told "a story of ethnic assimilation, a story in which both African and European Americans can be treated equally. . . . [I]t does what American discourse almost always does: it minimizes a critique of social class [and, I would add, racial inequality] in favor of a celebration of individual success."[80]

Other tourism websites likewise portrayed historical and contemporary New Orleans through the lens of a noncontentious multiculturalism that cultivated racial desire and ignored systemic obstacles to racial parity. NewOrleans.com's "History of New Orleans" describes the contemporary New Orleans as "a racially mixed city, with people of different backgrounds sharing many wonderful neighborhoods."[81] Another web page gushes: "They say it's a forever kind of a place. They say that the hundreds of years of mixing cultures, cuisines and international traditions has brought forth a smooth mixture of mysticism, style and an uncommon grace."[82] Gateway New Orleans shares in the romance: "Louisiana is blessed with a unique array of cultures not many states in America share. These diverse cultures complement one another, which makes Louisiana one-of-a-kind. We take great pride in Louisiana's diversity and enjoy sharing our culture with friends and neighbors all over the globe."[83] On New Orleans a la Net, Pamela Pipes takes the idea of multicultural New Orleans to its natural conclusion: "Once upon a time in 1718, in the new Louisiana Territory, a Creole Princess was born on the banks of the mighty Mississippi River. The small foundling on the waterfront was nurtured through many years of rich and diverse heritage, when Choctaw and Chickasaw settlements prevailed, swaggering pirates assailed her shores, Spaniards introduced flamboyant architectural splendors, and voodoo thrived as a religion. Then, in 1763 she warmly welcomed a group of French exiles from Canada, those charismatic Cajuns who blessed her with soul-stirring, foot-stomping music and intoxicating cuisine."[84]

This gumbo pot "history" diminished the reality of white privilege and the continuing legacy of racism in New Orleans and downplayed the potential and actual racial, cultural, gender, and economic conflict, divisions, and contests over power that have characterized New Orleans from its inception. Just as de Crèvecoeur's "melting pot" referred to the amalgamation of many nations into one American identity, the New Orleans gumbo pot motif suggested that all people—regardless of their national, racial, social, or cultural background—forge a new Creole identity once they become New Orleanians.[85] However, just as the image of the melting pot has been criticized for its underlying assumption that a new American race was in fact a Western identity available only to European immigrants, the gumbo pot's Creole identity often excluded the city's people of color and solidified the barriers a Creole identity was supposed to break down.

The term *Creole* has had a circuitous and contentious evolution. Contemporary historians acknowledge that its meaning has shifted over time and in relation to different political, historical, and economic developments. Throughout Louisiana's history, the word has been appropriated by different groups, at different times, and for different purposes to describe, variously, all native-born inhabitants of the early colony, irrespective of race; only those native-born colonists and their descendants who were of French or Spanish heritage; only white descendants of early colonists; native-born colonists and descendants of interracial unions among

French, Spanish, African, and American Indian settlers; and numerous combinations thereof.[86] As Gotham has argued, the racialization of *Creole* overlapped with the development of modern tourism in New Orleans. He explains: "As the social content of 'creole' became conflated with white culture, tourism boosters and advertisers attached a variety of pleasurable experiences to the category as a means of exciting consumer demand to travel to the city."[87] In the years preceding Hurricane Katrina, *Creole* was in fact being used to further entrench racial boundaries. Gateway New Orleans limits the term to "French-speaking white descendants of early French or Spanish settlers" or "less commonly" to "mulattoes speaking a creolized version of French and Spanish," based on an outdated bibliography lacking any of the African American studies scholarship that has substantially revised many of these exclusionary narratives.[88] The continued reliance on these outdated definitions of *Creole* perpetuated the racial exoticizing of the city for contemporary visitors. Although different racial and cultural groups claimed throughout the twentieth century that they alone were Creole, definitions of the term advanced in the tourist literature continued to leave little room for Afro-Creoles, whether poor or enslaved, or even for the much-touted free people of color. Instead, tourist literature often used the term to distinguish "the ingrown, aristocratic" (white) Catholic French colonists from the (white) Protestant Anglo-Saxons, whose "industry and drive" made them ultimately more successful, if less interesting, inhabitants of the city in the years following the Louisiana Purchase.[89]

Increasingly, however, by the 1990s many tours, succumbing to pressure to be more inclusive, began to sidestep criticisms leveled against the dominant narrative by supplanting a more racially exclusionary depiction of *Creole* with one that was entirely stripped of its racial, cultural, and historical meanings. Even on SoulofAmerica.com, a national black travel website, the term refers to "a city resident who claims to be of French descent and speaks French," which would eliminate many New Orleanians who consider themselves Creole. Today, according to the site, the designation includes "practically all residents who enjoy life and cooking and music of New Orleans. They truly believe in the art of sophisticated living, no matter how short their average life span."[90] Similarly, NOMCVB's website defines the term as a "temperament" found in the city's "food, its music, its French Quarter." "No longer . . . a specific race or breed," the website continues, "[Creole] defines that rather special New Orleans attitude toward life—*joie de vivre, laissez-faire, bon appetit*! In this sense, spiritually, all New Orleanians are

Creoles, *mes amis*."[91] Pipes likewise identifies the Creole spirit as "a fondness for having fun; a reverence for the aesthetic; a veneration of things vintage and traditional; a proclivity toward hospitality; and an unflappable attitude native to locals that most have to work furiously to attain."[92] GumboPages. com offers Creole as an empty signifier, meaning all that "is native to New Orleans. Whether it's Creole tomatoes, Creole cuisine, or a Creole debutante, they're all New Orleans."[93] Another page by Pipes attempts to avoid controversy by blurring and equating all categories: "Black Heritage . . . African Heritage . . . Greek . . . Caribbean . . . or Latin Heritage . . . the Swamp . . . the Gumbo . . . the Plantations . . . the Crawfish . . . even the Creole Tomato. Laissez Les Bon Temps Rouler, ya'll!"[94] These attempts to neatly obliterate the contests over meaning and power conceal the serious political, economic, and social connotations of the term.

Even when websites such as GumboPages.com acknowledge contests over the "much misunderstood term [Creole]" and identify "slaves, free persons of color, and whites" following the Louisiana Purchase as Creole, in the end they propose a stereotypical, oversimplified portrait of the city's Afro-Creole community. On GumboPages.com, free people of color are wholly portrayed as lighter-complexioned than enslaved black men and women and as using their Creole identity "to distinguish themselves from the (normally) 100% 'colored' folks now moving into the area [following the Civil War]."[95] This usage of the term sets up an impossible stratification of society and continues to mandate the purity of race as a legitimate means of classification. The myth of "100% 'colored' folks" who can be so easily and categorically distinguished from lighter-skinned Creoles is created only by ignoring a history of both inter- and intraracial unions; shared language and culture; familial and social bonds; economic, educational, and professional diversity; and a range of phenotypes among the free and enslaved black populations.

Until recently, New Orleans historians have offered a startlingly similar portrayal of the city's Afro-Creole population as a separate racial group, the members of which—because of their economic and political wherewithal—distanced themselves physically and philosophically from freed and enslaved African Americans.[96] The New Orleans writer and historian Grace King's 1895 history of New Orleans illustrates the longevity of this portrayal: "The *gens de couleur*, coloured people, were a class apart, separated from and superior to the negroes, ennobled, were it by only one drop of white blood in their veins. The caste seems to have existed from the first introduction of slaves. To the whites, all Africans who were not of pure blood were *gens de couleur*. Among themselves, however, there were jealous and fiercely guarded distinctions; mulattoes, quadroons, octoroons, griffes, each term meaning one more generation's elevation, one degree's further transfiguration in the standard of racial perfection; white blood."[97] This view, reproduced and popularized in literary and historical accounts of the city, is indicative of the problematic uses and portrayal of *Creole*, which has been used both as a metaphor for New Orleans's all-inclusive society and as a way to signify divisions and racial exclusions.[98]

In the past few decades, many historians have attempted to document the shifting meanings of *Creole* and to challenge the popular views of the term by emphasizing the in-group diversity and complexity of Creole society and the interclass and intercolor unions within New Orleans's free and enslaved Afro-Creole populations. The historian Jerah Johnson summarizes the recent proliferation of scholarship on Afro-Creoles in Louisiana:

> Acutely conscious of their legal rights and their group's interests as well as the tenuous and fragile nature of their position, [free Creoles of color] tended to act with an exceptionally high degree of cohesiveness. At the same time, individual members of the group freely associated with the European colonials, the African slaves, and the Indians, both free and slave. Work, service, trade, and *plaçage*, the developing institution of formalized mistress-keeping, brought them into close contact with the European community, while close cultural and family bonds tied them to both slave and Indian communities. Except for recently arrived islanders, there were few free people of color who did not have relatives, often immediate family members, among the African slaves and not infrequently among the Indians.[99]

However, in post–civil rights New Orleans, tours and tourist brochures adopted the conventions of the more entrenched literary and historical representations of African American and Afro-Creole New Orleans with their clichéd, oversimplified racial image of the city. In the end, the more recent multicultural strain of the city's tourism narrative promoted a vision that limited and distorted the actual black presence and experience in New Orleans. This vision cultivated a desire for a mythical southern past that depended on the faithful participation and performance of black New Orleanians in the perpetuation of racial and economic inequality. The tourism construction of black desire would ultimately set the stage for the post-Katrina portrayal of black disaster that prevailed in the aftermath of the storm. As I show in the following chapters, even tours devoted exclusively to multiculturalism and African American heritage had difficulty presenting an alternative to this predominant narrative.

Three. "Urbane, Educated, and Well-To-Do Free Blacks"

THE CHALLENGE OF A CREOLE WORLD IN LE MONDE CRÉOLE

FRENCH QUARTER COURTYARDS TOUR

What I like to show is basically the intersection between European and African cultures coming together in New Orleans. So it's not typically an African American tour. It's not typically a Caucasian, or white, or European tour. But this is what I think New Orleans is. It's the intersection between the two groups coming together—the good and bad aspects of it. Regardless, what we live in today is the legacy of this, and that is what we try to show. —*William Coble, interview*

The Real Story

As I sat across from Paul Nevski on a spring morning in 2002, I listened intently to his fervent advocacy of Le Monde Créole French Quarter Courtyards Tour that he had researched and scripted.[1] Captivated as much by his French accent as by his unapologetic dismissal of mainstream tours' "foolish nostalgia" and myths about "the grandeur of the South," I was primed for "the real story" that Nevski claimed distinguished the tours offered by Le Monde Créole (LMC) from other New Orleans tours. According to Nevski, since its founding five years earlier, LMC had illuminated New Orleans's past by connecting tourists to "places where people live," instead of "the monuments, the churches, the cathedrals" associated with traditional tourism narratives. In contrast, Nevski contended that by focusing on one family's history to provide an overview of colonial and antebellum Louisiana's history, culture, and society, LMC provided tourists with "a better, deeper, more authentic understanding of how life was here in New Orleans [by] using history as a tool to understand the present. And maybe to improve the present and the future for ourselves and our children." Though Nevski is a white European, his vision for the future called for a more pluralistic construction of the past, one in which he "talk[s] about the whole family, not only the white side of the family."[2] Of course, to talk about "the whole family" is to conjure up New Orleans's complex racial history, the institution of slavery, and sex across the color line. How these phenomena were portrayed had profound implications for the type of Creole world LMC created for New Orleans tourists in the years before Hurricane Katrina.

Nevski's characterization of the tour as markedly different from, and more authentic and more inclusive than, most other New Orleans tours was reiterated by LMC staff who consistently aligned the tour with the objectives of black heritage or multicultural tourism—namely, to incorporate African American and other neglected histories in a way that serves as a corrective to mainstream portrayals of history. For example, LMC's co-operator and tour guide Bill Coble stated that the tour's primary objective "is to show [tourists] the value, the contributions that African Americans have made in this city. It has been so long overlooked."[3] Jay, one of LMC's African American tour guides, concurred: "I guess it boils down to, you can't tell a story about New Orleans or this story without injecting African Americans into it. It's no place in the city you can't talk about African Americans and show what they have done. In everything you see—the iron work, anything you point out—I'm accomplishing that objective. The houses were built, the architect[ure], the furnishings, all done by African Americans."[4] Nevski added: "To be very blunt, I have a sense of justice. This city was built by people of African descent. That's a fact. It seems fair that you talk about the one[s] who built the city. When you look at the architecture, the way we eat, the way we live, it has a lot of similarities with West Africa. France in one way, Spain, but . . . West Africa. And I'm always shocked when I hear 'the French period, the Spanish period.' . . . Beyond all this there was [*sic*] a lot of people of African descent. And I think it's only fair to just talk about everyone that was involved. That's what I believe."[5]

These beliefs shaped LMC and made the walking tour a compelling case study to use in examining the multicultural framing of New Orleans tourism in the post–civil rights era that would shape the debates over New Orleans's destruction and recovery following Hurricane Katrina. Founded in 1997, a year after the creation of the multicultural branch of the Louisiana Office of Tourism and two years after the Republican Party regained the majority of both houses of the U.S. Congress for the first time in forty years and began implementing its conservative Contract with America, LMC epitomizes the incongruences of multicultural tourism in the post–civil rights era.[6] Such tourism capitulates to and capitalizes on demands for more authentic and inclusive versions of history. Yet, despite offering revisions inspired by the post–civil rights era to New Orleans's tourism narrative with the incorporation of African American images and stories, multicultural tourism obscures black New Orleans in both new and old ways.

Through my interviews and interactions with tour owners and operators, guides, other staff members, and visitors, analyses of LMC's newsletters, brochures, advertisements, and website; and ethnographic work on the tour from 2000 to 2004, it became clear to me that LMC self-consciously distinguished itself from other mainstream New Orleans tours in its inclusion of black characters and black history in the promotion of the tour and the presentation of its story lines. LMC centers on five generations of the Duparc-Locoul family and their New Orleans lifestyle, based on the 1936 memoirs of Laura Locoul.[7] Portrayed as the enlightened, racially moderate protagonist of the tour, this daughter of wealthy white Creole slave owners provides the impetus for LMC's historical narrative. The tour deviates from many mainstream New Orleans tours by explicitly discussing slavery; clearly defining Creole as non-Anglo, with West African, West European, and Native American cultural influences; acknowledging the contributions of free people of color to New Orleans; and highlighting the African branches of one family tree. These deviations from the dominant tourism narrative suggest that LMC's staff was sincerely trying to remedy past injustices by affirming the African presence and participation in the city's development. Nevertheless, the dominant tourism narrative's mythologies of New Orleans racial exceptionalism, relatively benign system of slavery, and unequivocal sanctioning of slavery and segregation by free people of color resurfaced in LMC's tours even as the company's owners and staff resisted or saw themselves as resisting clichéd depictions of the city's racial history. The disjuncture between LMC's stated and implied objectives and its actual product exemplifies the tension between the desire for black cultural inclusion and validation and the perceived disaster of black political agitation, resistance, and economic dependence. Ultimately, LMC's post–civil rights pluralist vision included black people but erased any challenges to, contradictions within, or contests over American history and identity that black people's experiences have so often illuminated.

LMC's pluralist vision has been influenced either directly or indirectly by the tour at Laura Plantation, located on the historic River Road, in Vacherie, Louisiana, about fifty miles upriver from New Orleans. Before founding LMC, Nevski was employed for four years as a tour director and chief interpreter at Laura Plantation, which is also based, in part, on Locoul's 1936 memoirs and makes similar claims of distinction for its attention to slavery and more inclusive approach to Louisiana history.[8] Both tours denounce the *Gone with the Wind* mythology that most area plantations profit from, and both purport to offer visitors a glimpse of a different world—the Creole world. While conducting research at Laura Plantation, Nevski learned about the family's French Quarter residences. He told me: "We realized—which was very common—in this family there was a European branch and an African branch. But, of course, this subject was a little taboo. I mean, I don't know any other company really [that would] talk about issues like slavery, you know like slaves [being] related to their masters most of the time. They were. It was one big family even though there was a lot of denial." With this revelation, Nevski said he became interested in "exploring the relations between the races here in New Orleans before, during, and after the Civil War." He said he "felt good about" Laura Plantation, where tours were not limited to descriptions of "an armchair and a mint julep."[9]

Nevski also talked about being influenced by African American visitors and workers at Laura Plantation. For instance, he noted that some African American visitors expressed discomfort about going to the plantation's slave quarters. Nevski responded empathetically: "I could not share that, being a white person from France, but I could certainly . . . understand and appreciate that those people would share their reluctance. So there were a lot of things that I was very unaware [of]." He gave an example of the depth of his unfamiliarity with U.S. racism when he referred to another Laura Plantation employee, a retired African American woman schoolteacher, who would not look him in the eyes when speaking to him. Nevski said that when he questioned her about it, she explained to him that "here in St. James Parish, 'til the seventies, you know, a person like me couldn't look a white person in the eyes." Nevski linked his naiveté to his French identity: "To tell the truth, I never heard of that before. I mean, coming from France where race was not such a big issue . . . like here with segregation and everything."[10] Inherent in Nevski's self-appointed status as a naive and innocent outsider is the premise that he is separated both physically and ideologically from a U.S. tradition of racism and therefore uniquely qualified to be an objective truth teller.

Consequently, Nevski crafted the LMC story lines to reflect this outsider perspective, unsullied by personal knowledge of or complicity in Louisiana's, or even American, slavery. Nevski, through LMC, established himself as the bridge between unenlightened white visitors and local black history. This logic presumes that white visitors—like Nevski, who was "unaware" of racial inequalities in the South but was able to empathize and change once he was educated—will be able to change once they are given the more complete and unbiased story that Nevski crafted into LMC's tours. It also presumes that knowledge alone—without necessarily questioning one's own racial privilege or reforming one's racist behaviors—is adequate for transformation.[11]

Similarly, Coble used his experiences to transform white visitors. He told me: "I grew up in the American South. I grew up in Mississippi. It was very Southern Baptist, very segregated, and I learned these things very slowly because when—and I love my family dearly, but when the general idea is, ever since you're a small child that you're taught 'these people are different; they're this, they're that.' So, what do you know better when you're a small child? This is what you're taught. And slowly I learned. And then I've learned, hopefully, as an adult to start to pass this information on." With his racial and social background, Coble claimed to be uniquely qualified to mediate the story of black New Orleans for LMC's primarily white audience: "Now, as a white man I will always give this story from a white perspective. There's really no way I can do that any other way. So, what I try to show—because we do have a large Caucasian population coming into New Orleans to take these tours—is . . . to show them what took place and how it blended together and how we're enriched by all this."[12] With Nevski poised as an outsider whose judgment is unclouded by racism and Coble poised as an insider whose intimate knowledge of and triumph over racism—complemented by the racial, regional, gender, and sexual diversity of the staff—LMC claimed to be especially qualified to present a postracial perspective on New Orleans's racial history.

Not surprisingly, the tour's attempt to revise the city's racial history met with some resistance. Nevski reflected on some of the possible reasons:

Race is not something that's easy to talk about, especially here in the United States, especially in the South. I found some reluctance from white people who don't even want to hear about black history. That happened. When they come to New Orleans, what do they want to see? They want to hear about the "good old days" and Miss Scarlett– *Gone with the Wind* type of story. Yes. At the same time, in the black community we found some reluctance because we talk about the free people of color . . . you know, they owned slaves. And this is something some black people are not comfortable with. For these reasons, what we talk about is not always welcome.[13]

Coble also talked about visitors who were insensitive to LMC's subject matter. He gave one example of the difficulty of conveying slavery to contemporary visitors:

One of the hardest stories I have to tell is about Laura's grandmother Elizabeth buying thirty female slaves for the sole purpose of making them a breeding factory. There are a lot of times, especially with men [who], when I tell that story, get a big smile on their face. All they can see is the sexual aspect of it: "Ooh, I would like to have thirty female slaves." And this isn't what I'm trying to tell them. This is stuff that is difficult. If I can really pull them into that place to see what it's really like, they won't have a smile on their face.[14]

LMC's efforts were made even more difficult by what Coble saw as a particular mind-set unique to New Orleans visitors. He explained that "it's the clichés that Americans know about New Orleans." LMC visitors are vacationing in a city that they perceive "is conducive for parties, so they think even the stories they're going to get is [*sic*] big jokes, big ha ha ha's."[15] Coble's observation suggests that visitors to the city arrive with preconceptions that have already been overdetermined by New Orleans's highly racialized and sexualized popular image.

Faced with the challenge of combating such entrenched narratives, Nevski insisted he was undeterred. He said that the history he presents "is a reflection of what really was taking place. Period. Some people don't want to hear it. That's their problem."[16] Of course, Nevski's bravado was a bit disingenuous. He and the other LMC staff members—whose success depends on visitors—were rightfully concerned about the way visitors perceived the tour. Nevski and his staff were clear that one of LMC's primary goals is to make a profit. At the time of my field research, visitors were charged eighteen dollars each for the tour. Nevski estimated that three or four of those eighteen dollars went to the homes and museums that allowed LMC tours access to their courtyards. Although some homes and museums did not charge any money, Nevski had separate financial agreements with other proprietors, ranging from thirty cents to a dollar per visitor.[17] Nevski portrayed this business arrangement "as living proof that if you find a way to work with people . . . they can make money with you" and, in the process, help expand the business.[18]

Not everyone was pleased by Nevski's and Coble's business acumen. Nevski recalled a Frenchwoman who, years earlier, had taken his tour of Laura Plantation and its slave quarters. She accused him of profiting off others' enslavement. Nevski recalled that he told her: "I'm not saying that I feel good about showing some painful part of the history, but I think the more we show that, the less there's a chance that something like this might happen again. It's better to show something like this than just pretend it never happened. And yes, you're right, I'll probably make money showing slave quarters, but I'd rather do that than making money and just saying that everybody was happy here." Nevski compared his tours to tours of the concentration camps in Eastern Europe, arguing that such confrontation with the past, even if painful, is an important part of an individual's identity and a community's ability to make progress without repeating the mistakes of the past. Nevksi's beliefs were validated by the financial success of LMC's tours. On the day of our interview, the 10:00 A.M. tour had already sold out, prompting Nevski to remark, "All I see is that we're doing good." He expressed surprise at his success, which he claimed was unexpected "because this was not like a mainstream subject. We were talking about something that was not really . . . it's not like a [snaps fingers] haunted house, ghosts [themed tour]. It's not the easiest thing to talk about. You hurt a lot of feelings . . . memories, denial, you know."[19]

LMC staff members were especially aware of their tours' potential to hurt feelings, evoke negative memories, and force visitors to confront suppressed histories, which works against their goal to challenge mainstream narratives. By Nevski's own admission, LMC's tours were not focused solely on history. They relied on a script that he continually readjusted "to find the balance between education and entertainment." Coble attempted to strike this balance by gingerly and gradually contesting New Orleans's popular image. He explained: "What I'm trying to do is to give [tourists] some good information about the human condition of New Orleans, but since it's a hard subject matter, you've got to give it to them in small doses and easily. Now as far as teaching people . . . you have to be careful with Americans. You don't want to give them the idea that you're trying to teach them something. They're on vacation. There's a bit of entertainment blending in, and basically you sneak in a history lesson while you're entertaining these people."[20] Yet, as the historian Michael Wallace illustrates in his study of the Walt Disney Company's failed attempt in the 1990s to construct "Disney's America"—a theme park chronicling even the most sensitive episodes of American history—the blending of education and entertainment could be rife with contradictions "between critical history and the interests of a . . . corporation with a considerable vested interest in the status quo."[21] These contradictions were perhaps most clearly illustrated in LMC's tours by the dissonance between the type of subjects covered and the methods used to convey those subjects.

Robin—who had been with LMC for three years after spending four years at Laura Plantation, where he continued to work periodically—described his own method as tour guide:

> When Paul [Nevski] and Billy [Coble] hired me, what they were looking for was someone who was from theater, who was dramatic. We are doing the stories, the life of Laura Locoul and the family, in a theatrical manner. So that people would be interested in the stories, they were done almost like one-act plays. They were done like you are doing a story. You are a storyteller. So, you emphasize the dramatic side of the stories. It was important for us to get people to see what New Orleans was about for this family, and how it was typical of other Creole families—what they went through. We like to get them emotionally involved in the characters' lives, so that they feel something about them.[22]

In this way, Robin used his background in theater to promote the entertainment value of the tour.

The tension between education and entertainment was especially pronounced around issues of race. Coble admitted that he is particularly sensitive about attempting to educate visitors about black history. He stated:

> I think in general, especially with southerners . . . if you were to tell . . . a white southerner, "Do you want to take an African American tour?"

they're going [to] be put off by that because they're afraid. Hopefully, what we bring in to them is . . . the way we tend to generalize the tour is we start to tell them this little information, so they're not fearful before they get this information. What I like to say is . . . , "I like to show off my city, warts and all," because . . . people understand we're all humans. . . . We have our frailties, our failures, but we can learn from this and become better people. That is the other thing I try to teach, but you have to do it in an entertaining way. You don't want to hit them over the head with this.[23]

Coble described his technique: "We have to slowly bring them into it. Start entertaining. . . . But slowly, I start to really feed that information. It has to be done, again, in little doses, so they come away with it. [Because] if you tell them some hard stories to begin with, they're going to become resistant. You can see that back arch up, and they turn that hearing off. And that's not what I want to do. So I have to sneak in some of that information."[24] Unfortunately, much of the information that was sneaked in—"in little doses"—was the very history of the city's black population that LMC's staff claimed is central to its alternative history of New Orleans. Like minstrelsy and other forms of racialized entertainment marketed to whites, LMC equivocated between vindicating and vanquishing black culture.[25]

LMC's attempt to maintain the precarious balance between the objectives of black history and multicultural tourism resulted in uneven or limited success in countering mainstream portrayals of African Americans. The company's French Quarter tour illustrates the ambivalent process of racialization shaping tourism in a post–civil rights, multicultural era in which whites' desire for and appropriation and consumption of black culture are taken as evidence of a meritocratic society no longer responsible for racial inequality. At the same time, African Americans themselves are alternately portrayed as natural or man-made disasters, either inherently inclined to criminal activity, laziness, and ignorance or misguidedly encouraged in these traits by the liberal policies of welfare, affirmative action, and other social programs originating from the civil rights movement's efforts to redress racial and class equality.[26] LMC exemplifies the failure of multicultural tourism to fully revise the predominant tourism narrative or to reenvision black New Orleanians beyond the tropes of desire and disaster.

Even before LMC's story lines announced the racial distinctiveness of its French Quarter tour, its advertisements, brochure, "heritage store," and newsletter self-consciously articulated an alternative racial history of New Orleans. A description of the tour in the brochure reads:

> Walk through the locked doors of the French Quarter and sur-rounded by the stillness of secluded, tropical courtyards, step into the mysterious and remarkable lives of 5 generations of one of New Orleans' oldest Creole families. Amid patios of profuse and entangled beauty, meet the spectors [*sic*] of those long dead; the European and African branches of this Louisiana dynasty. Discover their lives; their intimate secrets shared only with Voodoo queens of long ago and see this Creole world come alive and slowly dissolve as they struggle through changing society, slavery, civil war; the birth of Jazz, and fi-nally, the Americanization of Louisiana.[27]

Descriptions of LMC in *The Soul of New Orleans* depict the tour and heri-tage store as "specializing in Creole and African American New Orleans" and "exploring ties between the European[s] and African Americans of an old Creole *famille*."[28] The local entertainment guide *This Week in New Orleans*, evidently drawing on the brochure quoted from above, described the tour this way: "Hear about [five generations of a Creole family's] desires, fears, and unrevealed secrets shared only with Voodoo Queens as they tragically struggle to survive changing society, the Civil War, slavery and the Americanization of Louisiana. Relive compelling life stories of Creoles as recorded in the 'Memoirs of Laura,' tales of compassion and devotion that cross today's boundaries of time, race and moderation. . . . Le Monde Creole Shop is the starting point for a courtyards tour that explores the relations between Creole men, women, free people of color, and slaves."[29] These descriptions allude to the exotic imaginings of voodoo and sex across the color line that have come to engender desire for black New Orleans, but they also diverge from other representations in their inclusion of Afri-can American history and culture as an integral and constitutive part of the city's heritage.

In addition to incorporating the language of racial inclusiveness, LMC's brochure offers a visual representation of the city's fabled racial distinc-tiveness. With its sepia-toned photographs of whites and blacks in various costumes and poses, the brochure literally blurs racial, class, and social boundaries. The brochure features photographs of people who appear to be black, white, or racially mixed, titillating potential tourists with the promise of racial transgression, which is so intricately tied to New Orleans's popular image. One such prominent photograph on the brochure's cover of young Desirée Archinard—a character whose racial identity is never unequivocally clarified in the tour—was placed strategically to provoke potential visitors fixated on the subject's racial identity (see figure 3.1).[30] The fixation on racial boundaries and the threat of crossing them is especially intense in New Orleans, a city whose legal and cultural frameworks have been built on a complicated and contradictory set of racial demarcations.[31] In conjuring up this complicated racial past, LMC both hinted at the fiction of immutable racial categories and their corresponding social hierarchies and capitalized on the common myth of New Orleans's racial exceptionalism.

These competing ideas persisted once tourists arrived at LMC's French Quarter origination point on Royal Street, amid antique shops and art galleries. A sign on the nondescript exterior reading "Le Monde Creole, French Quarter Courtyard Tour and Museum of Les Objets Curieux" hinted at the curiosities awaiting visitors in the courtyard. Once there, visitors could purchase tickets for a tour or confirm their tour reservations in the heritage store.[32] The eclectic mix of merchandise in the heritage store, described by tourist brochures as "antiques, junk, books, music, and French and Caribbean imports," included a substantial amount of Afro-Americana among its music, books, and artifacts (see figures 3.2–3.3).[33] The items included nonfiction on slavery, race, and Creoles of color; fiction by African American authors; African American music in an assortment of music genres and periods, including blues, spirituals, zydeco, gospel, and jazz; cookbooks featuring African American chefs and cooking styles; and numerous items depicting African and African American images, culture, and people.

In fact, although no true inventory of items was kept, the store housed popular and academic literature in both French and English; the published memoirs of Laura Locoul, on whom the tour is based; cookbooks; folk crafts; antiques; gourmet foodstuffs; and even "contemptible collectibles."[34] Most troubling and perhaps most revealing was the heritage store's juxtaposition of scholarly and popular culture materials that paired slave narratives and W. E. B. Du Bois's *Souls of Black Folk* with refrigerator magnets featuring grotesque images of Mammy and Sambo on nineteenth- and twentieth-century household products (see figure 3.4). Unlike other displays of "contemptible

FIGURE 3.1 • Cover of Le Monde Créole brochure featuring a photograph of Desirée Archinard, one of the characters featured on the company's French Quarter tour.

LE MONDE CRÉOLE
French Quarter Courtyards Tour
Cemetery Visit • Voodoo Tales

"No existing place in New Orleans preserves more of her magical & haunting flavor than in her courtyards..."

624 Royal St. • Rear of Courtyard

FIGURE 3.2 • Le Monde Créole courtyard. Photograph by author.

FIGURE 3.3 • Eclectic merchandise for sale in Le Monde Créole's heritage store. Photograph by author.

collectibles" or "black memorabilia" that at least attempt to provide some context in which to understand the history of the African American experience or that frame the collecting as a lucrative financial investment, LMC's items were mass-produced reproductions that were scattered throughout the rest of the store's merchandise.[35] Hence, they were not historically contextualized, nor had they accrued any economic value. By reintroducing Jim Crow images to a contemporary audience, LMC's heritage store—foreshadowing the tour itself—became the site of a symbolic battle between the black liberatory practices of the civil rights and Black Power movements and the exploitative commodification of blacks during the antebellum and Jim Crow eras. This seeming disjuncture between LMC's merchandise and its claims is indicative of the conflicting, ambivalent ways that the French Quarter tour portrays New Orleans's black history.

Before taking the tour, visitors were given the four-page *Le Monde Créole* newsletter. Mimicking the shelves of the heritage store, the newsletter combined the kitschy and the intellectual with its articles, graphics, nineteenth-century Creole proverbs, quotations from Du Bois and Laura Locoul, advertisements, coupons, and articles on Creoles and free people of color. Its subtitle *Historical Topical Satirical Political Literary Theatrical* reflects the hodgepodge of ideas and materials it contained and anticipates the wide range of topics and themes presented on the tour (see figure 3.5).

Like the brochure, LMC's newsletter also depicted a racially exceptional city. An advertisement for preserves invokes popular multicultural rhetoric: "Don't miss our delicious *Le Monde Creole* and *Soumas Heritage Creole* preserves, all flavored with PRIDE by the SOUL of Africans [*sic*] slaves, the HUNT of Indians, the SPICE of the Spanish, and the ACCENT of the French" (emphasis in the original).[36] On the next page, a drawing depicting two Afro-Creole men in conversation is accompanied by a caption in Creole dialect written phonetically and translated in English as: "Heard said, that if you had to feed all the white people in Louisiana, you could do it with a bowl of rice; and have some left over!"[37] A quotation from Du Bois's *Souls of Black Folk*, lists of best-selling books that included African American authors and subjects, illustrations of Afro-Creoles, and an advertisement for the Musée Rosette Rochon—a museum honoring the accomplishments of the city's free people of color—further established an implicit argument that New Orleans is a racially diverse city that has been substantially influenced by the presence of those of African descent, who presumably fared better in New Orleans than elsewhere.[38] These racial markers differentiated

FIGURE 3.4 · "Fun-To-Wash Washing Powder" refrigerator magnet
for sale alongside other kitsch in Le Monde Créole's heritage store.
Photograph by author.

Le Monde Créole

624 RUE ROYAL
LA NOUVELLE ORLÉANS,
LOUISIANE 70130
USA

**HISTORICAL
TOPICAL
SATIRICAL**

**POLITICAL
LITERARY
THEATRICAL**

FOUNDER/PUBLISHER
PAUL NEVSKI

WELCOME!

We hope that you will enjoy your tour here today at Le Monde Créole. Walking along the streets of the old French Quarter you may have noticed those iron gates, barred doors, and archways that continually offer recurring glimpses into a secret world of private and intimate gardens. The way back into these private domains, through the gates and archways may be marked by a gas lamp or an iron bell and within the passageway, by a stairway that heads up to what may have been a slave quarter, or you will find a second gate, doors leading to another door until at last emerges a courtyard surrounded on 4 sides by high walls. But once inside, the most powerful impression of these hidden gardens is *green*. New Orleans is a tropical hothouse and things grow in profusion and fill the courtyard with fragrances. To go back in time, New Orleans was a hot, damp, muddy, unpaved city, whose inhabitants cast their garbage and sewage into the streets. Those who sought respite from the city turned inward, to their private, walled, and sweet-smelling gardens.

These gardens are called both courtyards (from the French *cours*) and *patios* (from the Spanish), although, strictly speaking, the two are not the same. Courtyards are larger than patios, are bounded by high walls, and have carriage entrances or wide corridors leading to them from the street. Patios are often completely enclosed inner spaces, entered through the house or sometimes by way of a small side entryway. Both are paved with flagstones

*"Que bel tignon, Madame CaBa...Laisse
vous pas tombé!"*
"What a fine head-dress, Madame Caba, be
careful it doesn't fall off!"
19th c. Creole saying - Louisiana

or bricks to provided solid paving for horse and carriage. The ideal of the French garden is everywhere evident: the hedges are placed just so, the walkways set down in basic geometries, the trees and plants set out with a highly refined sense of order. And yet the climate is such, and the vegetation, and the nature of things, that the vines and flowers cannot be entirely civilized; they are lush, luxuriant, almost wild. New Orleans was once a great cypress swamp, and the heat and humidity and rich soil still conspire to produce an astonishing variety of plants and flowers, from evergreens to tropical palms, shrubs, herbs, vines, oaks draped with Spanish moss. The place where New Orleans still nur-

tures the pleasures of private life.

So, to begin with, just what IS Creole? Creole is the non-Anglo Culture and lifestyle that flourished in Louisiana before it became the USA in 1803.

In Louisiana, Creole was an adapted, self-contained way of life that was created out of the blending of 3 very different ethnic influences: the West European, the West African, and with significant input from the native American.

Creole was a class system, based on family ties, position, wealth, and connections. It was more elitist than it was democratic. In its philosophy, economics and politics, much of European custom and modern thought (Enlightment) was thrown out and, in its place, was followed a strict, self-serving pragmatism, a conservative world-view formed out of the isolation and desperation that characterized Louisiana in its earliest years. Because of the the tragic lessons of survival learned in those first years in frontier Louisiana, the Creole was family-centered, not publicly oriented. Creole culture put no value in public education or public works and little value even in the rule of law.

cont'pg 2

LOOK!

Present this genealogy at selected museums and get a discount when you visit!

FREE ADMISSION
Pharmacy Museum / 514 Chartres

$1 DISCOUNT
Hermann-Grima House / 620 St. Louis
New Orleans Collection / 533 Royal
Gallier House / 1132 Royal

LE MONDE CRÉOLE • (504) 568-1801 • FAX (504) 945-6060 • WEBSITE LEMONDECREOLE.COM • EMAIL CREOLWRLD@AOL.COM

FIGURE 3.5 • Newsletter given to visitors taking Le Monde Créole French Quarter Courtyards tour.

LMC from other pre-Katrina mainstream New Orleans tourism portrayals of the city, which either diminished the role of African contributions in the city or shied away from discussing race at all. LMC tackled both issues head on, most notably through its attention to Creoles and free people of color.

The "Welcome!" article that commences the newsletter defines *Creole* as "the non-Anglo culture and lifestyle that flourished in Louisiana before it became [part of] the USA in 1803. In Louisiana, Creole was an adapted, self-contained way of life that was created out of the blending of 3 very different ethnic influences: the West European, the West African, and with significant input from the native American." The article ties New Orleans's Creole community together with other Creole cultures in the Caribbean, South America, and in the Indian Ocean, all of which share "similar histories of colonial liberalism, the same ethnic roots from West Africa, strong similarities in foods, architecture, music, folklore, life-styles [*sic*], family, and business values."[39] In this way, LMC acknowledged the centrality of West African culture to any definition of Creole and contested popular notions of Creole as exclusively European. Yet even as the article defined *Creole* as non-Anglo, it also limited the designation by class by defining *Creole* as an elitist "class system, based on family ties, position, wealth, and connections" and emphasizing that Creoles are a cultural group and social class with a pragmatic and conservative worldview.[40] Similarly, another article in the newsletter by Mary Gehman, the author of *The Free People of Color of New Orleans: An Introduction* (1994), focuses on the city's large antebellum population of "urbane, educated and well-to-do free Blacks" who became known as Creoles following the Civil War.[41] Both articles' definitions exclude Creoles who were poor, enslaved, or socially or politically progressive. "Welcome!" goes even further by assigning all culpability for any racism associated with the term to the Americans who arrived following the Louisiana Purchase. In its clearest differentiation between the European and the American colonies' understandings and practices of Creole identity, "Welcome!" asserts:

> In the 18th century before the Americans arrived, race, color, religion and national origin were not the main determining factors in the Creole class system, but, under the American regime, they quickly became so. By the 1870s, when American notions of race and color became paramount in Louisiana (and America [*sic*]) politics, "Creole" was transformed into a racial term. Over the last 100 years, it followed many varying Anglo definitions of race, meaning everything from

"descendants of French and Spanish aristocrats," to racially mixed or even to anyone of African blood. Anglos define people by these categories, but for Creoles, such distinctions were deemed irrelevant. And now, at the beginning of the 21st century, almost all Louisiana residents who call themselves Creole, regardless of race or color find themselves cousins by blood.[42]

This clear-cut distinction between a European color-blind society and an American racist one was a primary organizing principle of LMC. By claiming to focus on Louisiana's Creole—as opposed to American—world, LMC attempted to evade Louisiana's messy history of racism and racial conflict, except to more clearly demarcate individual—as opposed to systemic—acts of prejudice and discrimination. In the end, the French Quarter tour represented New Orleans as attaining the best of both worlds, combining the founding ideals of American democracy and egalitarianism with the conviviality, social elegance, and familial spirit of the Creoles and emerging untouched by the abuses and excesses of either world.

"Tour of Gossip"

Once the tour began, visitors were summoned from the heritage store or the wrought iron furniture and wooden benches in the shaded courtyard to gather more centrally around a tour guide for the introductory remarks. Although Nevski said that he encouraged tour guides to interpret the tour "according to their own story," there was a considerable amount of uniformity to the tour, irrespective of the guides' race, gender, and other characteristics.[43] The guides began by asking visitors where they lived. During my visits, the tour group generally contained visitors from throughout the United States, Canada, and Europe. With few exceptions, visitors were not residents of New Orleans. Following the introductions, the guides welcomed visitors to New Orleans and listed some of its many nicknames—including The Big Easy, The Crescent City, The City That Care Forgot, The City That Was Never Meant to Be Built. They described New Orleans as both elegant and decadent, mysterious and intriguing. In so doing, they capitalized on New Orleans's mystique in the popular imagination and further cemented its difference from the rest of the world, where the visitors lived. The tour's central themes and emphases were presented in this introduction. In particular, the guides attested that the tour's subject matter was both accurate and taboo; they provided a brief political and social history of New Orleans under French, Spanish, and American rule, including slavery in each period; and they began to define Creole culture. The guides translated *le monde créole* as "the Creole world" and invited visitors to explore this world through the material on which the tour is purportedly based: Laura Locoul's 1936 memoirs, her correspondence with relatives in France, and 5,000 pages of legal documents housed in the French National Archives.

Ironically, Laura Locoul's memoirs—written many years after she had married and raised a family in St. Louis—were allegedly penned in response to the publication of Margaret Mitchell's *Gone with the Wind*. According to the guides, Laura attempted to document over 250 years of the Duparc-Locoul family's history to educate her daughters about their Creole heritage and correct their misconceptions about the antebellum South. The guides imply that Laura's memoirs and the LMC tour that incorporates them are likewise employed to serve as a historical corrective for present-day visitors. Because Laura's life spanned 102 years, from 1861 to 1963, tour guides said that she had witnessed "history from Lincoln to Kennedy." In the tour, she was given the role of a credible firsthand witness of and expert on the topics covered by the tour, particularly Creole culture, race and gender relations, and class dynamics in nineteenth- and early twentieth-century New Orleans. Furthermore, Laura was presented as a renaissance woman. The guides described her as liberal in her desire to speak English and embrace the language of the Americans, in spite of her French-speaking grandmother's wishes. For Laura to speak both English and French was to breach the chasm between Creole and American societies, which had formed two separate worlds in the city following the 1803 Louisiana Purchase. Other anecdotes throughout the tour emphasized Laura's independent spirit, which often pitted her against the oppressive elements of Creole and American societies such as slavery, classism, and racism.

Visitors were invited to experience the Creole world that Laura Locoul inhabited by exploring the Duparc-Locouls' life in New Orleans, where the family resided during the winter social season. The tour stopped at several different sites throughout the French Quarter, where guides told stories about the tour's white main characters—including Laura; her parents, Emile and Desireé; and the black characters Anna and Toussaint—as well as minor characters such as Madame Delisle, a free woman of color. Most of the story lines were relayed in courtyards of historic buildings housing local businesses or residences or in a historic cemetery along the roughly

FIGURE 3.6 · Life-size cutout of Toussaint, one of the characters in Le Monde Créole's French Quarter Courtyards tour. Photograph by author.

half-mile tour route. Nearly life-size cutout representations of some of the characters were stored at some of these sites and sometimes brought out to illustrate their respective stories (see figure 3.6).

Before visitors were led to the first site, the guides told them that they were about to embark on a "tour of gossip." From the beginning of the tour, then, they were prepared to learn about the Creole world not from the documented or official historical record but from the rumor and innuendo of personal histories and stories. In this way, the tour served as history, mystery, and biography. This type of tour easily met the widespread demand for popular history. The rise of the heritage industry itself stemmed from consumers' demand for a firsthand experience of the past, an experience that many believed could be conveyed only through topics and sources that were ignored by traditional historiography.[44] One LMC visitor expressed this sentiment when she explained: "Diary history following people is always more interesting."[45] It seems that the appeal of this type of history is especially salient in the context of black heritage. After all, "gossip"—with its connotations of secrecy and marginality—parallels the oral, often clandestine and unsanctioned ways that African Americans have been compelled to reconstruct their histories and identities within and in opposition to dominant narratives. Even as gossip lends itself to a more subversive, liberal rendering of history, it also suggests inaccuracies, partiality, and even debilitating untruths. From the beginning of the tour, this struggle between liberation and loss is apparent.

"It Will Always Be a Black and White World"

Tour guides encouraged visitors to follow the Duparc-Locoul genealogy in the family tree printed on the back of the newsletter, which includes names, pictures, and dates and locations of births and deaths for sixteen members of the family from 1756 to 1963. Notably, the solid lines indicating familial relationships between the white members of the family are replaced by dotted lines to connect the black family members Anna and Toussaint (see figure 3.7). These dotted lines illustrate the equivocal relationship between the white Duparc-Locouls and their enslaved family members, one that is replicated by the uneasy relationship between LMC's pluralist vision and its portrayal of black characters.

LMC's two central African American characters, Anna and Toussaint, poignantly demonstrated this tension, despite tour guides' insistence that they were "the focus of the story."[46] During my interviews, the guides were candid about the limited information available on these two characters and their wish that more research be done on the lives of Anna and Toussaint.[47] Nevertheless, during the tour, this scanty information—supplemented liberally by anecdotes and conjecture—was often presented as verifiable history. By emphasizing Anna and Toussaint's acceptance of their slave status and their affection for their owners, the guides seemed to discount the African American characters' tenuous relationship with the white members of the family and their unequal position in Louisiana's Creole society. The guides missed an opportunity to deal forthrightly and truthfully with race and racism in New Orleans, instead reducing the tour's primary black char-

FIGURE 3.7 · Duparc-Locoul family tree in the newsletter given to visitors taking Le Monde Créole French Quarter Courtyards tour.

acters to stereotypes. They were used more readily to illuminate white characters' generosity and resolve, and perhaps to alleviate contemporary white visitors' guilt or apprehension, than to humanize Louisianans of African descent or shed any light on Creole Louisiana's racial caste system.

LMC used its characters to bring to life particular historical episodes and socioeconomic and political shifts in colonial Louisiana. Anna "represents slave history," according to Coble.[48] LMC's script portrayed Anna as a slave on the family plantation who did not get along well with the other bondsmen and -women because she was not Creole—born in Louisiana—and had a different language and culture. Tour guides suggested that Anna's estrangement from other bondsmen and -women made possible a closer bond between her and her white owners. This bond was exemplified by Anna's liaison with her white owner, Emile, that resulted in the birth of their son, Toussaint. LMC's interpretation of Anna as a valuable and, more important, trusted and respected member of the Duparc-Locoul family fails to consider the unequal system of power relations between slave owners and their human property.

One example is the guides' insinuation that Anna and her master were romantically involved, suggesting that their relationship may have been one of true love and passion. One guide stated that their liaison "may have been an arrangement in the family that may have been perfectly acceptable," given that marriage among wealthy whites was not based on love.[49] Anna's story was used to justify an interpretation of her as a loyal and well-loved slave, thus lobbying against an unequivocal condemnation of Creole slavery. Anna's story begins with Desirée, Emile's wife, intervening on her behalf. Desirée ran to tell Emile that his mother was trying to sell Anna to a slave trader. She begged Emile to prevent the separation of Anna and her son, Toussaint, comparing their loss to what it would be like for her and Emile to lose their own daughter, Laura. At his wife's behest, Emile pleaded with his mother to stop the sale, but to no avail. Emile pursued Anna and repurchased her from the slave trader for a higher price, predictably enraging his mother. Most guides said that Emile and Desirée were disparaged as "Negro spoilers" for their kindness to black people.

According to the tour's script, Anna was so thankful that she vowed to serve Emile until her death. When he returned from his service to the Confederacy, Anna was the first one to greet him, and she continued to serve the family after Emile's death. Anna was also the one who explained to her son, Toussaint, and his white half-sister, Laura, that they could no longer behave like relatives and must keep the secret of their kinship forever. She told Toussaint that he was black and had no place in the white world, and she encouraged Laura not to be embarrassed by her brother. Tour guides concluded Anna's story with the claim that Anna attended Laura's wedding, as a member of the family. One guide defended this portrayal of Anna as a loyal and faithful servant:

> The fact that she has an affair with Emile is interesting, because you have to say, "Did they have this affair because he was Elizabeth's son and he had power over her, or did they fall in love?" We present it kind of that it was hinted that it was a great passionate love affair, but that could have been Emile's side. This is the forbidden territory that we walk on. What is interesting is that when she lives in the house with Desirée and Emile, and then Emile dies, Desirée doesn't throw her out as the mistress, and she doesn't move out on her own. Obviously one of Desirée's friends, she is a member of Laura's wedding party, one of her bridesmaids. She obviously gets along with Laura. I find this a very complex relationship between these people, one that people don't understand. Most women, particularly the white women, can't understand how Desirée could tolerate the situation. It's hard to explain how a wife puts up with a mistress living in the house with her. And then you think, "well, fine, she should get rid of her." Then you think, "well, they are best friends." Laura really says at one point that her mother and Anna are best friends. I kind of believe that they probably were. I find that very interesting.
>
> To me, I think her history tells us that somehow she loved Emile and Desirée. They were good to her, and somehow she was a part of this family. . . . She felt accepted in the house with Laura, and all that. . . . Otherwise, when the [Civil War] was over, and Emile died, she would have left on her own. We know that Toussaint sent his mother money, so she didn't need money then. I mean he sends her checks. That's . . . information we know. When he's got his band in New York, supposedly there was always money coming in from her son. But she still stays in the house.[50]

This guide and the rest of LMC's staff used the limited information they had about Anna to support a predetermined interpretation of her character, one that invoked the type of paternalism and condescension central to mainstream nineteenth-century proslavery arguments.[51] Any information that

contradicted or weakened this interpretation was either ignored or rational-
ized away. As a result, Anna was not as complex and interesting as the guide
proposed. Instead, her story was used to make the tour's white characters
more complex and interesting by illustrating Emile's and Desirée's compassion toward their slaves and black workers.

Outside of the tour, the guides were more apt to depart from this sim-
plistic characterization of Anna as a devoted, satisfied slave. During an interview, Coble reenacted his answer to the periodic question from visitors,
"How do people treat their slaves?"

> You have to understand. These people were considered property. No
> more, no less than horses, cattle, your carriage. Now whoever owned
> you would probably understand that you are going to make money
> for them. Because of the full spectrum of humanity, you can have ev-
> erybody who was absolutely wonderful toward you to the people who
> were like Simon Legree, who would whip you every day for nothing.
>
> The vast majority, the bigger part of it . . . all they had to do was
> threaten you—to sell you off. Understand that. It may not sound like
> a lot, but at any moment in your life, you could be separated from
> your husband, your wife, your children, your parents—all because
> you didn't do what they told you to do. That is a big psychological
> threat, and that kept a lot of people under control. You don't have to
> be physically cruel to someone when you can just be mentally cruel
> to someone. There are all aspects.[52]

However, Coble admitted that he did not volunteer this information unless
visitors asked "because of the time limitation," leaving one to wonder about
the potential for this more nuanced depiction of slavery to compete with
the tour's script.[53]

Nor does one find a more nuanced depiction in the tour's portrayal
of Anna's son, Toussaint. Toussaint's story begins with Laura's childhood
memory of his apparent disappearance from the family's plantation. No one
could find him until Laura discovered him hiding under her piano. When
she explained to Toussaint that everyone was looking for him, he retorted
that he would stay and listen to the beautiful music no matter how many
whippings he received. Laura began to teach her illegitimate half-brother
how to play the piano and purchased sheet music for him with her own
money. Despite the potential awkwardness of their association, the two developed a loving relationship that ceased only on Anna's insistence. Tous-

saint was freed with the South's defeat in the Civil War, and—according to some tour guides—his father, Emile, educated him and financed his musical training.[54] Given Toussaint's classical training, tour guides suggested that he might have been one of the originators of jazz, the new musical genre that was emerging at the end of the nineteenth century. Guides claimed that Toussaint played the piano at Laura's wedding, reading from the very sheet music that she had purchased for him as a child. Following Reconstruction, as race relations worsened in New Orleans and Creoles of color left the city or passed for white, Toussaint changed his name to Toots Lockwood and left to pursue his musical career in Chicago.

Given Toussaint's biracial heritage and his diverse musical influences, Coble described him as caught between the worlds of blacks and whites.[55] Another guide elaborated on this idea:

> I like Toussaint a lot. I present him, being an artist, as the artist of the family. I think it's amazing. What he went through, too, is another good story. . . . Here is a person who has a natural, God-given talent, and in the old slave system, that would have gone completely unacknowledged. It would have gone to waste. It would have died on the vine. But because of the time he was born, the fact that his father was a little bit more open-minded than most in the time, and the fact that he was able to be brought to the city to grow up, as opposed to the plantation, he's going to end up with all those influences, even though they were in a brothel, where jazz is growing.[56]

Toussaint, portrayed as an outcast from both the white and black worlds, is predictably LMC's tragic mulatto. His characterization relies on the same formulaic construction that sustained this character type in popular literature, art, and film beginning in the nineteenth century.[57] Toussaint was descended from whites but was not afforded the same privileges and possessions as his white half-sister, Laura. At the same time, he fared better than other former slaves because of his relationship with his white family. Though born a slave and never emancipated by his white father, Toussaint was educated by him and trained classically in music.

Despite having very little information about Toussaint's life, LMC's staff used him to make inferences about the racialization of jazz in New Orleans. Tour guides suggested that his musical tutelage changed the contours of his own life as well as the course of American music, as free people of color and former bondsmen united to create jazz. The development of jazz serves as an allegory for the city's shifting race relations. Coble explained:

> From my understanding, musicians were one of the best things in the nineteenth century. When you had Creole men and sons of ex-slaves—as far as this American New Orleans was concerned—they all had to play in the same venues. From what I've read, they could not tolerate each other because they considered themselves different classes, but they really didn't have much other choice.
>
> And it's from working together that they're going to create slowly—it takes a long time—an alliance, because they realize it will always be a black and white world. There's no in-between. Creoles of color in the nineteenth century will begin to make alliances with African Americans because white society will never fully let them in. So that's where the choice is. Because before the Civil War, always people of color—because they would always try to align themselves with white society. They want to move up, and they realized afterwards it's never going to happen. The divisions were always too black and white in this city and in the South, in general.
>
> Becoming a musician was also important because it allowed them to blend together. Jazz music is going to be born from this. But [Toussaint]'s going to make that transition. No longer is he a person of color who's . . . middle class. He is going to have to start identifying himself as an African American from this point on.[58]

Coble portrayed Toussaint as a character symbolic of the postbellum transition from privileged status as a free person of color (FPC) to African American—or, more accurately, disfranchised Negro. However, what Coble and other tour guides failed to consider is the fact that Toussaint was never part of the FPC community. According to the LMC time line, Toussaint was only seven years old at the end of the Civil War. Nor are we told that Emile left Toussaint any property or assets in his will. Consequently, Toussaint never had the social or economic status of an FPC. Furthermore, it seems unlikely that Toussaint would be aligned with whites before the Civil War because he would have followed the status of his mother, black and enslaved. Somehow, Toussaint's enslavement gets lost in the LMC narrative. Coble's insistence that all FPC aligned themselves with whites until whites disavowed them undermines any idea of racial cooperation or agency on the part of blacks to choose their own racial identities or alliances. It also fails to recognize the fact that many members of the FPC community were related to or associated with slaves. Without this agency, LMC's black characters become part of the background, not the focus of the story.

The discussion surrounding a life-size photograph used to depict Toussaint exemplifies the privileging of stereotype over typical experiences. For Coble, the photograph LMC chose for Toussaint did not fully capture the irony of Toussaint's tragic status. Coble explained: "Since we, again, know [only] a little about him, we have no images of him. Those images are what we think he would look like. Personally, I've tried to convince Paul [Nevski] to . . . pick a photograph of a black man who would pass for white, which would make it even more ironic. Simply because he is listed as a black man, he's going to be treated very differently. Though to view him, he would look like he would be in the same place where Laura was."[59] Coble's campaign for a more ironic story line is indicative of LMC's use of racial melodrama to obscure the historical realities of an oppressive and violent slave system, which affirms the film scholar Linda Williams's claim that melodrama is "the fundamental mode by which American mass culture has 'talked to itself' about the enduring moral dilemma of race."[60]

The tour's most melodramatic and perhaps its most revealing scene centered on Toussaint's father and master, Emile, who was forced to leave the family's plantation after the Civil War because of deteriorating health and financial ruin. As Emile prepared to leave, all of his former slaves lined up to bid him farewell. Tour guides described in detail a tearful departure—on either the part of the former bondspeople, Emile, or both. Some guides described a long line of black workers spontaneously waving their white handkerchiefs and weeping openly, which created such a stirring sight that Emile was also moved to tears. Of the six tour guides whom I interviewed or with whom I took the tour, five interpreted this emotional farewell as an indication that Emile was well loved and respected by his former bondspeople. Only one guide, who was outspoken during our interview about the lack of institutional support for black heritage tourism, offered an alternative reading of LMC's script.[61] This portrait of Emile, doomed yet beloved, is symbolic of the tour's romanticism of a dying way of life for white Creoles, a portrait that is identical in form and function to the myth of the antebellum South. Emile's story ends on his deathbed as he bestows a final gift on his white daughter, Laura—the choice to determine her own path. She would be the first fully realized American of the family, shunning the acts of brutality and capriciousness associated with the family plantation.[62] LMC's black characters, on the other hand, were employed more for the consumption of whites—as entertainment, transforming agents, and/or redeemers—than as a way to accurately reflect and record black history and culture.[63]

LMC's failure to vindicate and empower its black characters was nowhere more salient than in the silence around Toussaint's name. Tour guides discussed Toussaint's name change to Toots Lockwood, suggesting that the name was better suited for his new life and identity as a jazz musician bound for Chicago. However, the guides completely missed the significance of the name that his mother gave him. Toussaint had the same name as the Haitian revolutionary who led the overthrow of France's colonial regime in Saint Domingue nearly seventy years prior to Toussaint Locoul's birth. Toussaint Louverture's defeat of Napoleon's forces in 1803 ultimately resulted in the establishment of Haiti, the Caribbean's first independent black state, as well as Napoleon's sale of the Louisiana Territory to the United States, thus changing the history of both Haiti and the United States. Many scholars have documented the effects that these actions had on black thought in the nineteenth century, including acts of slave resistance, blacks' rhetorical and symbolic appropriations of the events, renewed hope and dignity among African Americans, and the ascension of Toussaint Louverture to the status of hero in nineteenth-century black discourse. Louverture's story would have also coincided with the activism of New Orleans's radical black Creoles and their militant demands for citizenship, particularly in light of the influx of FPC following the 1809 migration of Saint Domingue refugees to New Orleans.[64] Given this historical context, Anna's naming her son Toussaint seemed to be a comment on Louisiana's slave system, in general, and her relationship with Toussaint's white Creole father, in particular. The child's naming, at least on a figurative level, served as an act of resistance against his status as slave.

Although a minor character on the tour, Madame Delisle is in some ways a more problematic character than Anna or Toussaint. She was represented as a free woman of color who formed a friendship with Emile's mother, the matriarch of the white branch of the family, following the Civil War. Like other LMC characters, Delisle was used in the tour to exemplify a particular set of values and experiences. Coble explained that LMC used her to "talk about what a free woman of color, what her role was in New Orleans, the good and the bad of it."[65] However, LMC's selection of "the good and the bad" aspects of New Orleans's FPC fortified and glorified a range of troubling clichés and racial stereotypes already embedded in popular discourse, while tempering and glossing over any distasteful elements of colonial and antebellum history.

More specifically, Delisle, a woman of means and culture who owned slaves, was used to illustrate a central theme of the tour: Creole identity was not based on race but on class and religion. FPC were portrayed as identifying with their French heritage instead of their African one as the only way they had to further their social mobility. When discussing FPC, tour guides emphasized that they constituted a quarter of the population of colonial New Orleans; they were mostly the children of white planters; they were Catholic; they were classically educated in Europe; they owned slaves, land, and other property; they were class-conscious; and they had a vested interest in the maintenance of a separate Creole identity and, by extension, a vested interest in the maintenance of slavery. Consequently, Creoles of color had more in common with white Creoles than they did with black slaves or other non-Creole blacks.

LMC reinforced this depiction by sensationalizing quadroon balls, which were used to arrange common-law marriages—*plaçage*—between white men and women who had varying degrees of African ancestry. Tour guides presented these arrangements as a socially acceptable and appropriate way to ensure that the men provided for their *plaçées* and any offspring, even sug-gesting that the unions were more authentic than marriages among white couples. To substantiate this claim, guides emphasized that during the colo-nial period most marriages were arranged, and white couples rarely married for love. Two guides represented white women's lack of concern about their husbands' black mistresses with the quip: "You can have the honey, 'cause I got the money."[66] Hence, these interracial unions, represented as legitimate and relatively egalitarian relationships, were presented during the tour as benefiting nearly everyone concerned. White women were relieved of their unpleasant sexual marital obligations, giving them more time to pursue their own economic and political interests; fair-skinned black women and their offspring received education, culture, and wealth with the possibil-ity of a loving, interracial relationship even in the midst of a slave society; and white men were able to satisfy their racial and sexual fantasies without relinquishing their status and standing in their communities or in the an-nals of history. What this portrayal neglects is the severely circumscribed options for black, Creole, and free women of color that placed slavery and plaçage in a dialectical relationship.[67]

LMC's use of Delisle in the tour was not a problem because the portrayal was unflattering or politically incorrect. Rather, the problem stemmed from LMC's misrepresentation of Delisle, as well as her unrepresentativeness. On the one hand, Delisle was disingenuously portrayed as an actual historical figure. In an interview, Coble commented that "we're not sure if we know any of that," yet Madame Delisle's character was used "to tell those stories."[68] LMC fabricated a name, a life-size portrait, and a connection to the Duparc-Locoul family without ever revealing to tourists that Delisle's identity is fictitious. On the other hand, these manufactured facts and artifacts authenticated her existence and potentially conflated LMC's fictional Delisle with the historical Henriette Delille, founder of the black Catholic religious order Sisters of the Holy Family, with whom visitors to the city may be familiar. Such a conflation obscured Henriette Delille's spiritual activism and the distinctive tradition of feminine Afro-Catholicism that empowered New Orleans's women of color.[69] Only during our interview did Coble divulge that the Delisle character was not included in Laura's memoirs but only referred to in her correspondence. He claimed that "since we don't have any information on her, she is a composite character of, generally, free women of color."[70]

Despite this misrepresentation of Madame Delisle, LMC certainly had the right and perhaps even the responsibility to include black characters or to create them, particularly when the available information about their lives is limited. What was far more insidious, however, was LMC's choice to create and promote particular types and stereotypes of black characters while simultaneously advancing a more authentic and revisionist approach to black representation, a hallmark of post–civil rights racial discourse. In other words, the tour fulfilled visitors' desire for black representation and multiculturalist rhetoric while also maintaining a vision of black emancipation and equality as a failed social experiment with disastrous consequences. In the case of slavery, LMC guides seemed eager to assuage any residual guilt or misgivings on the part of visitors by justifying many elements of New Orleans's slave system and presenting it as exceptional, if not enviable. In general, guides desisted from moral, ethical, or even juridical considerations to focus on the practical motivations and impacts of slavery. For instance, one guide used the introduction of the black characters to discuss, without irony, how European men encouraged interracial unions as a means to reduce the number of heirs and as a form of (white) birth control that resulted in a new class of individuals: the FPC.[71] Even more remarkably, guides claimed that racism and racial boundaries did not have any place in the colony until the Americans arrived following the Louisiana Purchase.[72] One guide even posited that because of these favorable conditions, violence against slave masters was rare until the Louisiana Purchase. This guide blamed the 1811 slave uprisings on the British, who allegedly either agitated or manipulated slaves into rebelling, thereby discounting blacks' agency and historical struggles for freedom.[73] In the process of diminishing the impact of race and racism in New Orleans, LMC's narrative disregarded more than half a century of U.S. historiography that argues that resistance and rebellion, not acquiescence and acceptance, characterized North American slavery.[74]

Tour guides hinted at very few possible drawbacks to New Orleans's racial caste system. One such allusion was to the 1786 Spanish law mandating that black women wear *tignons*—a type of headdress—in public to differentiate very light-skinned free women of color from white women. The guides explained how free women of color began to wear such beautiful and elaborate tignons that the headdress was adopted by white women, effectively thwarting the law. However, the story operated more as a modern-day allegory of cultural diversity and the triumph of multiculturalism than as a critique of a racist government's attempt to keep black women in their places or an acknowledgment that black women had united to resist and reduce racism in New Orleans.[75] LMC's treatment of the 1724 French Code Noir was similarly problematic. Tour guides attributed New Orleans's community of FPC to the Code Noir, which granted more rights and privileges to slaves and free people of color in the French and Spanish colonies than was the case in British or American territory. Guides emphasized that the code prescribed less strict treatment of African bondsmen and -women, with rules mandating that slaves be baptized or converted to Catholicism and that they be allowed to sell their own products, be allowed permission to hire themselves out, and be given Sundays off for their own entrepreneurial and social pursuits. As a result, slaves had the ability to purchase their own freedom; be educated as Catholics; and develop a surprising level of economic, religious, artistic, and cultural independence and stability.

Ironically, the Code Noir was used to launch a discussion about New Orleans's black history and the contributions of its Afro-Creole population. Tour guides explained that because of the Code Noir's favorable provisions, a growing FPC class was augmented by West African bondsmen and emigrants from Haiti and other parts of the Caribbean who were skilled artisans and purchased their freedom by producing wrought iron products and working as architects and builders. Guides conceded some limitations to FPC's freedom, including proscriptions against owning a saloon or marrying a white person and requirements to carry identification papers. Guides also acknowledged that during times of suspected insurrection, whites feared that FPC would form alliances with bondsmen and -women and revoked many rights. Yet tour guides immediately undercut this potential criticism by insisting that whites' fears were unfounded because FPC would never align themselves with enslaved black New Orleanians. The guides explained that many FPC owned slaves themselves and that their interests were more closely associated with those of whites than those of slaves.[76] Indeed, the single most offensive element of the Code Noir cited by all tour guides—that it expelled Jews from the colony—disingenuously represents the Code Noir as a proto–civil rights act for those of African descent.

What guides failed to mention was that the Code Noir also solidified and codified the slave system in colonial Louisiana, institutionalizing a multitude of strictures and limitations on black freedom. It is important to note that the Code Noir's articles—both the punitive and the protective ones—were ignored or enforced selectively at different times, depending on the different priorities of the colonial government, shifting political and social contexts, and varied practices of local municipalities and individual slave owners. For instance, Gwendolyn Hall notes that beginning in 1769, Spain extended certain rights to slaves, such as the right to complain of mistreatment and the right to be informed of their monetary value, while simultaneously weakening the protection of slave families by allowing their separation at sale.[77] By focusing on passages that stipulated relatively fair or benevolent treatment of slaves, LMC's discussion of the Code Noir was deceptively misleading: after all, the code favored those who were profoundly invested in the maintenance, regulation, and continuance of slavery, not its abolition. Ultimately, LMC's recognition of FPC and their economic, social, and cultural contributions to the city came with a heavy price. In many instances, LMC's revision of New Orleans history to incorporate the city's black history rewrites that history to distort the experience of those of African descent and to disempower them.

The tour's melodramatic conclusion exemplifies this rewriting of history. Once they returned visitors to the LMC's courtyard, tour guides related a tightly scripted story of Laura Locoul's final connection with her Creole past. They described in detail how, by the early twentieth century, the adult

Laura Locoul had married, had children, and moved to St. Louis, where she became a prominent figure in that city's high society. At her daughter's debutante ball, Laura approached the African American band leader who had been staring at her all evening. When confronted, the young man revealed that he was the son of Toussaint, or Toots Lockwood, who had died in Chicago. On hearing the news, Laura wept openly, creating an uncomfortable scene because the white guests assumed the young black man had committed some sort of impropriety. Toussaint's son extricated himself by feigning unfamiliarity with Laura. He formally introduced himself as Ashiel Locoul from New Orleans and kissed the hand Laura extended to him. When she asked if his father had revealed the secret of Laura's kinship, he replied, "No . . . but my grandmother [Anna] did," a phrase that generally produced laughter from those taking the tour. After assuring Laura that he had kept the family secret, Toussaint's son returned to the band, and Laura returned to her family for the remainder of the evening, telling them only that the man was someone from the old plantation.

Despite its carefully detailed exposition, this tearful reunion was completely fabricated by LMC to build drama at the end of the tour. Coble defended this fictional addition by explaining the tour's objectives: "We are using [the family] in a general, broad way to explain the history. [The genealogy] is not important to me. If I was just going to do the family genealogy, I'd just give them a little boring genealogy and say, 'take that home with you.' It's just like *The Titanic*. Everybody's seen that movie. You know it's all based on true stories, but we all know that love story did not exist. And for most people, that doesn't bother them. They don't go home [saying], 'Well, it wasn't true. She didn't really exist.' That's what we are."[78]

Coble's assessment pertains to the tour's final story, as well. The tour ends in the corridor of LMC's courtyard, which was lined with photographs of family members and property, maps, and other documents and mementos. One photograph was always singled out by the tour guides, that of Marie Cephalide Metoyer—Laura's maternal grandmother. Guides referred to the photograph to explain that records indicated that two girls with the same name were born on the same day in the same parish—one black and one white. They proposed that these two girls were in fact the same person, a child born to a black family with the means to purchase a white identity for the child, which guides described as a common practice in New Orleans. They concluded that if this was the case, then Marie Metoyer would be considered a *passant blanc*, or a black person passing as white, and according to the laws of the time, her daughter and her grand-daughter, Laura, would also be black.

In addition to providing a dramatic twist in the plot, this theory had the potential to critique the destructive consequences of whiteness by ex-posing the constructedness and ideological nature of race.[79] LMC's script suggested that Laura's virtue, intelligence, and wealth were not, in the end, biologically ordained but were accrued because of the political, economic, and social benefits associated with white skin. Yet this critique was largely neutralized by the overriding message of the preceding two hours of the tour, which reiterated the idea that certain blacks in colonial New Orleans were already more white than black. Therefore, the subversive potential of a story line exposing the Duparc-Locouls' black ancestry was mitigated by the fact that this ancestry was never truly black in the first place. Another reading, equally disconcerting, is also possible: Laura and her mother, as exemplars of black women's success, demonstrate the unique and abundant opportunities for blacks in colonial and antebellum New Orleans to realize their full potential and enjoy relatively unobstructed freedom. LMC missed an opportunity to challenge the city's racialized image by reaffirming New Orleans as the nation's most racially exceptional city. Furthermore, even this moment of latent critique dissipated once the white descendants of the Metoyer family threatened legal action if LMC continued to intimate that Marie Metoyer and her descendants may have had black ancestors. Accord-ing to Coble, the family, in its zealousness to maintain their progenitors' racial purity, contended in letters that the tour's unsubstantiated claims did a disservice to the white and black branches of the family. Tour guides were since instructed to change the tour's ending, and by October 2002 at least two guides claimed to have already altered the tour's surprise conclusion.[80]

Although critical of the Metoyers' overreaction to LMC's racial conjec-tures, Coble admitted that LMC's own research suggested that Laura's bi-racial ancestry was doubtful or at least impossible to prove:

We tried to look into it. . . . What we think, because there's really no ev-idence that shows [a relationship], [is] that they were probably distant cousins—one coming from the family of color Metoyers that owned Melrose [Plantation] and then ones that were descendants from the other Metoyer family. That seems to fit in all the instances. But what we're trying to do on the tour, and this is so you can understand, most important of all—I am not trying to give an actual portrayal of these people. That is not the purpose of this tour. The purpose of this tour is to use this family to explain the history. That's more important. There are times when we take artistic license.[81]

Yet LMC did not use its artistic license to complicate New Orleans's racial mythology or to create more fully human and autonomous black characters. Instead, LMC perpetuated the sensational truisms already associated with the city, but in such a way as to present them as historically accurate. The distribution of the family genealogy, the display of portraits, and the narration of detailed biographical sketches—all allegedly verified in Laura's firsthand accounts—lent credence to often dubious and sometimes wholly fabricated claims and inferences about black New Orleans. Even references to blacks' contributions to the city's culture and history were filtered through the lens of a problematic multiculturalism that uncritically celebrated difference without acknowledging conflict or inequality and that emphasized personal choice and responsibility at the expense of systematic forms of oppression and the role of power in shaping race relations. In the end, LMC's black characters were skewed to create a very particular image of New Orleans's black community—both slave and free—that was misleading and melodramatic.

Because New Orleans was portrayed as a site of relative freedom and flexibility for blacks, and blacks themselves were presented as largely content and productive in the city, LMC's black characters served as justification for and even endorsement of the city's slave system. All subsequent references to black contributions to the culture and history of New Orleans were necessarily filtered through this lens of black complicity and culpability, often culminating in the triumphant rhetoric of contemporary multiculturalist discourse. For instance, a discussion of voodoo during a stop at the New Orleans Pharmacy Museum focused on the ways that nineteenth-century voodoo was adopted into mainstream New Orleans society, which made the pharmacy an acceptable and safe space for (white) Creole ladies to purchase voodoo potions. In this construction, the nineteenth-century pharmacy—and, by extension, the city of New Orleans itself—was a racially neutral space where whites and blacks came together to exchange knowledge, culture, and traditions. Voodoo priests and priestesses were neither threatened by nor threatening to elite white Creoles who valued them, evidently as equals, for their expertise in herbal medicine.[82] Any conflicts between a potentially insurrectionary African religion and a proslavery

Christian society; enslaved and free blacks' demonstrated desire for legal, spiritual, and economic autonomy and whites' economic and psychological interests in a slave society; or Western and non-Western ideals and values were largely ignored in LMC's script.

These underlying conflicts were never acknowledged by guides even when the tour brought them into sharp relief. Guides pointed out examples of architectural influences and wrought iron artisanship by FPC on colonial and antebellum structures and then pointed out where the slave quarters were in many of these same types of buildings, without remarking on the irony.[83] Standing across from the former site of the Storyville red light district—then the site of the Iberville public housing development[84]—guides romanticized it as a place of sexual and racial freedom where famous black jazz musicians honed their musical craft in officially sanctioned brothels. They did not, however, even hint at the direct correlation between the rise of Storyville and the escalation of racial segregation, which resulted in the formation of two Storyvilles and prohibited these black musicians from playing elsewhere in the city.[85] Most tour guides directed visitors to the tomb of Marie Laveau, queen of voodoo, in St. Louis Cemetery No. 1 and the adjacent tomb of the city's first black mayor—descended from a prominent Creole family—and remarked on their influence and acclaim in the city, while overlooking the tomb of Homer G. Plessy in the same cemetery.[86] Guides insisted that, consistent with Creole values, New Orleans cemeteries were not segregated by race but by religion, with Protestants buried in the back of each cemetery. This suggestion of racial equality even among New Orleans's dead denies the fact that burial practices mirrored the city's antebellum and Jim Crow customs, which relegated slaves and poor African Americans and Afro-Creoles to segregated sections of older cemeteries or to haphazard underground plots, where bodies were washed away or exposed to the elements. It also fails to acknowledge that even the city's most elite FPC during the city's most progressive eras were constrained by race, class, gender, color, and connections.[87]

LMC's unwillingness to stray from a narrative of New Orleans's racial exceptionalism is epitomized by the Hermann-Grima House, where tour guides identified the location of the slave quarters without any substantive discussion of slavery in the city. Instead, on the tour the home's architecture and first occupants served as symbols of New Orleans's multicultural meritocracy. Built in 1831 for Samuel Hermann, the Hermann-Grima House was constructed in the American Federal style with Creole influences.

During his tour, Coble described the home as indicative of American culture. Reminding tourists that originally the Code Noir banned Jews from the colony, Coble concluded that the ability of Samuel Hermann, a Jewish German immigrant who married a white Creole woman and achieved prominence in the city, illustrates the fulfillment of the American Dream.[88] At another point in his narration, Coble pointed out that Hermann owned a considerable number of slaves, accommodated in two stories of the home that served as slave quarters. Yet by failing to make a connection between Hermann's attainment of the American Dream and his reliance on the oppression of blacks to do so, Coble and the other guides missed yet another opportunity to comment on the complexity and contradictory nature of New Orleans race relations. Throughout the tour LMC guides made inferences and conjectures about the city's unique and favorable racial climate, yet they were unable or unwilling to draw conclusions about the evidence or events presented in their own tour that challenged or called into question the mythical idea of New Orleans.[89]

Despite LMC's ultimate failure to significantly revise or reenvision New Orleans's racial mythology, my own observations and interactions with the company's owners and staff members led me to surmise that their efforts to offer alternative, more inclusive, and historically accurate racial representations in New Orleans's tourism industry were indeed sincere. Unlike other mainstream tours, LMC's brochure and newsletter prominently featured people of African descent and consistently included them in descriptions of New Orleans. Likewise, the historical, cultural, and material contributions of people of African descent were incorporated into the tour's narrative of the Duparc-Locoul family. Without exception, LMC staff members to whom I talked criticized other tours that excluded or distorted the city's black presence to sustain an old South mythology; emphasized the tour's educational objectives; and praised LMC for offering and encouraging a space for narratives that have long been excluded from New Orleans tourism. By deviating from the accepted topics of most mainstream tour companies, LMC promised an alternative vision of New Orleans history. However, although LMC's vision differed, the company often reproduced the traditional tourism version of New Orleans history. It simply adapted the nineteenth-century tourism narrative to a late twentieth-century and early twenty-first-century emphasis on a multicultural yet color-blind society. What resulted was a disjuncture between LMC's stated and implied objectives and its actual French Quarter tour. This disjuncture within LMC parallels the schism inherent in New Orleans's contemporary tourism narrative, which simultaneously promotes the city as distinct from the rest of the South and uses imagery and rhetoric to unite it to the myth of the old South. LMC's inability, despite its noble intentions, to break from this mythology illustrates the tenacity of the organizing themes of desire and disaster even in multicultural tourism.

Four. "Wasn't Nothing Like That"

NEW ORLEANS'S BLACK HERITAGE TOURISM AND
COUNTERNARRATIVES OF RESISTANCE

The fact that [Anna] has an affair with Emile is interesting because you have to say, "Did they have this affair because he was Elizabeth's son and he had power over her, or did they fall in love?" We present it kind of that it was hinted that it was a great passionate love affair. —*Robin (pseud.), in an interview*

Wasn't nothing like that. Anna was raped. She had to deal with it. She knew where her bread was buttered. She didn't want to be sold, so she kissed ass.
—*Jay (pseud.), in an interview*

"Kissing Ass" and Other Performative Acts of Resistance

The two divergent interpretations of the African American character, Anna, in Le Monde Créole French Quarter Courtyards Tour (LMC) and her relationship with the white slaveholder, Emile, that appear above suggest the possibility of a counternarrative to New Orleans's racialized tourism narrative in the years preceding Hurricane Katrina.[1] In an interview when she discusses Anna's tenuous position in the Duparc-Locoul family, Jay clearly identifies "kissing ass" as a performative act of resistance, not only for enslaved black people attempting to protect themselves and their families, but for contemporary African Americans like Jay herself, who were compelled to operate within the conventions of the popular tourism narrative to eke out a living.[2] Throughout her version of LMC's two-hour French Quarter walking tour, Jay emerged as something of a renegade tour guide by strategically revising pivotal descriptions and scenes. By referring to the alleged "love affair" between Anna and Emile as merely a "liaison," by omitting the melodramatic scene of handkerchief-waving black laborers moved to tears by their former master's departure from the plantation, by treating voodoo as a legitimate religion and spiritual practice, and by providing a historical context for black slave ownership, Jay made subtle revisions to LMC's script that had significant implications for the way that LMC's black characters were portrayed and the limited avenues available to New Orleans's black population to combat hegemonic discourses. Of course, by employing the strategy of "kissing ass" to manipulate the French Quarter tour, Jay did not incite an overthrow of New Orleans's racial and class systems or even a revolution in the tourism industry, nor did she intend to. Jay's performance, however, did demonstrate the existence and transformative potential of the oppositional narratives crafted by New Orleans's black communities.

Jay's efforts to claim and construct her own historical narratives were part of a broader heritage movement. By the 1960s the movement had been transformed into an industry that incorporated historical trends and events to resuscitate material and cultural elements from the past. In both Britain and the United States, the way history was written and conceptualized changed from a purely formal, academic endeavor to a more populist concern for the recovery of the past, as marked by a proliferation of living and open-air museums, historical reenactments, and heritage tourist sites.[3]

However, unlike other heritage movements that emerged primarily as a response to postmodern distancing and dislocation, the black heritage movement appeared simultaneously with the modern civil rights and Black Power movements. This was a period of renewed optimism and possibility, when African Americans gained some control in and over the institutions that could validate and affirm their own narratives, histories, and memories. In an essay on nineteenth- and twentieth-century African American preservation efforts, the historian Fath Ruffins outlines the changing contours of African American memory, history, and mythos. She argues that African American preservation efforts have been motivated by narratives steeped in personal experience, spirituality, recorded history and scholarship, and collective memory. Since the 1950s, African American preservation efforts have synthesized elements of these narratives at the same time that African Americans have gained more access to traditional institutions, marking a defining moment in the way black culture and history were both preserved and presented. Ruffins argues that nineteenth- and twentieth-century notions of racial uplift, black nationalism, pan-Africanism, Afrocentricity, and the special destiny of black people have converged to create an African American mythos.[4]

Within the past fifty years, the black heritage industry has inspired and responded to public and scholarly demands for a more inclusive representation of history and tried to capitalize on this mythos by targeting a growing number of African American travelers who, by the 1960s, were decreasingly encumbered by the indignities and dangers of navigating through the Jim Crow South. By the mid-1990s, the growth of domestic tourism prompted the creation of national task forces to promote tourism and generated renewed interest in harnessing the economic potential of the tourism industry for local markets. These local markets were forced to acknowledge the economic impact of African American spending, which had increased from $304 billion in 1990 to $469 billion in 1997, a 64 percent gain in merely seven years. Citing a 1994 Travel Industry Association of America survey, a *New Orleans Tribune* reporter calculated that $34 billion of this amount was spent annually by African American vacationers, who represented 64 percent of African American households. Through the early twenty-first century, African American travel continued to rise at a higher rate than that of the rest of the population. Other studies showed that African Americans are three times as likely to take part in group tours than other groups of Americans, and more likely to travel as part of a family reunion.[5]

In the late twentieth century, these trends signaled new development in all facets of tourism that mandated from tourism marketers and tourists themselves a reevaluation of African Americans' historical past. These numbers also proved that cities could no longer afford to take African American travelers for granted and were compelled, often with the threat of economic boycott, to show greater sensitivity to African American concerns and to include more African American vendors in the visitor and convention trade.[6] A proliferation of guidebooks, tours, travel agencies, and tourist sites and destinations erupted in response to this emerging market. In cities throughout the United States, a growing interest in black heritage prompted the identification and reinterpretation of numerous individuals, institutions, and locales. Together these black *lieux de mémoire*—physical, imaginary, and symbolic sites that African Americans have imbued with cultural, political, and social significance based on their personal and collective memories—claim to portray a more inclusive, authentic representation of the past.[7] As a whole, in their articulations of a collective heritage, they incorporate memories and narratives that counter and comment on the images and myths of the mainstream tourism industry while making claims to reinterpret and rewrite history.

A *"Top Minority Tourist Destination in the South"*

In response to these national trends, New Orleans soon emerged as a favorite destination for black tourists. This shift signaled the city's transformation from an exclusionary and inhospitable locale for black visitors to a black heritage site. The city's designation as a black heritage site was due in large part to the efforts of local African Americans who, for several decades before Hurricane Katrina, fought valiantly to challenge the racialized tourism narratives and harness the city's tourism industry for their own advancement. Buoyed by the hard-won political and social gains of the civil rights movement, black New Orleanians were ready to translate these advances into full inclusion in the city's political and economic structure. The 1965 Voting Rights Act ushered in a new era of black political influence in New Orleans, marked by the mobilization of black voters, the proliferation of black political organizations, and the election of African Americans to political office. Black political agitation coincided with—and helped precipitate— the city's growing interest in and dependence on the tourism industry in the latter half of the twentieth century, but not until the 1980s did this political influence translate into a more racially inclusive tourist image.[8]

By the mid-1980s, disproportionately high unemployment and poverty rates among black New Orleanians prompted many of them to turn to the booming tourism industry for a remedy as the city's African American business community attempted to capitalize on the growing number of African American travelers.[9] In July 1986 local African American business and civic leaders established the Greater New Orleans Black Tourism Center (GNOBTC), a nonprofit agency, to provide "guidance" and help "prepare Black businesses to compete for bids and contracts," to develop expertise in professional advertising and marketing among African American business owners, and to market the city to African American visitors during the summer months when the local tourism industry slumped and visitors could take advantage of deep travel and lodging discounts.[10] In 1987 a delegation of Louisiana's African American mayors formed a special committee to identify and preserve black historic landmarks and lieux de mémoire throughout the state. These early efforts were designed to coordinate a statewide black heritage industry designed to rescue predominantly black, economically strapped cities. Ironically, like other postindustrial cities, New Orleans turned to black heritage tourism during a time when urban cities were facing public disinvestment, white flight, and increasing racial polarization. As the historian Elizabeth Grant aptly notes, "having to meet African American needs for improved employment opportunities and political representation without the state-backed programs of the postwar era, black leaders . . . turned to speculative development projects based in service provision and tourism to provide their constituents with a source of income and capital."[11]

Hence, in 1990 the Greater New Orleans Black Tourism Network (GNOBTN), which had evolved from the GNOBTC, was incorporated by the city of New Orleans. Differing from its predecessor by having a regular operating budget, formal membership structure, and a more clearly defined relationship with the Greater New Orleans Tourist and Convention Commission (GNOTCC)—the city's primary and predominantly white tourism confederation—the GNOBTN was poised to capitalize on the nascent black heritage industry. The relationship between the GNOTCC and the GNOBTC was strained, with the mainstream tourism industry providing only tepid support for the GNOBTC. In contrast, the more clearly defined relationship between the GNOTCC and the GNOBTN helped alleviate tension between the organizations. Unlike the city's mainstream tourism organizations, the GNOBTN dedicated itself to facilitating the full inclusion of mostly small black-owned businesses into the city's billion-dollar tourism industry through training, marketing, and networking opportunities. In the absence of affirmative action policies and government set-asides, the GNOBTN attempted to help these small black-owned businesses compete with larger, national firms, with the goal of eventually including them in the mainstream tourism commission.[12] At the same time, as Phala Mire, the GNOBTN's executive director, explained in a 1996 letter to potential members, the organization attempted "to link small businesses with the vast and largely untapped African American meetings/convention market." She boasted: "No other organization provides you with as much detailed and timely information on the African American meetings market—the fastest growing market segment in the industry."[13] In order to tap into this market, the GNOBTN first had to redefine New Orleans to African American groups that had complained of racist encounters, hotel rate hikes, and other discriminatory practices in the past. The GNOBTN served as a mediator between the GNOTCC and African American organizations that were considering New Orleans as a meeting site.[14]

The GNOBTN not only helped transform the city's image, but it expanded the city's promotion of ethnic tourism nationally through the organization's annual multicultural tourism conference from 1991 to 1999. Held in New Orleans for all but the final year, the Multicultural Tourism Summit and Trade Show convened tourism professionals from all over the country interested in developing or expanding their black heritage and ethnic tourism markets.[15] By "provid[ing] education and awareness to both the local and external markets of the organization," the GNOBTN conference provided information about the economic and social impact of multicultural tourism, offered workshops on how to access capital for heritage tourism ventures, and promoted family reunions as a growing African American market.[16] The GNOBTN's attempt to meet the growing demand for this new niche market dovetailed with national tourism priorities, exemplified by the U.S. Travel and Tourism Administration's ethnic and cultural tourism development program and a new trend among major organizations to mandate that conventions be held only in cities that demonstrated an appropriate level of minority participation.[17] By responding to, if not precipitating, the shift in market expectations, the GNOBTN helped distinguish New Orleans as a leader in black heritage and cultural tourism. According to the GNOBTN, a partnership between the U.S. Travel and Tourism Administration, the U.S. Department of Commerce, and the Minority Business Development Agency "resulted in a designation of New Orleans as a 'top minority tourist destination in the South.'"[18]

The "Essence" of New Orleans's Black Heritage Industry

A key success for the GNOBTN was facilitating the city's hosting of the first annual Essence Festival in 1995. The event was cosponsored by Essence Communications and the New Orleans–based Festival Productions, best known for producing the annual Jazz and Heritage Festival.[19] The three-day music festival and motivational symposium, held during the July 4th weekend, began as a commemoration of *Essence* magazine's twenty-fifth anniversary. Marketed primarily to the magazine's black female readers, the festival attracted 142,000 primarily African American visitors, raked in $70 million, and filled hotels to nearly 100 percent of capacity in its first year. These numbers were especially welcome during the habitual tourist slump in July.[20] The Essence Festival's success heralded the arrival of the black middle class in the national marketplace and was viewed by many as "a wake-up call to the industry about the power of the Black consumer dollar."[21] African American businesses benefited from the festival as well. One restaurateur exulted: "The people who came with the Essence [F]estival were black and Afrocentric. They wanted to patronize black business."[22] According to some estimates, they also were prepared to spend more money than whites with the same income (see figure 4.1).[23]

The following year, when Essence threatened to pull out of Louisiana following Governor Mike Foster's repeal of affirmative action initiatives, the GNOBTN joined forces with Mayor Marc Morial and other African American business and civic leaders to broker a compromise between Essence officials and the Republican governor. Their warning that "a national convention boycott would have a catastrophic impact on our city and state economies and would damage our national image" resulted in Foster's commitment to a program for economically disadvantaged business owners.[24] Foster's concession demonstrated the strength of the GNOBTN and the city's African American business and political communities' ability to manipulate the city's tourist image for their own gain. Despite this controversy, festival attendance and spending increased in subsequent years. The Essence Festival accounted for a significant portion of the city's annual $300 million–$500 million African American tourism market and helped boost the number of African American tourists to over a quarter million. Essence Festival contributed to an increase in the percentage of African American travelers to New Orleans from twelve percent to twenty-two percent in 1996, then down to seventeen percent the following year. Still, both figures reflected the fact that the percentage of African American tourists to New Orleans was more than twice the national average of eight percent. During its first four years, the festival broke attendance records in two consecutive years and brought 450,000 visitors and $235 million to the city. By highlighting New Orleans as a distinctly African American destination, the Essence Festival helped the city attract dozens of other African American groups, including church conventions, fraternity and sorority conferences, professional meetings, and family reunions. The GNOBTN recorded a surge in overall black tourism spending from $120 million in 1993 to $500 million three years later.[25]

The festival's success quickly made it a mainstay of the New Orleans tourism industry, guaranteeing its acceptance, according to one article, into the "elite fraternity of tourism spectacles that includes Mardi Gras, Jazzfest [sic] and The Bayou Classic."[26] Because of its economic impact, the festival validated the GNOBTN's status as a viable partner in the tourism industry, encouraged greater sensitivity to the needs of African American tourists,

Coca-Cola Presents The Essence Music Festival celebrates the finest in every music genre, including rhythm and blues, jazz, classic soul, hip-hop, world music and the blues, and has become a must-do for the Fourth of July weekend.

Lauryn Hill

The Festival, now in its fifth year, presents multiple one-of-a-kind evening concerts in the Superdome.

On the eve of the new millennium, Coca-Cola Presents The Essence Music Festival will be an extraordinary event for all music lovers to enjoy, featuring international, multi-platinum and Grammy Award-winning superstar talent. The 1999 concert lineup includes the dynamic Lauryn Hill, R. Kelly, Erykah

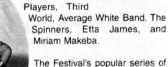

Erykah Badu

Badu, Brian McKnight, Monica, Deborah Cox, Dru Hill, Will Downing and Gerald Albright, The Temptations, Patti LaBelle and Maze featuring Frankie Beverly. The Superlounges will present acts such as

Brian McKnight

Bobby Blue Bland, The Ohio Players, Third World, Average White Band, The Spinners, Etta James, and Miriam Makeba.

The Festival's popular series of empowerment seminars will be held once again at the Ernest N. Morial Convention Center. The seminars will offer new topics in the form of lectures and roundtable discussions by many dynamic African-American leaders and intellectuals. Convention Center activities also feature a major crafts fair, a variety of down-home cuisine and a book fair with author signings. Coca-Cola Presents The Essence Music Festival has become a tradition that will

Frankie Beverly

return to New Orleans in 2000 and 2001, bringing its unique mix of music, culture and inspiration.

EVE OF THE MILLENNIUM CELEBRATION

July 2 - 4, 1999
For ticket information call
(800) 488-5252 or visit
the ESSENCE Web site at
www.essence.com.

FIGURE 4.1 • Essence Festival advertisement in the 1999 *The Soul of New Orleans* guidebook.

and led to more cooperation between the different tourism agencies.[27] Phala Mire, the former GNOBTN director, recalls: "Originally we had no relationship with the [Conventions and Visitors Bureau] where we worked together, and frankly, it was a bit confusing, because it looked like two separate entities were doing the same thing. . . . Now we work together and there are very distinct differences in what we both do. The bureau brings its long-standing hotel relationships to the table, and we market all the additional services that New Orleans provides."[28] The GNOBTN's success ultimately led to an increase in African American sales managers at local hotels, a strong national presence for the city—as revealed by its relationship with the National Coalition of Black Meeting Planners—and a growing influence on local mainstream tourism organizations that increasingly sought to attract African American travelers.[29]

Despite the growth of African American tourism, the success of the Essence Festival, and the influence of the GNOBTN, many of the city's African Americans questioned the soundness of the organization's mission and expressed dissatisfaction over the continued paucity of African Americans in management or under contract with major hotels, restaurants, and other tourist-related ventures. They cited institutional racism, inadequate marketing practices, and lack of training as impediments to black businesses seeking to gain a foothold in the tourism industry.[30] Their criticisms echoed an ongoing debate over the exclusive reliance on tourism to remediate racial inequality and to foster African American economic and political empowerment.

At least as early as 1987, some people were dubious of the economic turnaround for the city promised by tourism advocates. Tom Dent, who served as executive director of the New Orleans Jazz and Heritage Foundation from 1987 to 1990, warned that unless "Black tourists and convention groups . . . [are] directed to the service and products of Black-owned companies, . . . Black New Orleans will never see a profit from tourism."[31] Citing the industry's seasonal nature, the glut of hotels, the mobility of employers, the prevalence of layoffs, the lack of benefits and unionization, and the predominance of low-paying "back-of-the-house" jobs for African Americans, one reporter for the city's African American weekly *New Orleans Tribune* argued that "the industry is a 'boon' for owners and managers and a boondoggle for the city and its citizenry."[32] By the mid-1980s, tourism was increasingly being sold to New Orleanians based on its ability to create jobs and bolster the city's struggling economy. Yet with a poor system of public education, inadequate training for employees, and no evidence that the economic boon was trickling down to the city's working-class and poor residents, some African Americans would have agreed with the *New Orleans Tribune* reporter, who concluded: "The bottom line is that, as it stands now, the city of New Orleans is getting the shaft and the citizenry, which is over 60% Black and makes up the majority of the hotel industry's workforce, is hosting a party to which it hasn't been invited."[33]

Although some, like Dent, expressed "serious doubts" about whether tourism could be "the panacea for all our economic ills" or whether it could in fact "save Black New Orleans," an increasingly more common sentiment was expressed by Brenda Marie Osbey, the future Louisiana poet laureate, who said that "while it is unlikely that tourism or the port or oil and gas, *or any one industry* can resolve all of the persistent poverty of Black New Orleans, Black participation at every level, and especially at the management levels of these combined industries can do much to alleviate the economic problems facing Black New Orleans" (emphasis in original).[34] Osbey seems to concur with Dent, however, on the need to recognize and market New Orleans "as a Black cultural site" to ensure that the city's African American population reaped the economic rewards of the burgeoning tourist industry. African Americans, critical of the mainstream tourism industry and its disregard for the African American contributions that made the city such an attractive tourist destination, agitated for the integration of black businesses, historic sites, and cultural traditions into the city's promotional efforts. Like Dent, they charged the GNOBTC (later the GNOBTN) with "bring[ing] Black New Orleans to the fore of this whole tourism picture."[35] Yet the GNOBTC did not have the budget to commit to projects that could reframe the tourism picture and could only facilitate interactions between black-owned businesses and potential visitors.[36]

In the next decade, even those who had supported the city's tourism efforts grew frustrated that African Americans were still largely relegated to low-paying jobs in the service industry. Despite the high number of ethnic and racial minorities working in the hospitality industry, few had positions in upper management. As late as 1998, there were no general managers in any major hotel, very few women, and only a nominal representation of Latinos and Asian Americans.[37] Some placed the onus on African Americans themselves to take advantage of the potential windfall. Caletha Powell, the former president of the GNOBTN, lamented: "We don't own black hotels. We own very few restaurants in tourism districts. We own very few tourism products like black museums, site attractions, black resorts. . . . We've got to do something besides being a consumer in this market in order to hire our youth. . . . I am trying to get people to think beyond hamburger-flipping."[38] Others blamed institutional racism and corporate greed for exclusionary practices that ignored New Orleans's black community.[39] Madeline Jones, who served as director of the Tourism and Economic Development Program at the University of New Orleans's Metropolitan College in the late 1990s, pointed out: "New Orleans has a population that is over 70 percent African American and has a tourism industry that is approximately three billion dollars, and at this point, the two are not making a happy marriage."[40] Irrespective of the causes, African American proponents and critics of the city's tourism industry could agree on one point: after years of city- and statewide initiatives to diversify the local tourism industry and change its image, in the years preceding Hurricane Katrina, New Orleans tourism continued to be dominated by whites.[41]

Segregated Tourism in a Segregated City

The predominantly white GNOTCC and its successor, the New Orleans Metropolitan Convention and Visitors Bureau, slowly came to appreciate the economic value of the city's black heritage market; however, the white-dominated mainstream and black heritage industries remained segregated, as exemplified by the divergent walking and driving tours published by the GNOTCC and the GNOBTN (see figures 4.2–4.5).[42] When reporting on the GNOTCC in the late 1980s, Osbey charged that "there is no indication of a local Black presence in any of the material generated by the government-funded agency."[43] Not surprisingly, the pages of "New Orleans," a GNOTCC brochure published in the early 1990s, continued to promote the tropes of black desire and disaster in its visual and textual representation of the city, while the brochure's back cover alerted African American visitors that "special services for minority meetings and conventions are available in New Orleans through the Greater New Orleans Black Tourism Network, Inc. [the GNOBTN]."[44]

In the years before Hurricane Katrina, the city's black heritage industry offered one of the strongest challenges to dominant representations of the city's history and identity as predominantly and metaphorically white. By the late twentieth century, the voice of New Orleans's black heritage tourism emanated from a variety of sources. The GNOBTN and its print and online tourist guide, *The Soul of New Orleans*, were perhaps the most obvious and comprehensive sources of information pertaining to local black heritage. In addition, national black travel websites and publications, such as SoulofAmerica.com, often featured New Orleans attractions and information. Finally, African American tour guides such as Jay, who had either developed their own tours or had usurped in some way the script of mainstream tours, used black heritage to resist and reinvent New Orleans's dominant tourism narratives.

Unlike the brochures published by the GNOTCC and the New Orleans Metropolitan Convention and Visitors Bureau, the GNOBTN's tourist guide and website, *The Soul of New Orleans*, appealed directly to African American visitors with its Afrocentric tone, revitalization of black history, identification of black lieux de mémoire, and introduction of counternarratives to the predominant tourism representations of the city (see figures 4.6–4.8).[45] Despite the fact that early editions of the guidebook included a welcome from the city's second—and more conservative and accommodationist—African American mayor, Sidney Barthelemy, that avoided any references to African history or culture while adopting the business community's preoccupation with the French Quarter and the city's "old world charm," the tone of the guide was set by Caletha Powell, the GNOBTN director whose "Visitor's Welcome" describes *The Soul of New Orleans* as "a magazine that highlights our afrocentric culture" and celebrates the city's "cultural diversity that is unmatched any place in America."[46] Once Marc Morial succeeded Barthelemy as mayor in 1994, the mayor's "Greetings" in *The Soul of New Orleans* reflected the Morial administration's commitment to reshaping the city's tourist image to reflect its racial and cultural diversity and to use the tourism industry to push for economic equality by more closely mirroring the style and content of *The Soul of New Orleans*.[47] Averaging over a hundred pages each, the 1990s editions of *The Soul of New Orleans* were crowded with little-known facts and histories; profiles of neighborhoods, institutions, and individuals; and articles on a wide range of black cultural practices, rituals, and traditions in the city. Years before the mainstream tourism industry had begun to embrace a more multicultural vision for the city's tourism promotion, *The Soul of New Orleans* paid homage to a dizzying assortment of African American musicians, artists, politicians, entrepreneurs, community activists, historical sites, schools and universities, fraternal and benevolent organizations, monuments, recreational facilities, churches, communities, and local traditions. Regularly featured article topics ranging from the academic to the didactic educated visitors about the city's African heritage and retentions, affirmed

FIGURE 4.2 • Cover of the Greater
New Orleans Tourist and Convention Commission's "New Orleans:
America's European Masterpiece, Self-
Guided Walking and Driving Tours"
(November 1982). The map inside,
along with the brochures and guidebooks pictured in figures 4.3–4.10, reflects the segregated tourism practices
of the Greater New Orleans Tourist
and Convention Commission and the
Greater New Orleans Black Tourism
Network in the late twentieth century.

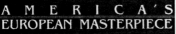

FIGURE 4.3 • Cover of the Greater
New Orleans Tourist and Convention
Commission's "Black Heritage of New
Orleans" (February 1988).

FIGURE 4.4 • Cover of the Greater New Orleans Tourist and Convention Commission's "New Orleans Self-Guided Walking and Driving Tours" (1988).

FIGURE 4.5 • Cover of Greater New Orleans Black Tourism Network's "'Soul of New Orleans': African American Heritage Map" (n.d.). Maps such as this illustrate the segregated tourist market that persisted in late twentieth-century New Orleans.

the vitality and importance of the city's contemporary African American community, and challenged the spatial and cultural mapping of tourist New Orleans. This remapping was evident in "A Message from GNOBTN" included in the early editions: "Every facet of this city, including its churches, schools, architecture, folklore, music, and food has been touched and gilded by the people of the African diaspora. New Orleans is possibly the only city in North America which has not only retained the vibrancy of its African, Caribbean and Native American ancestry, but which revels in it."[48]

The article "New Orleans Culture" typified *The Soul of New Orleans*'s Afrocentric sensibility during its first decade. The article linked the Louisiana Purchase with the Haitian revolution "in political, economic and social ways" by asserting that, as was the case with many slave societies, New Orleans's African laborers "fed the engine of society," which resulted in African culture "permeat[ing] every style of New Orleans Culture [*sic*]." "From its inception," the article continued, "New Orleans held a special place in Africanamerican [*sic*] history. Africans created song, practiced magic, rewrote religious catechisms, explored the limits of freedoms, and challenged the racial order."[49] In addition to extolling New Orleans's African past, *The Soul of New Orleans* paid attention to the contemporary black city. The articles "New Orleans Culture" and "About New Orleans," for example, specify the percentage of the city's population that was African American, a figure that remained above 60 percent throughout the decade. "About New Orleans" designates New Orleans as "America's most afrocentric city," in part because "a majority of the city council is African American as well as many other elected officials and judges [and] our city has had over fifteen years of administration by black mayors."[50] According to "New Orleans Culture," the city was indebted to Africa not solely for the history, music, and food—what Kevin Fox Gotham has described as New Orleans's urban brand[51]—but for ongoing "African retentions of close kinships, the ability to bounce back after a crisis, the value of education, the strength of the extended family and community, habits and mores, i.e., the Friday night fish fry, the chicken and gumbo supper, the jazzy funerals, bingo, Mardi Gras Indians, second line parades, social aid and pleasure clubs, and artists and craftspersons." In contradistinction to the mainstream tourism industry, the article emphasizes that these retentions emanate "from the people and their communities who validate the culture rather than [from] popular culture coming from universities, museums or media."[52]

The GNOBTN clearly often rejected the city's mainstream tourist image altogether, opting instead for an alternative iconography to signify place. An unlikely article on the New Orleans Recreation Department that appeared in *The Soul of New Orleans* proclaimed that the "number one resource in New Orleans is our children," proposing that, contrary to popular belief, New Orleans's "greatest resource is not the music . . . or the food . . . or the multitude of wonders" that predominated in the mainstream tourist literature.[53] Though seemingly out of place in a work aimed at tourists, the article expressed a commitment to the city's predominantly African American youth and families and to post–civil rights government assistance targeted to poor and minority communities as one way of ameliorating decades of social and economic inequality.[54] Through *The Soul of New Orleans*, its advocacy for black-owned businesses, and its elevation of marginalized voices, the GNOBTN helped forge a discursive space for "New Orleans's strong African American presence" that could be used to attract the "visitor seeking an afrocentric and historically enlightening vacation, business trip, or convention."[55] As one GNOBTN director put it, "our aim is to increase ethnic tourism in New Orleans while identifying sites, events, and attractions of cultural interest to visitors."[56] In this way, the organization staked a claim on New Orleans, as both a city and a tourism image.

By the beginning of the twenty-first century, the city's packaging of black heritage had undergone significant changes. A redesigned, streamlined print *The Soul of New Orleans* vied with the organization's updated website and numerous other local and national online resources emphasizing multicultural tourism (see figures 4.9–4.10). Most significantly, in 1999, the GNOBTN changed its name to the New Orleans Multicultural Tourism Network (NOMTN), signifying a new focus on being "more inclusive of people of color from all ethnic backgrounds."[57] These efforts to broaden the focus and the audience of the city's black tourist initiatives would ultimately reshape both the mechanisms and meanings of the city's black heritage industry. They would also help to popularize the city's black lieux de mémoire through the development of specific counternarratives to the city's tourist image.

One such lieu de mémoire is the Faubourg Tremé district, historically notable as one of the oldest African American neighborhoods in the United States. Adjacent to the French Quarter, the Tremé was founded in the eighteenth century and became a thriving neighborhood of property-owning freed African slaves and free people of color (FPC) who influenced the city's political and social culture for two centuries. Because the Tremé was generally excluded from the mainstream tourist literature before Hurricane

FIGURES 4.6–4.8 • Covers of *The Soul of New Orleans*.
Top, left: 1993. Top, right: 1994–95. Below:1996.

FIGURE 4.10 · Cover of *The Soul of New Orleans: Official Multicultural Visitor Guide* (2002).

FIGURE 4.9 · Cover of *The Soul of New Orleans: Official Multicultural Visitor Guide* (1999). The new subtitle reflected its publisher's name change from the Greater New Orleans Black Tourism Network to the New Orleans Multicultural Tourism Network.

Katrina, its inclusion on black tourist sites comprised part of a black heritage counternarrative. The NOMTN's "History" web page focused solely on the Tremé district, while SoulofAmerica.com included the Tremé neighborhood among familiar areas such as Uptown, French Quarter, University District, Garden District, and Faubourg Marigny.[58] The article "Faubourg Tremé: America's Oldest Black Neighborhood" in *The Soul of New Orleans* suggests both the significance and the marginalization of the district: "Tremé is not only America's oldest black neighborhood but was the site of significant economic, cultural, political, social and legal events that have literally shaped the course of events in Black America for the past two centuries. Yet, few outside of New Orleans except for scholars and historians know its enormous importance to Americans of African descent."[59] Only in the late twentieth century, through the efforts of New Orleans black heritage promoters, did the Tremé begin to receive any attention by the mainstream tourism industry. Before Katrina, it remained a neighborhood relegated to the margins of the city's tourist identity.[60]

Nevertheless, a black counternarrative endured on the margins. SoulofAmerica.com's New Orleans page has evoked a countermemory of the Tremé. What SoulofAmerica.com includes that no other source mentioned is that the Tremé was home to the famed Storyville red light district in the early twentieth century. Unlike other websites' more charitable, even celebratory, tone regarding Storyville, SoulofAmerica.com offers a different perspective: "As [was] customary for the powers of that era, they chose a vulnerable neighborhood within the emerging Black community to become a red-light district." We learn from other sites that Louis Armstrong and other jazz musicians honed their craft playing in the clubs and bordellos of Storyville, yet SoulofAmerica.com claims that these musicians—"Buddy Bolden, Sidney Bechet, Jelly Roll Morton, King Oliver and Louis Armstrong"—lived and worked in the Tremé, which offered "steady work and better than average social conditions," suggesting that Storyville provided one of the few spaces of economic and social autonomy in the segregated city.[61]

In addition to being critical of white politicians' and patrons' use of the Tremé neighborhood to provide sanctioned gambling and prostitution, SoulofAmerica.com is critical of the city's failure to preserve Tremé's heritage. Its article on the neighborhood criticizes the "classic case of failed urban redevelopment in the mid 20th century" that replaced original Storyville structures with "the infamous Iberville Housing Projects" and the ill-conceived design plans that cause Armstrong Park to be largely abandoned by locals instead of being a thriving jazz center.[62] The article does commend efforts in the part of Tremé nearest the French Quarter, such as the opening of the African American Museum of Art, Culture, and History and signs of redevelopment in the neighborhood. Yet these small strides did little to secure Tremé's position in the city's past or future.[63]

A black heritage counternarrative to the traditional narrative about New Orleans's antebellum FPC, also known as Creoles of color, similarly challenged the mainstream tourism representation of this group as practically white in genetic makeup, physical appearance, status, individual freedoms, and disdain for dark-skinned blacks. An article by Gregory Osborn, a librarian and tour guide, in *The Soul of New Orleans* complicated this classification. The first paragraph of the article explained that the city's FPC are a diverse group of "Africans, Creoles of Color (New World-Born People of African descent), and persons of mixed African, European, and/or Native American descent" and traces the genealogy of the term *Creole* to slaves in Spanish colonial Louisiana, decades before whites used the term to describe themselves.[64] This sequence directly challenged the prevailing notion that the term was originally used to describe European settlers in the colony and only later, if at all, used to include those of African or mixed racial ancestry.

Whereas other tourism narratives emphasized the system of *plaçage* by which white men cared for and often emancipated their common-law mulatto, quadroon, and octoroon wives and the children they had with those women, Osborn located the most dramatic growth of FPC during Spanish colonial rule between 1769 and 1803, generations before plaçage became commonplace. During this period, New Orleans's FPC community increased by 2,500 people, most of whom were "Africans and unmixed Blacks who bought their freedom."[65] Others were emancipated for service in war or for saving the lives of their masters. New Orleans's FPC community was later augmented by immigrants from Haiti, the Caribbean, Mexico, Central and South America, and other parts of the world.

Having set the historical framework for a much more culturally, educationally, and phenotypically diverse group of FPC, Osborn corroborated other portrayals of the group as industrious, skilled, and enterprising: "Free People of Color were highly skilled craftsmen, business people, educators, writers, planters, and musicians. Many free women of color were highly skilled seamstresses, hairdressers, and cooks while some owned property and kept boarding houses. Some F.P.C. were planters before and after the

Civil War and owned slaves." Yet, although Osborn conceded that some FPC owned slaves, he stopped short of characterizing the entire group as more tied to white interests than to those of enslaved blacks: "Although shocking and incomprehensible to many people today, the fact that some F.P.C. owned slaves must be viewed in its historical context." Osborn portrayed the legacy of FPC as a positive one that resulted in "jazz, Creole cuisine, and numerous artists, politicians, and educators," such as Henriette Delille, who founded the Catholic religious order Sisters of the Holy Family for black women.[66]

The article "What's Creole? What's Cajun?" in *The Soul of New Orleans* also subtly revised persistent tourist conceptions of Creole identity. On the one hand, the language of the short piece reverted to the melting pot motif by referring to Louisiana's "gumbo of cultures." On the other hand, the article affirmed three viable definitions of Creole: a descendant of an early French or Spanish settler born in the colony; a descendant of a mixture of Africans and French or Spanish settlers born in the colony; or the children born to settlers in Louisiana. Despite noting that "no one seems to be able to agree on one single definition of the word Creole," the article acknowledged that "today people who identify themselves as Creole live in many parts of the state, including Cajun Country and the New Orleans area."[67] Unlike other tourist explanations of Creole identity, this statement legitimized these competing claims to the term instead of rendering all claims insignificant or obsolete.

SoulofAmerica.com also referred to African American institutions and individuals who were rarely if ever mentioned on mainstream websites. In the process, it informed visitors to New Orleans about the city's contemporary African American culture and invited them to participate in it. One passage boasts that "more than 470,000 African American residents, and the Historically Black Colleges [*sic*] of Xavier, Dillard and Southern ensure that the city keeps its flava'" and creates an alternative black tourist geography wherein "Congo Square within Louis Armstrong Park, nightclubs in Faubourg Marigny and on the edge of Tremé, the Jazz Museum, and African American Museum & Cultural Center are sites worth visiting."[68] In addition, the site lists native-born African Americans on its "Famous Residents" page. Although the list includes many jazz musicians whose names appear elsewhere, too, it also includes Reconstruction and contemporary politicians, a golf-course designer, a Broadway composer, and national television broadcasters.[69]

Even when New Orleans black heritage websites focused on the readily acknowledged cultural contributions of blacks, such as the Mardi Gras Indians, jazz, or the second line that were included in mainstream representations of the city, the heritage websites often portrayed these contributions differently. For instance, although many other pre-Katrina websites described New Orleans as "the birthplace of jazz" and even claimed particular world-renowned musicians as the city's sons and daughters, few emphasized the African and African American roots of the musical form. Nor did these descriptions present jazz funerals or second lines as living, viable expressions of working-class black culture that themselves reject or signify on white, elite values.[70]

This difference is notable with black heritage representations of Mardi Gras, which emphasized local, grassroots expressions of the celebration that diverged from the bacchanalian extravaganza of international repute. For instance, both *The Soul of New Orleans* and SoulofAmerica.com included histories of the Zulu Social Aid and Pleasure Club, which originated as an African American benevolent society. The article in *The Soul of New Orleans* emphasized the integral role the Zulus played in the city's black community. The members were laborers whose dues paid for each other's insurance and burial expenses. Even as the organization established itself as a Mardi Gras krewe, the article maintains that the Zulus continued to be closely linked geographically and thematically with New Orleans's working-class black communities and continued to "march to their own drum beat."[71] Whereas *The Soul of New Orleans* article is more reticent about the Zulus' critique of white Mardi Gras clubs, the SoulofAmerica.com page on Mardi Gras clearly asserts that the Zulus' "costumes and themes mocked dominant White society of the time."[72] The page also included information on Mardi Gras Indians, describing the neighborhood "tribes" as "a mixture of Native American and African American cultures."[73] The inclusion of these African American cultural practices and acts of resistance created an alternative image of Mardi Gras in the decades before Katrina.

New Orleans's jazz funerals were also portrayed differently in black heritage sources. SoulofAmerica.com suggested that they resulted from blacks' combining West African and European musical traditions and social processions in the early eighteenth century "to give folks a proper sendoff in New Orleans." The website even highlighted the Original Illinois Club, founded in the nineteenth century, as "the oldest known African American social organization and cherished for it [sic] participation [in] Second

Linin' and Jazz Funerals [sic]."[74] "The Jazz Funeral," originally printed in *The Soul of New Orleans*, cited the late jazz musician Danny Barker's explanation of the jazz funeral and its roots in Africa. Barker traced the procession to the sixteenth-century practices of the West African Dahomey and Yoruba, who pooled resources to ensure that fellow tribe members would be afforded a proper burial, an antecedent to New Orleans's social and pleasure clubs. The article explained: "As time passed, these very same concepts that were rooted in African ideology became one of the basic principles of the social and pleasure club. The social and pleasure club guaranteed proper burial conditions as did many fraternal orders and lodges to any member who passed. These organizations were precursors to the concept of burial insurance and the debit insurance companies."[75] Barker also attributed to Africa the addition of music to the funeral, drawing a parallel between Africa and New Orleans as lieux de mémoire where music commemorates and celebrates both life and death.

Similarly, SoulofAmerica.com focused on the African American roots of the second line procession. "Social Traditions and Cemeteries" marked the origins of the second line in the late 1800s with black youth mimicking the parading of white musicians and band leaders. Using the black vernacular, the web page does some signifying of its own, asserting "*Ya' know the brothers had to get funky with it*" (emphasis in original).[76] In the article "Second Linin': A New Orleans Soulful Experience" in *The Soul of New Orleans*, the jazz musician Michael White linked "the social and spiritual dimensions of the jazz culture" with their basis in the distinct black urban culture of social aid and pleasure clubs, church parades, and funerals. White contended that the second line became "an almost religious-like 'celebration' to commemorate special events and occasions (or just to gather in revelry 'for no reason at all')." The article began with a description of a typical second line by Jelly Roll Morton that differed drastically from white celebrations of the period: "Those parades were really tremendous things, the drums would start off, the trumpets and trombones rolling into something like 'Stars and Stripes' or 'The National Anthem' and everybody would strut off down the street, the bass drum player twirling his beater in the air, the snare drummer throwing his sticks up and bouncing them off the ground, the kids jumping and hollering, the grand marshall [sic] and his aides in their expensive uniforms moving along, dignified women on top of everybody—the second line, armed with sticks and bottles and baseball bats and all forms of ammunition to fight the foe when they reached the dividing line. It's a funny thing that the second line marched at the head of the parade but that's the way it had to be in New Orleans." White, however, downplayed the irreverent or potentially insurrectionary tone of the procession, focusing instead on the unifying, celebratory aspects of New Orleans music "that makes you just want to dance."[77] This transition to the trope of black desire that characterized mainstream tourism was not uncommon in black heritage websites and print sources.

This tension between promoting a distinct black heritage version of New Orleans's history and culture and relying on the customary tourism conventions regularly surfaced in the city's black heritage literature. For example, with its allusions to "the many cultures of our past," "so many cultures," "a delicious gumbo of cultures," and its "melting pot culture," SoulofNew Orleans.com reproduced the same clichés of New Orleans's unproblematic multicultural past that appeared in mainstream tourist literature.[78] Likewise, on its "Historical Context" page, SoulofAmerica.com endorsed the mainstream tourism representation of Creoles of color as uncompromisingly conservative and allied to white interests. Its history of New Orleans was overtly critical of the city's "complex, but nonetheless racist society," particularly the light-skinned Creoles' separation from "their African and Native American brethren." The article argued that Creoles did not "publicly advance the human rights of their blood ancestors" and, "regrettably," some Creoles owned slaves. As a further indication of New Orleans's complicated race relations in the nineteenth century, the website pointed to the fact that "hundreds of free African Americans, not just Creoles, fought on the side of the Confederacy!"[79] Yet by failing to acknowledge the complex reasons why black men joined the Confederate army—including fear, coercion, economic interests, desire to prove their patriotism and worthiness to be accepted as equal citizens—or the white supremacist practices and policies that limited their full participation, SoulofAmerica.com and other black heritage sites and sources reinscribe the dominant tourism discourse.[80]

Even the ostensibly more inclusive nomenclature adopted by the NOMTN illustrates the tension between facile mainstream models of multiculturalism and black heritage models of resistance and economic, political, and social parity. The renamed organization rhetorically shifted its focus from a black to a multicultural New Orleans and a corresponding mission to promote cultural diversity and incorporate people of color at all levels of New Orleans's tourism industry. However, it is unclear how the organization defined people of color because, in addition to its former focus on the city's African heritage and the inclusion of the city's Vietnamese population, the reconceptualized organization featured the city's European heritage, including articles on Germans, Italians, and Spanish *Isleños*. This shift to a multicultural New Orleans that indiscriminately included every group and every activity subverted the NOMTN's mandate to provide previously underrepresented people of color with leadership opportunities and resources in a largely white-dominated tourism industry.[81] Nevertheless, the city's black heritage sources often subverted these tropes even as they embraced them.

For instance, the same "History" page that SoulofNewOrleans.com used to describe a raceless pluralism also strayed from the expected tourist clichés with its exclusive treatment of the Tremé district.[82] Even the "Food" page credited African and Caribbean influences with making the Creole and Cajun cooking styles distinctive. Furthermore, in a discussion of cooking, the site referred only to two chefs, both African American—Leah Chase and Armand Olivier—suggesting that the two are representative of New Orleans chefs who "have influenced generations with their culinary magic."[83] In the same way, SoulofAmerica.com's "Historical Context," while alluding to "interracial liaisons," "a collage of cultures," and "multicultural society," made those of African descent—and their alliances with Native Americans, resistance to colonial racial strictures, and continuance of African cultural practices—central to the history of New Orleans. This African-centered portrait of the city deviated in subtle but important ways from the mainstream tourism narrative and corresponded more closely to recent historiography. "Unfiltered" African culture, Congo Square, and "Voudon religion" were the main components of, not ancillaries to, New Orleans history on this site. Furthermore, SoulofAmerica.com's history did not erase the slavery and racism that existed "in and around New Orleans."[84]

Most significant was that SoulofAmerica.com's history proceeded beyond the Civil War to include the erosion of Creoles' relative privilege and independence; the enactment of "many local laws tinged with white privilege and racial separatism"; the 1900 race riot "in which European Americans terrorized all people of color"; and the subsequent coalition between Creoles of color and other black residents of the city.[85] The inclusion of the 1900 race riot—a symbol of both the institutionalization of racism and the resistance to it by African Americans at the beginning of the twentieth century—clearly disrupted the prevailing depiction of the city's racial exceptionalism.[86] In addition, the website used the riot to complicate the iconic representation of Creole identity. Recognizing their common interests and foes, Creoles and black New Orleanians channeled their efforts toward their mutual interests. SoulofAmerica.com claimed that this history of uneven conflict and cooperation—not a harmonious blending of cultures—resulted in jazz: "This environment of racial mixture, abrupt cultural separatism, social turmoil then cooperation, and then entrepreneurial zest created a gumbo of ingredients for the birth of jazz."[87] Hence, although the site's "gumbo" terminology was similar to that of the predominant tourism narrative, its characterization was strikingly different.

For SoulofAmerica.com, the birth of jazz did not mark the end of difficult times for the city. Instead, the site claims, "Jim Crow was alive and kicking in New Orleans. Police harassment was a constant. White flight began with the arrival of freeways and malls."[88] Instead of attributing New Orleans's desegregation to white tolerance and amicable race relations, SoulofAmerica.com credited local and national African American organizations and leadership for the city's civil rights gains, which culminated in 1978 with the election of "Dutch" Morial, the city's first African American mayor—who was also descended from the city's Creoles of color.[89] SoulofAmerica.com, like other black heritage sites and sources at the turn of the twenty-first century, proffered an alternative tourist vision of New Orleans that undermined New Orleans's representations as either old South or melting-pot city. Instead, these black heritage sites presented a contemporary New Orleans with a majority African American population whose leadership had actively sought black conventions and tourist events, such as the Essence Festival and the Bayou Classic.[90]

Tropes and Triumphs: Touring Black New Orleans

Perhaps black heritage tours most clearly demonstrated the multiple goals of the GNOBTN (later called the NOMTN) and the city's black heritage industry—namely, to nurture and promote African American businesses; to incorporate African Americans into the mainstream tourism industry; and to create and disseminate new, more racially inclusive narratives of the city that paid homage to its African heritage. Although there had been earlier, more sporadic attempts to document and create black heritage maps and tours of the city in the post–civil rights period, the appearance of regularly operating black heritage tours in the mid-1980s marked a more concerted, consistent effort to meet the growing demands of tourists and local church, school, and social groups for information about African American history, culture, and artistic production.[91] These tours took up Dent's charge to showcase "the immense cultural and political impact of the African presence in New Orleans" by identifying "the many historic sites of regional and national importance to Afro-American life."[92]

In the next two decades, several local, black-owned tour companies offered black heritage maps and tours of the city that deviated from the standard tourism script by identifying black lieux de mémoire and offering oppositional narratives and images of the city.[93] Black heritage tour guides hijacked the format of the mainstream three-hour bus tour and rerouted it through African American neighborhoods to highlight centuries of achievements and contributions by enslaved Africans, FPC, and African Americans who built and sustained the city; created wrought-iron furniture and grillwork; established a Catholic order of nuns; influenced mainstream musical and religious trends; founded militias; served honorably in battle; attained positions at the highest levels of politics, business, education, and the arts; and made an indelible imprint on New Orleans culture and society.[94] As one reporter noted about a pioneering black heritage tour, its surveys of the city did not "bypass the ghettos" but instead took "unconventional routes through Black neighborhoods that are filled with history, but are seldom seen by tourists."[95]

In addition to expanding New Orleans's physical and imaginative landscape, black heritage tours claimed to dispel the lies of black desire and disaster that characterized the mainstream tourism narrative. For example, an advertisement for Le'Ob's Tours boasts: "Do You Want to tour New Orleans? There's only one company that can show you the Real City. . . . Le'Ob's Tours. . . . Known Nationwide, and rated best by the Travel Channel, Le'Ob's Tours doesn't cater to wild stories, they dig hard for the truth and facts! Only after they do their homework, do they began [sic] tours. Le'Ob's Tours, for the best all truthful tours in the city."[96] These claims criticized mainstream tourist websites and tours that trivialized the past by packaging history as entertainment or cloaking it in "wild stories." At the same time, black heritage tours, such as Le'Ob's, invoked a countermemory of New Orleans that claimed to tell the truth about the past—particularly the black past—that is integrally linked to the present. Le'Ob's Tours' emphasis on "the truth and facts" is substantively different from the flawed view of history as "just the facts" that the anthropologists William Handler and Eric Gable criticize in their assessment of Colonial Williamsburg's black history program.[97] Unlike the historical site's dismissal of undocumented, unwritten history that presented African American history as unverifiable and less authentic than stories about white elites, Le'Ob's insistence on "the truth and facts" served as a corrective to the historical myth making associated with mainstream tours of New Orleans and suggested a more egalitarian, democratic story that included black history.

In the years preceding Hurricane Katrina, several local black heritage tours continued to construct a black countermemory of New Orleans history. An analysis of websites of Africans in Louisiana Tours, Loews Express Bus Charters and Tours, and Williams Tours and Transportation illustrates the different opportunities and challenges of such a historical revision.

Africans in Louisiana Tours presented a tour about slavery in Louisiana that was only "available during special seasons."[98] Its website, Africans inlouisiana.com, outlined the main theme of the bus tour "dedicated to bringing the voice of the slave back to life." With photographs of enslaved children and slave cabins at St. Joe's Plantation, the site's visual representation of Louisiana was far different from most other websites. Narrated by Leonard N. Moore, the former director of the African and African American Studies Program at Louisiana State University, the six-hour tour focused on the "slave experience along the Old River Road in Louisiana where thousands of Africans labored on some of the wealthiest plantations in the United States." The site presented itself as a teaching tool, informing visitors that "when you tour with us you will learn." Topics of instruction included the institution of slavery, with particular emphasis on the Middle Passage; life in America; the domestic slave trade; slave religion; gender roles in slavery; and slave revolts.[99]

Specifically, the tour proposed to take visitors "past the New Orleans Slave Market and through the French Quarter where slaves worked in a variety of skilled occupations. Passengers will travel along the banks of the Mississippi River past African-designed and constructed plantation homes, above ground cemetaries [sic], former slave cabins, sugar plantations, and other sites pertinent to the slave experience in Louisiana." The "African-centered" tour focused on the African and African American influence and contributions to the city of New Orleans and its environs, which were generally absent from mainstream tourist websites. Even when using the cliché of prompting visitors to "step back in time," Africansinlouisiana.com did not promise the wealth and grandeur associated with much of New Orleans's old South romanticism. Instead, the website promoted a return to "the daily life of the enslaved African through compelling stories and by viewing the slave quarters that still stand" at Laura and St. Joe Plantations. At these sites visitors were given an opportunity to see beyond the tourist-sanctioned New Orleans, both literally and figuratively, to a place "where thousands of slaves created a vibrant community life and culture as they labored on some of the nation's largest and wealthiest plantations."[100]

Following stops at River Road plantations and the River Road African American History Museum, the bus tour retraced the path taken by Charles Deslondes and his followers in the 1811 slave revolt in St. John Parish, described as the "largest slave revolt in American [h]istory." The website's description of Haitian-born Charles Deslondes and the five hundred members of his slave army, who killed whites and freed black slaves in a failed attempt to capture New Orleans "and free thousands of slaves," recovers the violent history of slavery in the region and reclaims African Americans as significant, and potentially sympathetic, historical agents. The tour also highlighted slave owners' brutal execution of eighty-two suspected rebels and staking the decapitated heads of the revolt's leaders on pikes along the road to New Orleans "as a warning to other slaves."[101] This episode, which graphically illustrates black resistance and institutionalized white violence even before the Louisiana Purchase, was not referred to on other tourist websites that featured a history of New Orleans.

As was common with black-owned tour companies attempting to compete with mainstream tours, Loews Tours featured a black heritage city tour in addition to its standard city tours. On its website, the company described its city tour as "a driving tour 45 miles long narrating the contributions of the French, Spanish, American, Irish, Italians, Greeks, Germans and Native Americans from the 1700s to the present in New Orleans." Focal points included the customary New Orleans bus tour destinations: the French Quarter, a cemetery, City Park, Bayou St. John, Lake Pontchartrain, the mansions of St. Charles Avenue, the Garden District, and the University section.[102] Its black heritage tour, the site explained, "is incorporated into the traditional city tour with added emphasis on numerous Black achievers and their accomplishments. Extensive research has been done on over 50 topics of interest. You are exposed to the entire city while absorbing the Black culture that contributes to the fabric that is New Orleans." Yet this claim is problematic, given that the description for Loews's traditional city tour does not include any reference to the city's black culture. It seems that only on the black heritage tour were visitors able to "hear the history of free people of color, slaves, Negro iron workers, Sisters of the Holy Family, Black Indians, jazz musicians, voodoo, our first Black governor and the Black Republicans of 1865."[103] This clear-cut separation of subject matter into traditional (white) and black heritage (black) tours relegated the black heritage tour—even within a black-owned company—to the margins of New Orleans's tourism industry. Representationally and structurally, these segregated tours reproduced a separate and unequal New Orleans.[104]

Williams Tours similarly presented African American history through a separate black heritage city tour. Covering three hours and forty miles, the tour included the standard city tour highlights: the French Quarter, cemeteries, City Park, Lake Pontchartrain, and St. Charles Avenue, including the university section. In addition, and of black historical significance, the tour stopped at the French Market, Armstrong Park for a "guided walking tour," Amistad Research Center, the Gallery art exhibit located uptown "in the hood," and a black-owned restaurant for a drink. The tour ended with visitors' "transport . . . back into the 20th Century [sic]," presumably after having visited New Orleans's black past.[105] Clearly, this version of New Orleans's past revised the prevailing tourism narrative by incorporating not only black history but also contemporary black cultural productions and institutions. The presentation of black heritage as both past and present attests to the longevity and viability of the city's black culture. Unlike mainstream narratives that presented the best of the city's black contributions as part of the segregated past—in the form of a thriving FPC community, the birth of jazz, and the zenith of voodoo—these black heritage tours argued for a black presence that remained significant well into the twentieth and twenty-first centuries. These tours were consistent with a comment on a GNOBTN heritage map: "It has been said that New Orleans lives with its past better than any other place in America. We don't live for the past with our heads in the sand, nor do we relive the past like an amusement park. In New Orleans the past will always be present."[106] By reconceptualizing the city's past and its legacy for present generations, these pre-Katrina black heritage tours purported to give a more authentic, inclusive portrayal of the city's history and to provide an alternative vision for a predominantly African American city beleaguered by crime, poverty, and racial inequality.

Black heritage tourism faced a range of obstacles in its quest for a better future for New Orleans. First, black heritage tour guides who charted new territory by veering from the standard tourism narratives were left to create their tours anew, without adequate training or resources from the mainstream tourism industry. Many tour guides recounted supplementing information from Louisiana history and tour guide courses with their independent research, volunteering, and travels.[107] Because of their independent studies and varied work experience, African American tour guides often developed an uncommon level of expertise on African and Afro-Creole culture.

Gregory Osborn—who in 2002 was employed by the city's public library as a specialist in local history and genealogy—had honed his skills as a graduate research assistant for the historian Gwendolyn Hall as she edited the comprehensive *Databases for the Study of Afro-Louisiana History and Genealogy, 1699–1860*.[108] Yet, despite Osborn's expertise, he found himself on the same employment path as many other African American tour guides who moonlighted with tour companies or in other occupations due to the sporadic, unreliable nature of the industry. On weekends, Osborn conducted cemetery tours with Save Our Cemeteries, an organization devoted to preserving and protecting the city's historic cemeteries. He had consulted with the African American Museum in St. Martinville, Louisiana, and was sometimes hired by mainstream tour companies for black conventions and family reunions. Once a year, Osborn was commissioned by the Tennessee Williams Festival to conduct its "African American Legacy Heritage Tour." The research-based tour emphasized the contributions and culture of enslaved black people and FPC during the colonial and antebellum periods. In his narrative and the way he answered visitors' questions, Osborn consciously corrected and reinterpreted the prevailing tourism narrative with which visitors were familiar. For instance, he used Hall's definition of Creole, which includeed people of African descent, and he deemphasized the prevalence and significance of the renowned quadroon balls. The tour's black lieux de mémoire included the former slave auction house at the corner of St. Louis and Chartres Streets (now the Omni Royal Orleans Hotel); French Quarter architecture, including slave quarters and FPC craftsmanship; the original location of Henriette Delille's Sisters of the Holy Family convent; Congo Square; the contemporary Voodoo Spiritual Botanical Temple; and a site of nineteenth-century quadroon balls (the current site of Bourbon Orleans Hotel).[109] Similarly, LMC's renegade tour guide, Jay, was a self-described history buff who had been a New Orleans tour guide for over twenty years before Hurricane Katrina. With very little support and few resources from the tourism industry, she operated her own black heritage tour company based on her research about the city's black furniture makers, maroon societies, and the 1811 slave uprising. Using these black lieux de mémoire, her counternarrative to the predominant tourism mythology reclaimed New Orleans as the nation's "most African city."[110]

Second, despite their expertise and positive reviews, Jay, Osborn, and other African American tour guides found it difficult to market their black heritage tours in a city enamored of its European heritage. They relied primarily on word of mouth and black tourism venues for most of their patronage. As a result, Jay found it necessary to freelance as a tour guide with mainstream tour companies, such as LMC, to supplement her income, while one of Osborn's African American tours was ultimately canceled because of marketing problems.[111] Lucille Le'Obia, owner of Le'Ob's Tours, recalled getting the news that the tourism brochures that she had left with a concierge at a downtown hotel had been peremptorily discarded, "as if the tour is not important enough to tell all people about it." Le'Obia viewed the insult as part of a systematic exclusion of African Americans from the mainstream tourism industry, with at most token representation during events targeting African American travelers. She explained: "In New Orleans, tourism is a billion dollar industry. African Americans spend a lot on tourism, but the hotels do not support our businesses or restaurants. The only time they call me and ask me to bring my brochures down is during the Essence Fest."[112] In an interview, Jay also identified institutional obstacles facing African American tour guides and owners: "It starts, I think, because of the marketing. From the state to the local government. When they send out materials promoting tourism in Louisiana, they omit blacks. So, there is a well-planned effort to eliminate the African Americans' existence in New Orleans. Tourist commissions, Chamber of Commerce, State Department of Tourism. Remember, this has been a Jim Crow city. We just started celebrating Louis Armstrong, and he didn't want to be buried here because of the discrimination he experienced. You know, we've had the Perezes, the David Dukes . . . Catholic Church . . . It's been an effort to eliminate [black New Orleanians]."[113]

Finally, as I have shown in earlier chapters, Jay and other African American tour guides were forced to operate their tours within a tourism market that was in many ways inhospitable to black heritage. Ironically, in pre-Katrina New Orleans—a predominantly African American city with a rich and enduring African history and culture featuring jazz, Creole cuisine, voodoo, different forms of architecture and artisanship, the largest antebellum FPC population in the United States, significant civil rights activism, and countless resources dedicated to historic preservation and tourism marketing—African Americans contended with the glaring omission of New Orleans's black history and community by the white-dominated mainstream tourism industry. In many ways, New Orleans's African American tour owners, guides, and others dependent on the city's tourism industry were placed in an untenable position, forced to conform—because of economic necessity—to the very conventions of a tourism mythology that promoted their own distortion and negation.

Osborn contended with this reality when he attempted to revise New Orleans's tourism narrative to reflect the historical record. He admits that his efforts were sometimes impeded by white visitors' feelings of guilt and discomfort in acknowledging New Orleans's history of racism and bigotry, as when he showed Homer Plessy's tomb in St. Louis Cemetery No. 1 and related the significance of the *Plessy v. Ferguson* case for the deterioration of African American rights.[114] Like Osborn, Jay used her tours to counter the predominant popular narrative in which "African Americans [were] left out of the history of the city of New Orleans." Yet, she recalls with frustration, "sometimes, even when we were doing the Gray Line [Tour] course, blacks were never mentioned except Louis Armstrong. And if they were mentioned, some [tour guides] would call them 'servants,' not 'slaves.' And the real story was not being told, as if they [whites] had guilt, which they should have, or [as if to say], 'we'll just eliminate part of the history.' And people [were] too much sacrificed. . . . We need to be educated on what we're all about, the contributions."[115]

With this goal of education in mind, local black heritage guides and companies fought for inclusion in New Orleans's tourism industry, both economically and representationally. In order to do so, they found alternative ways to identify audiences and tell their stories. Osborn, for example, included his own genealogical research, thereby revising the dominant tourism narrative according to his personal history in an effort to appeal to contemporary visitors. He recognized that in the age of the Internet, accessible archives, and growing interest in tracing one's roots, people seek history that was previously the domain of historians. In appealing to these visitors, Osborn claimed his primary goal was to educate them by providing a more complete, inclusive history of the city. Jay and other tour guides tried to meet the same goal by giving tours to New Orleans public school students and testing them to evaluate what they had learned.[116]

Despite these innovations, New Orleans black heritage tourism remained embattled. In fact, on the eve of Hurricane Katrina, the touristic preoccupation with black desire and disaster, the construction of nontourist spaces as unsafe, and the preservation movement's neglect of potential black lieux de mémoire ensured that there were few permanent or regularly operating tours or tourist sites in New Orleans dedicated to portraying the city's black history and culture. Furthermore, the French Quarter, the city's central tourist district, had few black-owned restaurants and no black-owned hotels for tourists to patronize. Black heritage bus and walking tours were seasonal and peripatetic, materializing in response to family reunions, conventions, or special events attracting large numbers of African Americans to the city. During these times, such as the annual Fourth of July weekend's Essence Music Festival, independent black tour guides either offered their own tours or were employed by larger, mainstream tour companies. As has been the case historically with black institutions, which generally receive limited financial and institutional resources, these smaller outfits often had difficulty competing with larger tour companies.[117] As a result, many black-owned businesses were left to promote themselves or to forgo the tourist business altogether. One African American restaurateur lamented: "I'd die waiting for tourists. Local clientele is the basis and mainstay of our business. Of course, we seek tourists; we welcome them; but local patronage is our bread and butter."[118] Her assessment reflected the precarious state of black heritage tourism before Hurricane Katrina. Although black spending power in the United States had risen exponentially since the 1970s, black businesses and neighborhoods failed to benefit from—and were ultimately hurt by—white corporations' class and geographic segmentation of African American consumers.[119]

New Orleans's black heritage tourism highlighted this paradox. On the one hand, the GNOBTN (later called the NOMTN) and African American leadership substantively changed the economic and political terrain of the local tourism industry with demands for more participation and equal opportunity for African Americans. On the other hand, many black businesses found that in order to attract and retain tourists, they would have to capitulate to market demands for a familiar—and often racist—tourist iconography. This dilemma reflected the extent to which New Orleans's black heritage tourism industry was itself implicated in the desire-disaster binary. As Grant contends in her study of African American tourism in Atlanta and Philadelphia, "African American history and culture have become commodities within the urban symbolic economy." She explains that this tourist commodification vacillates between "cultural expressions of the urban experience" and "projections of an urban decline that continues to justify the redevelopment of city centers, gentrification, and segregation."[120] The former is invoked by a desire for blackness, while the latter portends its disaster.

Nevertheless, the city's black heritage tourism did offer an important, if not always successful, critique of the city's tourist image. Corresponding to the structural changes effected by the creation and financing of African American– and multicultural-focused tourism organizations was a representational shift that attempted to revise the predominant image of New Orleans as a "white" city. At times the incorporation of New Orleans black history directly challenged the more dominant tourism narrative. By foregrounding black resilience and resistance to racial violence and systemic inequalities, black heritage tours attempted to subvert pre-Katrina tourist tropes of desire and disaster to express a desire for racial justice and to condemn the disaster of historical and contemporary racial injustices. More often, however, these challenges failed to substantively revise the dominant tourist tropes because they were overtaken by a conciliatory multiculturalist rhetoric, produced only ephemeral changes, or were so peripheral to the mainstream tourism representations that they struggled to survive, let alone overhaul the city's touristic culture. Such an overhaul would come in the wake of Hurricane Katrina and its devastation to the city's infrastructure and reputation. For better or worse, following the storm, New Orleans's tourism industry was forced to contend with the city's black past and future.

Five. "Starting All Over Again"

POST-KATRINA TOURISM AND THE RECONSTRUCTION OF RACE

It's really hard because it's almost like time stopped, and we're starting all over again.
— *Toni Rice, in an interview*

This shows you the topography of the city . . . and then this shows you the number of people who died—and they're still dying, by the way. — *Tour guide, "Post-Katrina City Tour," Tours by Isabelle, July 30, 2007*

This is what it looks like when you gut a house. Nothing left. The windows, the doors, everything's gotta come out, brought to the swamps. They crushed the appliances, took the Freon out of the refrigerators, brought them to Bayou Steel on the river. They ground up all the trees in a mulch, giant piles of mulch—look, a ray of hope.
— *Tour guide, "Katrina Recovery Tour," Celebration Tours, August 1, 2007*

Given the marginalization of New Orleans's black communities following Hurricane Katrina and the distortion of what happened to them, it seems that most observers failed to heed the warnings of the city's black heritage industry and the performative acts of resistance that sustained it. Nevertheless, Hurricane Katrina also thrust the images and stories of black New Orleanians into the national imagination, forcing past and potential New Orleans tourists to confront a black New Orleans that existed outside the tourist construction. As a result, post-Katrina tourists expected and even sought out different stories of the city that might help them make sense of the devastation and tragedy and that incorporate alternative images and ideas—of African Americans, the Lower Ninth Ward, poverty, and racism— that have become a part of the national discourse about New Orleans. Almost immediately after the storm, a new dominant tourism narrative was being created and revised in response to—and as a way to profit from—these different expectations.

This emerging post-Katrina tourism offers an opportunity to assess the perseverance of performative struggles of resistance and whether they might be a vital part of recovering and reclaiming New Orleans history and culture. The number and range of tours and tourism messages contributing to this tourism revision call for not simply an analysis of a single tour or tour company, but a reexamination of New Orleans tourism as a whole.[1] What is at stake in this battle over the historical memory of Hurricane Katrina is the very future of black New Orleans and its place in the nation. In describing the process of national healing following the trauma of the Civil War, the historian David Blight contends that "how people . . . would come to define and commemorate that tragedy, where they would find heroism and villainy, and how they would decide what was lost and what was won, would have a great deal to do with determining the character of the new society that they were to build."[2] Likewise, at a time when the rebuilding of New Orleans is uneven and incomplete, how we come to remember and forget the tragedy of Hurricane Katrina has far-reaching political and social implications, particularly for racial justice.[3]

Narratives of Forgetting

In the first few years after Hurricane Katrina, the tourism industry redoubled efforts to regain visitors lost since the storm with a series of new initiatives and ad campaigns.[4] Often these efforts were directed at shielding visitors from post-Katrina realities. In various ways, tourists were prompted to replace uncomfortable associations of New Orleans with black poverty, residential segregation, or African American unrest with pre-Katrina tropes of racial harmony and tourist-sanctioned performances of blackness. These narratives create what the scholar Marita Sturken has identified as a culture of comfort: "a sense of reassurance that mediates the fraught, painful, and difficult world in which the United States finds itself at this moment in history." Yet, although consumerism, memorialization, and tourism may provide meaningful ways for communities to work through emotional pain and vulnerability, Sturken's work on the memorialization of Oklahoma City and New York City's Ground Zero demonstrates that "much of the culture of comfort functions as a form of depoliticization and as a means to confront loss, grief, and fear through processes that disavow politics."[5]

This disavowal is achieved in post-Katrina New Orleans through tourism narratives that compel visitors to forget the racial and class injustice illuminated by the hurricane.

One example is the 2007 ad campaign "Fall in Love with New Orleans All Over Again." The brainchild of the New Orleans Tourism Marketing Corporation, the campaign tried to create or rekindle fonder, more innocent recollections of New Orleans, free from the troublesome images of a forsaken black community that predominated in the storm's aftermath. This campaign suggests, in fact, that instead of destroying New Orleans's vibrant culture and community, Katrina may have enhanced it. In the 2007 *Official Visitors Guide to New Orleans*, an interracial group of celebrities with New Orleans ties contend that "the food seems to taste better. The music sounds *more exuberant*. The art and ambience feel *more poignant*" (emphasis in original).[6] The presentation of an interracial coalition around New Orleans's food, music, art, and ambience jarred with the contemporaneous political battles over rebuilding and economic recovery along racial and class lines.[7] In other words, by emphasizing the shared values of all New Orleanians, irrespective of ongoing racial and class disparities, the 2007 advertising campaign advanced a postracial understanding of New Orleans recovery. To use words describing another contemporary tourism narrative that offer balanced presentations of blacks and whites, the campaign "downplay[ed] the hierarchical relationship (white over black) of the two groups in favor of a type of benign multiculturalism in which group differences are all similar and therefore unthreatening."[8] In New Orleans, the reality of systemic racial and class inequality threatens the racial fantasy that propels the city's tourist image.

The New Orleans Convention and Visitors Bureau responded by encouraging tourists to return literally and imaginatively to the fantasy of pre-Katrina New Orleans. A year after the storm, its website reassured potential tourists that "the most celebrated and historic core of the city—including the Faubourg Marigny, French Quarter, Central Business District, Warehouse and Arts District, Magazine Street, Garden District, Audubon Park and Zoo, and St. Charles Avenue—not only remains intact, both physically and spiritually, but is thriving. The cultural riches, sensual indulgences, and unparalleled service that define the New Orleans experience continue to flourish, as they have for centuries. We are open, fully prepared, and eager to welcome all of our visitors again."[9] This statement, since adopted by countless vendors and travel sites, evokes the tension between desire and disaster characterizing the pre-Katrina narrative. The description omits New Orleans's significant black historical sites as well as its contemporary black communities and our ongoing struggles for survival. The predominantly black neighborhoods of the city that are not "intact," one may assume, are disaster zones, safely removed from the predominantly white, elite "historic core of the city." Although African American neighborhoods are absent from this core, African Americans themselves can be viewed as providing the "cultural riches, sensual indulgences, and unparalleled service" that distinguish New Orleans's tourist economy. New Orleans's twenty-first-century tourism construction of Afro-Creole culture has remained mired in nineteenth-century ideas of blacks as entertaining, licentious, and subservient.

Another example of the tenacity of this narrative was the promotion of the Forest Products Machinery and Equipment Exposition, which was held in New Orleans in 2009. The marketing of the exposition relied on a subtext of desire for black tourist culture and service that conflated real African Americans with disaster. The exposition's website enjoined viewers: "Forget the images of streets swamped by Hurricane Katrina. New Orleans has worked 24/7 to restore its ability to host conventions and exhibitions in a way no city can duplicate. And this famous Southern city—known for its food, music and hospitality—is ready to host EXPO 2009."[10] This reassurance demanded the willful forgetting of the natural and man-made disasters that had devastated New Orleans and its most vulnerable communities. The performance studies scholar Joseph Roach's conception of culture as a process of both memory and forgetting suggests that the EXPO's appeal to conventioneers was part of a larger performance by which "improvised narratives of authenticity and priority may congeal into full-blown myths of legitimacy and origin." Often in the face of calamity, Roach observes, "selective memory requires public enactments of forgetting, either to blur the obvious discontinuities, misalliances, and ruptures or, more desperately, to exaggerate them in order to mystify a previous Golden Age, now lapsed."[11] Tellingly, the EXPO's return to a pre-Katrina tourism narrative required the erasure of black New Orleans, except insofar as blackness was used to perform, through the "food, music and hospitality," a romantic mythology of the antebellum South, landscaped with cooking, dancing, singing, and serving black stereotypes.[12]

Not all post-Katrina tourism, however, so unambiguously asked tourists to ignore "the streets swamped by Hurricane Katrina" or the people who lived and worked on those streets.[13] Although most post-Katrina tours paid special attention to environmental issues, such as coastal erosion and disappearing wetlands, this environmental turn did not displace a racial critique, as some scholars have suggested.[14] In fact, some tours required visitors to come face to face with post-Katrina New Orleans and the histories and memories of a painful past. Unlike the narratives of forgetting, these tourism narratives conjure up the literary conceptualization of "rememory," whereby communal healing depends upon the "re-membering of a dis-membered past."[15] The rapid development of bus and van tours conveying visitors from the French Quarter directly to the most ravaged hurricane sites, and the international controversy that they created, responded to and generated interest in a different type of New Orleans tourism.[16]

Although Gray Line Tours' "Hurricane Katrina: 'America's Greatest Catastrophe'" may have garnered the most attention, it is not the only, or even the first, company to participate in the post-Katrina repackaging of tourist New Orleans.[17] In fact, by 2007 just about every tour company, across a broad spectrum of tourism genres, was offering some type of Hurricane Katrina–related tour, including but not limited to Airboat Adventures, Louisiana Swamp Tours, Cajun Encounters, and Old River Road Plantation Adventure. Most tour companies attempted to incorporate a post-Katrina narrative into a conventional, preexisting three-hour city tour format.[18] In the standard pre-Katrina city tour, tour guides narrated the history of the city, identified historic neighborhoods and architecture, interpreted New Orleans's customs and traditions, and described unique features of the city's physical and cultural geography as they drove through the French Quarter, Faubourg Marigny, Lakeview, Central Business District, and Garden District or stopped at one of the city's aboveground cemeteries. Tours developed in the aftermath of Hurricane Katrina added stories and sites that mandated literal and metaphorical travel to the heart of the Katrina-ravaged city. Along the way, tour guides provided a timeline of the hurricane and subsequent flooding, gave emotional accounts of human suffering and loss during and in the aftermath of the storm, explained the intricacies and indignities of the post-Katrina bureaucracy, enumerated the ongoing lack and inadequacy of essential services, and introduced tourists to the new technologies and terminologies—for example, "T-wall," "MR-GO," "house markings," and FEMA trailers—that have become a part of the local lexicon since the storm.[19] Augmenting the customary pre-Katrina tourist sites were construction sites at the 17th Street, London Avenue, and Industrial Canal levee breaks; a sampling of flooded structures in various stages of rebuilding, demolition, or atrophy; and volunteer projects. Furthermore, whereas pre-Katrina city tours strategically circumnavigated the city to avoid most historically and predominantly African American neighborhoods, post-Katrina tours consistently remapped tourist New Orleans to include African American spaces in the Upper and Lower Ninth Wards, parts of New Orleans East and Gentilly, and the Tremé. At the very least, this spatial rerouting of the tourist map forced visitors to physically and psychically confront both the presence and absence of African Americans in the city.

Most apparent following Katrina was the new imperative to identify and describe communities outside of tourist New Orleans. Tour guides referred to the city's slave history and West African heritage and pointed out sites—such as Congo Square, Louis Armstrong's childhood neighborhood, the Zulu Social Aid and Pleasure Club headquarters, and other African American lieux de mémoire—that were widely unacknowledged before Hurricane Katrina. As part of this revisionist narrative, tour guides emphasized that the Ninth Ward and Tremé are historic neighborhoods, implicitly increasing their value in a city that pays special homage to the past. Most tour guides refuted the media representations of black criminality, destitution, and shiftlessness with counternarratives that stressed shared humanity, industry, and national identity. For instance, in her study of Gray Line's post-Katrina disaster tour, Phaedra Pezzullo notes how tour guides compared the tragedies of Hurricane Katrina and 9/11 to emphasize New Orleans's significance to the nation. She explains: "Implicitly, one can hear the echoes of 9/11 again haunting the tour, attempting to invoke a similar 'structure of feeling' identification and national pride."[20] Gray Line Tours was not alone in its invocation of 9/11. A tour guide for Tours by Isabelle illustrated the magnitude of flooding in the city by using Manhattan as a yardstick. As the tour left the French Quarter for areas of the city that flooded, she explained: "That's where 80 percent of the city—the people in the city live. Now, what is that 80 percent? What does it refer to? It's seven Manhattans. A hundred and forty-four square miles was under two to fourteen feet of water, and in some sections [for] up to eight weeks. So the city marinated."[21] Like the nationalist discourse and iconography evoked in the Gray Line tour, this guide's statement "is emblematic of how important some have felt it has been to imagine Katrina as an [*sic*] *national* tragedy, one in which rebuilding and rebirth will require addressing not only material needs, but also symbolic wounds of alienation" (emphasis in original).[22]

Ironically, the circumstances that alienated New Orleans from the rest of the nation sometimes helped create understanding and common purpose between previously disparate and even antagonistic groups within the city. The local tour guides—all presumably white and from predominantly white areas of the city or metropolitan area—whom I encountered on the bus and van tours shared their own stories of struggle and survival that resonated with the narratives they presented about African American storm survivors.[23] Some tour guides had not left the city even after the mandatory evacuation and used the tour to explain and justify New Orleanians' common practice of vertical evacuation, in which people sought shelter in French Quarter hotels instead of subjecting their young, elderly, or infirm family members to the inconvenient and usually unnecessary motorcade away from the city. One guide, a self-described eighth-generation descendant of the Isleños who migrated to St. Bernard Parish, Louisiana, between 1778 and 1783 during Spanish colonial rule, guided the tour van past her own Chalmette neighborhood and narrated her family's personal tragedy:

> I was in Buccaneer Villa [a community in Chalmette, Louisiana]. [My house] was [under] fourteen feet of water for six weeks, and it was skewed on the foundation . . . so it's down. I had to have it demolished, so it's just gone—because it was not structurally sound. And the sad thing—but my whole family—we all lived in an area, my mother's side, my dad's side, everybody lived within earshot of each other, but everybody's house is down. Not one house on my mother's side, or my dad's side, the family—extended family, I have cousins, not one of us was able to save any of the houses. So you couldn't go to a neighbor or a friend and say, "Can I stay with you while I'm rebuilding?" You're renting up in Paulina, or Gramercy, or Lutcher, and you're making the trip, forty-five miles in, forty-five miles out. You know, you have your job, but you still—and my family isn't unique. That's how all the families are. People are living somewhere else and coming in and work[ing].[24]

Another guide, who had moved from the disproportionately white and wealthy Lakeview neighborhood in New Orleans to the predominantly white suburb of Metairie before Katrina, considered himself fortunate to have evacuated to relatives' homes in Canton, Mississippi.[25] Despite having evacuated, he shared with survivors the agony of returning to the New Orleans area after Katrina:

> We didn't get back for one month. They wouldn't let anybody in the city. All the roads were blocked, National Guards. Trees were everywhere, helicopters, power lines—the smell was horrific, dead animals, 500,000 refrigerators had food in them without electricity. No cell phones, no way to communicate, pitch dark, no lights, National Guards everywhere.
>
> When we got to our house, it was destroyed. A mini tornado took the roof off. Eighteen inches of water came in because they shut down the pumps in Jefferson [Parish]. Mold grew over everything. We couldn't save anything. It was dark. It was late in the evening. I couldn't see in the house. We had to go around looking for somebody we could stay with. We were homeless. We never had that much clothes. We just took what we needed for two or three days. We were buying clothes in Wal-Mart in Canton, Mississippi.
>
> [In Canton], everybody was very nice to us, churches. We just didn't know what to do. We were traumatized. When you're traumatized, it's similar to losing a close loved one. At first, you don't believe it. Then you believe it, but you don't accept it. Then you accept it, but you're angry. You wanna blame somebody.[26]

In going off script to share their feelings of alienation, trauma, and confusion, tour guides at times deviated from tour company policy and disrupted the national discourse about those affected by Katrina. Tour guides' agency and indignation recast Katrina victims (or, worse, opportunists) as Katrina survivors and national citizens.

Another way that tour guides attended to the symbolic wounds of alienation was by contextualizing the scenes of deserted African Americans that tourists had encountered in the media. One guide reiterated the absence of aid at the Ernest N. Morial Convention Center for days after the storm struck: "Over by the Convention Center, nobody. Nobody in—a policeman never passed there, a National Guard, nobody. Those poor souls were out there for those—until Friday morning, and that's when [Lieutenant] General [Russel L.] Honoré hit the city and he started moving things. That's when the buses appeared, the trucks, food, water; they pulled the people from the Convention Center and brought them over here to the Superdome for the staging of getting everybody out."[27] The guide also described the contemporaneous debate over public housing between tenants and social justice organizations protesting for the tenants' right to return in opposition to the Department of Housing and Urban Development (HUD) and the Housing Authority of New Orleans (HANO), which were proposing to replace poverty-concentrated developments with mixed-income units.[28] In the process, she explained that "all of the tenants are back" in the Iberville Housing Project. Her persistent refrain that "they pay rent, it's not a free place, rent is paid" made another attempt to humanize and legitimate poor and working-class black New Orleanians as rightful American citizens by portraying them through the convention of the deserving poor instead of the equally familiar, yet castigated, trope of welfare recipients.[29] When driving past the fenced St. Bernard Housing Project, the guide was even more insistent on portraying poor African Americans as sympathetic American citizens who were unjustly and inhumanely treated by powerful government interests. She explained: "The mayor is on TV saying, 'Come home. Come back.' To what? They can't live if they have it all fenced off. HUD and HANO arrested the people when they came back. And they had their key, they have never been evicted, they've paid rent—they haven't paid rent here because they're getting, they're paying rent where they are, but they still have their personal things here. They have their furniture, they have children's pictures, all their personal belongings. So the ones that were able to come back to take a look, evaluate, and leave. When they came back they were arrested for trespassing on their property, but HANO and HUD say, 'No, that area, you can't. That's trespassing because that project is due to come down.'"[30]

On a different tour, another guide was equally critical of political and business elites who exploited poor and marginalized communities: "The top-level people provide jobs and housing. They came back, but the entry-level people couldn't come back. They never had no place to live. They brought in 70,000 Hispanics from Honduras and Mexico to clean up the city. They paid them $17.50 an hour in cash every day, no income tax as an incentive to do a dirty, stinking, dangerous job."[31] These narratives substantiated one tour guide's indictment that "we were done in by an act of man" and another's claim that "the weak link in the chain, in your flood control, flood protection system, turned out to be the poorly designed, poorly built levees on the outflow canal," presented as evidence that "the government let a lot of people down."[32] These instances of rememory countered the prevailing "self-image of the United States as innocent" that has been justly criticized by Sturken for its positing of the United States as "a country of pure intentions to which terrible things can happen, but which itself never provokes or initiates attack."[33] Instead, tour guides' criticisms typified the post-Katrina narrative's shifting of blame from the victims of the storm to the government authorities and private corporations—particularly local and national government leaders, the U.S. Army Corps of Engineers, the Road Home grant program, and insurance companies—that had violated the public trust. A recurring theme was that Katrina hit all classes and races of New Orleans, and that the dismal recovery efforts did not reflect the character of the people—or, more specifically, the deviance of black people—but the failures of political and business authorities. Tales of U.S. citizens left stranded without food or water; public-housing residents who were unjustly prohibited from retrieving their belongings from structurally sound units; and the exploitative employment practices targeting people of color jarred with pre-Katrina tourist images of the city.

Symbol and Spectacle: The Lower Ninth Ward

Perhaps more than any other post-Katrina lieu de mémoire, the Lower Ninth Ward became the city's most conspicuous tourist icon. As such, the Lower Ninth Ward holds the French Quarter, long presented as the physical and spiritual center of the city, up to "a cruel hyperbolic mirror."[34] To the neglect, and perhaps relief, of other neighborhoods and racial and ethnic communities, the Lower Ninth Ward became a tangible symbol of black desire and disaster almost immediately after the hurricane. Although some tour companies attempted to minimize the exploitation of Ninth Ward residents by limiting tourist access to certain neighborhoods or prohibiting tourists from taking photographs, they all participated in the spectacularization of the disaster and recovery in the neighborhood.[35]

However, spectacularization is not an altogether cynical approach; instead, it embodies the tension between reproducing and remedying structural inequalities. The media spectacle of Hurricane Katrina both exacerbated social disparities and initiated new ways of thinking about how to redress them. Post-Katrina bus tours, while profiting from the continued desolation of New Orleans neighborhoods, might also offer opportunities for societal reassessment and change.[36] The sociologist Kevin Gotham contends that these tours convey "a subtle form of immanent critique to build global awareness of New Orleans's plight, appeal to peoples' empathy and generate public support to rebuild the city. Bus tours use spectacle to showcase physical destruction to transmit information, provide background and context, and expose people to the devastation of urban and suburban neighborhoods."[37] In numerous ways, post-Katrina bus tours have employed the spectacle of destroyed black Lower Ninth Ward neighborhoods to stress the commonalities between New Orleans's black communities and the rest of the—that is, white—city and nation.

One tour guide's reminiscence that the Lower Ninth Ward "was predominantly Caucasian when [he] was a teenager" probably helped reincorporate the predominantly African American neighborhood into a more palatable and recognizable past for mostly white tourists.[38] More important, tour guides' descriptions of the contemporary neighborhood dispelled myths about African American vagrancy and delinquency. The same guide reassured his tour group: "Now [the Lower Ninth Ward is] predominantly African American—hard-working people, pay taxes, serve in the military, vote, send their kids to school. Seventy-five percent own their own house, older houses built in the 1800s out of cypress trees, well kept. They took care of their houses."[39]

Although offering a divergent set of statistics, another guide nonetheless painted a similar portrait of industriousness and community pride to elicit a compassionate response from tourists:

> Lower Ninth is a working poor community. Over 60 percent of these homes were owned by the working poor. These homes were built in the 1940s for maybe $5,000, $8,000. They're 1,000, 1,100 square feet. To rebuild today it's $125 a square foot basic, for the little art squares, or that linoleum stuff on the floor, not granite tops, not hardwood floor, just basic rebuild[ing], what the people are being charged $125 a square foot [for]. They're gouging the people. And this is the working poor.
>
> It wasn't that the people in this area were just sitting back getting the welfare check. They were working—making just enough money that took them off the welfare roll—but they were working, and they were proud of their little homes. Now you did have a little small section back here at the end of Caffin Avenue, where you had a little bit of drug activity, but that's in all neighborhoods, but that was—[the

media] focused in on this. But the majority of the people were working people. They worked in the hospitality industry, they worked in the culinary industry. They were waiters, they were cleaners, they worked for the hotels, the restaurants, the Convention Center.[40]

In this case, tourists' compassion for displaced Lower Ninth Ward residents is dependent on recognizable tropes of African Americans serving mostly white tourists in the hospitality industry. Nevertheless, these familiar images were transmuted outside the city's traditional tourism zones, where tourists were forced to encounter the vestiges of African American lives removed from their tourist performances.

In addition to historicizing and contextualizing the Lower Ninth Ward as a vibrant African American community before the storm, tour guides also used the neighborhood to present counternarratives to portrayals of African American criminality and irresponsibility in the wake of the storm. One tour guide retorted: "Nobody is for a free ride. So again, there's nothing wrong with the character of the people. It's not that you're just waiting for somebody else to help you, it's home."[41] Another tour guide's explanation that the people in the area were "actually on high ground close to the river. I'm sure most of them didn't have flood insurance" refuted criticism that residents were foolhardy to inhabit such a potentially dangerous natural environment and recast them as unfortunate but sympathetic casualties of the flood and poor public policy decisions. His anecdotal reference to people who drowned after "not getting in a helicopter, refus[ing] to get in because they don't wanna leave their dog" became a heartrending story of caring pet owners who contemplated a terrible dilemma: "If I can't bring my dog, I'm not leaving. I couldn't live with myself knowing I let my dog drown." In another instance, this guide rebutted the media spectacle of lawlessness and profligacy: "A few people set their house on fire. A few people stole guns out of Wal-Mart, shot at the police, the helicopters, a few people [were] looting, but most people weren't. The majority of people were good. The news media picks it up and slants it to sell commercials. They sell bad news up north saying we're still shooting at each other and all that. That's not true. They have drugs. That's gonna go on forever unless the people of America stand up and say we're not gonna take it anymore. It's an $80 billion industry. They're not gonna shut down drugs. All those people are buying it, and a lot of rich people buy it, and a lot of rich people get kickbacks from the drugs."[42] His rebuke of the news media, wealthy profiteers, and apathetic

U.S. citizens posited post-Katrina social ills as a national problem affecting all segments of U.S. society, including "up north." Yet most of his tour was dedicated not to exposing Lower Ninth Ward problems but to vindicating the neighborhood in the wake of the sensational stories most familiar to tourists. He countered those accounts "1,000 horrific stories, maybe 10,000, but also 1,000 or 10,000 heroic stories. So many wonderful people helping each other. People needed to talk to survive. They were traumatized."[43]

Even the acknowledgment of trauma in the lives of black New Orleanians was an important response to the vilification—or, perhaps worse, abandonment—of the post-Katrina city. As the sociologist Emmanuel David notes in his study of the elite New Orleans–based organization Women of the Storm, such an intervention "helps move our understandings of suffering, violence, and loss out of the recesses of the individual psyche and into the body politic."[44] Like these women, who used their cultural and financial capital to resuscitate the memory of a devastated New Orleans and to reframe the city's cultural trauma as a national tragedy, post-Katrina tour guides also "sought to shed light on the ongoing crisis in New Orleans by keeping the catastrophe in public discourse, collectively endowing the events with heightened meaning and engaging in affective and expressive reactions to fears of being forgotten."[45] This fear prompted one tour guide's lament about diminishing evidence of the devastation: "Every house looked like this or worse. Every day, they clean up. There's not gonna be much left to see except the houses."[46] Another tour guide conjured up the memory of displaced Ninth Ward residents for tourists gazing on the barren landscape: "Now the people in this area, all this vacant land, this used to be houses, those houses are all gone. Over here on the left is a memorial to the Ninth Ward people who lost their homes. . . . You'll notice the blue columns give you the depth of the water and then the red chairs for the people who used to sit out, that one blue chair is for the 139 who died, drowned, in this area. Now you see those brick pillars, that was the foundation at one time of homes; they're gone."[47]

Tour guides' appropriation of the Lower Ninth Ward as a "disaster memory site" offers another way for everyday citizens to reflect on and potentially shape the national response to social injustices that are magnified by disasters, such as the 1927 flood to which one tour guide compared Hurricane Katrina.[48] She encouraged her passengers to read John Barry's *Rising Tide: The Great Mississippi Flood of 1927 and How It Changed America* as an unheeded cautionary tale of how greed, corruption, and arrogance create "natural" disasters for poor, disfranchised groups.[49] In perhaps the most forthright correlation I heard between the devastation caused by Hurricane Katrina and the legacy of New Orleans's history of race- and class-based oppression, the tour guide predicted: "You'll get the same reasoning why Lower Ninth is where it is today with the levees are about nine feet, and all the levees coming to them are fourteen and nineteen feet high. It's a natural spillway because you wanna protect the economic hub, which is the city of New Orleans. And you're going to see it. I don't have to say a word. I'm going to show you that natural spillway that's there even today."[50] Her incrimination of U.S. economic and political policies is enabled by an appropriation of the Lower Ninth Ward.

In thus appropriating the Lower Ninth Ward, tour guides embarked on a difficult balancing act, attempting to straddle the line between notions of exceptionalism ("The Lower Ninth Ward got the worst") and representativeness ("But it wasn't just the Ninth Ward. You've been through Gentilly, Broadmoor, Central City, Lakeview; it was all sections of the city").[51] Tour guides presented the Lower Ninth Ward as a distinctive lieu de mémoire, but they simultaneously challenged tourists' preconceptions about the area's singularity. One guide emphasized: "I don't think people realize from outside this area the extent of the devastation. It's like Ninth Ward, that's all."[52] Another said: "They got all these expensive homes out in the East, but people get the idea that it was only the poor people.... But everybody got hit. And in the East, as you know, we've got some very expensive homes and subdivisions out there, and they were very badly flooded."[53] This tension manifested itself in the way that tour guides talked—and were silent—about race and class in the pre- and post-Katrina city.

Touring Race and Class

Sometimes the counternarrative of communal tragedy and national belonging complicated racial and class misconceptions and opened up space for unheralded stories of solidarity and diversity within and between races and economic classes, as well as critiques of entrenched power structures. One tour guide was especially attentive to the economic implications of rebuilding and recovery. She interpreted visual cues of class differences and disparity with her observation: "Now notice how—see this is the street we turned off on, this is Harrison. You notice the income here—I mean the housing.

It's upper middle class, middle class, right in the shadow of lower-income people. Well, that's how the city is, it's a little checkerboard community. You have low income, high income within whispering distance of each other, but that's how it is."[54]

Later in the tour, she alluded more directly to the stark difference in recovery efforts between the lower-income, predominantly African American neighborhoods on the tour and the affluent, predominantly white Lakeview neighborhood. While driving through Lakeview, she reported: "Now these people have services. You see big houses; this is not your lower-income area as you can see, but they have their streetlights. They have all of their services."[55] The guide did not limit her focus to the discrepancy between the rich and poor, however. She also explained the impact of the storm and governmental neglect on the city's professionals, many of whom constituted the city's sizable black middle class:

> But look at these homes. Overnight—overnight they have professionals who are jobless and homeless. They have doctors that have no patients. They're trying to pay rent for their office, they have to pay a mortgage, they're trying to hold their staff together. Well, you can put money aside for about two months, but then after the second month you're running low if you don't have any income coming in. You have dentists that lost out, you have lawyers that lost all their clients because there was nobody in the city, everybody left. And these homes, as I mentioned before, it wasn't just Katrina hit Ninth Ward, the working poor. Katrina hit everybody.[56]

This rare discussion of middle-class loss and dislocation directs attention to the tremendous toll on the city's most educated and accomplished citizens who depended on the poor and working class, not only as clients and employees but also as neighbors, family members, and caretakers.[57]

Despite being more inclusive of black spaces and stories, the post-Katrina narrative often placed black communities in the preexisting framework of New Orleans racial exceptionalism. The idea that all black and white New Orleanians were unified and undifferentiated in their pre- and post-Katrina struggles obscures a history of racial and class inequalities and denies the persistent role of race and racism in post-Katrina policies. The political scientist Robert Lieberman explains the contradictions inherent in such notions of a "color-blind" society:

Hurricane Katrina and its aftermath constitute, in effect, a metaphor for the deep tension between color-blind and race-conscious models of politics and policy that has been one of the central defining themes of U.S. political culture, dating back to the founding of the American republic and even before. On the one hand, American politics is founded on the basis of a set of egalitarian liberal principles, which imply that race, like any other ascriptive category of social relations, should be irrelevant to public life and that the racial distinctions that often structure public life, for whatever purpose, are anomalous or invalid. On the other hand, even a cursory glance at U.S. history reveals that color blindness has more often been the exception than the rule and suggests that racial hierarchy and inequality are central to American political development.[58]

The illogic of a color-blind society extends to issues of class, as well. One tour guide went so far as to discredit New Orleans's disproportionate rate of poverty: "We don't have poverty. The Lower Ninth Ward ain't poverty. They might have a little less, but they're not poverty. There's lots of opportunity in New Orleans to evolve if you want to. Some people, they're happy where they are, but anybody needs help in New Orleans will get it. It's a Judeo-Christian community. You'll get more help than you can handle."[59] His statement relies on what the black studies scholar Clyde Woods describes as the dominant definition of poverty: "a combination of impersonal economic forces, cultural and moral flaws, and personal failings" that ignores causative historic or systemic inequities.[60] Furthermore, the guide's assessment belies the facts that more than a third of the city's black population lived below the poverty line before Katrina and that since Katrina, a lack of affordable housing and stalemates with insurance companies and the Road Home housing recovery program contributed to a 100 percent increase in homelessness.[61]

If the idea of a color-blind society obscures New Orleans's racial hierarchy, the corollary construction of the white savior glorifies this hierarchy. Tour guides often invoked this trope when presenting Musicians' Village, the Habitat for Humanity musician-themed community in the Upper Ninth Ward, or Brad Pitt's Make It Right Foundation and its architectural innovations in the Lower Ninth Ward. In these instances, New Orleans's post-Katrina narrative presented African Americans as victims awaiting the action and expertise of whites to intervene on our behalf. Stories heralding the racial, economic, human rights, and environmental justice activism of local grassroots organizations, cultural centers, and religious institutions went untold.[62]

Conspicuous Absences

Still, it was not difficult to find examples of African American agency in the post-Katrina narrative. One tour company had its tours make a restroom stop at Stewart's Diner, a black-owned restaurant in the Ninth Ward whose owners generously answered tourists' questions and shared photographs of President George W. Bush's visit to the restaurant and their family's subsequent visit to the White House, as his guests.[63] The displayed photographs of a smiling President and Mrs. Bush, Mayor Ray Nagin, and the Stewart family and employees, coupled with the renaming of the Monday red-beans-and-rice dinner as the "president's special" in honor of Bush's 2006 visit, garnered positive press for the president after his abysmal response immediately following the hurricane. Yet the restaurant's co-owner, Kim Stewart, while unexpectedly charmed by the president in real life, said she planned to hold him accountable for his promises that "help is on the way, that he is working to make sure it goes into the right hands."[64] More important, perhaps, is the Stewart family's implicit incrimination of the Bush administration and its failure to provide assistance to their family or community even two years after the storm. Before the lunch-hour rush when I visited with a tour, Kim Stewart gave sole credit for the reopening of the restaurant and the ongoing rebuilding of neighborhood homes and businesses to the generosity of family and friends. Her acknowledgment exposed the lack of accountability by government agencies and private insurers and, in turn, testified to the resilience and resolve of New Orleans's black community.

Even when visitors were not given the opportunity to talk to black residents, the tours provided other, sometimes unintentional, opportunities to witness the city's black presence and participation. Along the redirected routes, tour buses drove past pre-Katrina murals and post-Katrina memorials depicting black life and loss throughout the city's history. For instance, guides directed tourists' attention to the North Claiborne Avenue underpass, where the interstate supports had been painted by local African American artists. One tour guide said: "Now if you notice these pilings that have decorations on them. If you start on Orleans Avenue and go all the way down to St. Bernard Avenue, and you look at these paintings, that will give you the history, the culture, the important people, moments in time of the enslaved and the free people of color in the New Orleans area. The city was paying $1,500 per column to the artist to paint. And your painting had to be approved; it had to be related to the enslaved and the free people of color."[65] These visual markers reference both the historical and cultural contributions of the city's African American population. Yet they also betoken a deeper subtext of black desire and disaster.

Following Hurricane Katrina, this section of the North Claiborne Avenue underpass in the Faubourg Tremé neighborhood served as a makeshift dump site that one guide noted "was filled with cars that were dragged from all over the city."[66] Unfortunately, this was not the first or the worst disaster to befall the neighborhood, which had been bereft by the construction of Interstate 10 decades before. The urban geographer Richard Campanella's terse description poignantly captures the effect on the neighborhood: "From St. Anthony to the Pontchartrain Expressway is what one might call *lost Claiborne*. Once described as the 'Main Street of Black New Orleans,' this oldest portion of the street, serving Faubourg Tremé and the Sixth Ward, was dealt what some deemed a crushing blow in 1966–1969 when its beautiful oak-alley neutral ground was bulldozed and overlaid with Interstate 10. The street below, shadowy and thunderously noisy, is utterly devastated as a historical streetscape" (emphasis in original).[67] While homes, businesses, and the natural landscape were sacrificed in the name of development and modernization in the Tremé, white preservationists waged a fierce, successful battle to stave off a riverfront expressway that would have cut through the neighboring French Quarter. Their achievement in securing the neighborhood's federal designation as a historical landmark cemented the transformation of the French Quarter from a decaying, disreputable neighborhood into a revered, romanticized heritage site where black desire could be centralized and sanitized.[68] The irony, of course, is that city leaders opted to preserve a fictionalized past and stereotyped representations of blackness while refusing to sustain the living cultural traditions and folkways created and practiced in the Tremé. Their choice had broader implications for the development of the city's modern tourism industry. In the ensuing years, as the city's white-centered tourism industry became more entrenched, the French Quarter was instantiated as a sanctioned site of black desire, while once-vibrant African American neighborhoods, such as the Tremé, became symbols of urban disaster, purposefully removed from the tourist gaze.[69]

Despite the alienation from tourist New Orleans, such neighborhoods and the cultural innovations that they produced endured. Even on the "shadowy and thunderously noisy" Claiborne Avenue where Interstate 10 had physically and spiritually scarred the Tremé, African American culture continued to thrive. In the decades before Katrina, black New Orleanians congregated beneath the overpass to shop at local markets, join in second line parades, celebrate Mardi Gras, and sing and chant with processions of Mardi Gras Indians.[70] By driving through and narrating the history of African American neighborhoods, post-Katrina tours bridged the gap between the artificially constructed tourist New Orleans and the unscripted living city, which was more difficult to contain. The physical and cultural remnants of this living city, as reflected in the interstate murals, referenced the practices and performances of New Orleans's pre-Katrina black community.

These indicators of a once-vibrant black community provide what the cultural anthropologist Helen Regis refers to as "a critical moral consciousness" that questions or challenges powerful institutions and narratives.[71] On the post-Katrina bus tours, visitors were confronted by the literal signs of this challenge that were brought into relief against the physical and tourist landscapes. A sign in front of the St. Bernard Housing Project unsuccessfully protested the demolition of that public-housing complex. As one tour guide drove past, she painstakingly explained the significance of the protest: "It's the black sign with white writing on it, and you see—and the white writing are the names of the people who—some—some of the people who lived in the project here, and they're saying they wanna come home, let us decide. And you're gonna see their names, and I'll stop so you can see it on the left. 'The people must decide. Survivors' village, until we come home.' Can you see it over there on the left? And these are the names of the families that lived over here in the project, but they wanna come home."[72] Another sign in the Lower Ninth Ward—"We want our country to love us as much as we love it"—resisted the designation of evacuees as refugees and silently claimed citizenship for those who had been displaced by the storm and government negligence. Similarly, the sign "Roots Run Deep Here," posted on a house in the Lower Ninth Ward, attested to a history and community in New Orleans not often acknowledged in popular narratives about the city (see figure 5.1).

FIGURE 5.1 • "Roots Run Deep Here" sign in front a house in the
Lower Ninth Ward (July 2009). Photograph by author.

Nevertheless, there is no denying that the absence of African Americans was conspicuous on these tours. At the time that I took them, two years after the storm (and as subsequent visits have revealed), the drive through predominantly black neighborhoods was often a drive through a desolate landscape of razed houses, dilapidated structures, piles of debris, and impassable streets and sidewalks overtaken by weeds and decaying trees (see figures 5.2–5.3). Only occasionally did I see even paltry signs of life or rebuilding. One Gray Line tour guide, referring to New Orleans East, said matter of-factly: "I don't think much is going to come back here. I think it's just going to go away."[73] Other tour guides intimated as much for portions of the Lower Ninth Ward and Gentilly. Still, even the absence of black residents and signs of recovery in black neighborhoods eerily and powerfully critiqued the exclusion of African Americans from the rebuilding efforts in New Orleans and from the local and national narratives that precipitated that exclusion. In her justification for not including the voices of poor women in her study of Puerto Rican women and U.S. colonialism, Laura Briggs admits that "silent subalterns are troubling, and should be; they haunt texts as the victims of violence, the bad conscience of imperialism and racism."[74] In a similar way, New Orleans's African American population, disproportionately displaced following the storm, continued to indict the city and the nation.

After the Katrina Tour: Narratives of New Orleans's Future?

No sooner was this indictment made than most tours completed the "Katrina portion of the tour" and headed uptown to the palatial mansions of the Garden District.[75] Although the visual and thematic transition between neighborhoods was abrupt and usually unacknowledged by tour guides, one tour website's description unintentionally revealed the dissonance of the scheduled route: "Along the way we will also show some of the devastation caused by Hurricane Katrina in 2005. From there we head to the 'American Sector,' the New Orleans Garden District. Alive and well with its live-oak tree lined St. Charles Avenue, you will get a great sense of the luxury and extravagance of old New Orleans. This is a true step back into the antebellum era."[76] The journey along St. Charles Avenue lacked any social history or commentary and apparently did not deviate from pre-Katrina tours of the area. As tour guides pointed out marble stairways, Grecian columns, and Victorian cottages, the tour catapulted passengers back to a period preserved in time that, according to one guide, is bound by the years

FIGURE 5.2 · Dilapidated structures and overgrown vegetation in the Lower Ninth Ward symbolize the neglect of many predominantly black neighborhoods in post-Katrina New Orleans (May 2013). Photograph by author.

FIGURE 5.3 · Even nearly eight years after the storm, many streets in the Lower Ninth Ward are conspicuous for the absence of the African Americans who once inhabited the neighborhood (May 2013). Photograph by author.

1803 to 1848. The guide's pronouncement that "the whole city's a museum" accurately reflected the tourism industry's enshrinement of a racialized fantasy.[77] The retreat into the sanctity of the antebellum white city from the trauma of the abandoned black city signified a retreat from the difficulty of redressing racism into the security of a white mythical past. Even when tour guides referred to the present during this portion of the tour, they did so often to promote the frivolity and joie de vivre so closely associated with the city. For instance, one tour guide played Benny Grunch's song "There Ain't No Place to Pee on Mardi Gras Day," and another handed out Mardi Gras beads to passengers.[78]

Adding to the disconnect between the exigencies of post-Katrina recovery and the tropes of pre-Katrina tourist fantasies was the constant fear that tourism, and hence the city, would not rebound if tourists were not entertained and reassured by the familiar tourist conventions. Before passengers disembarked, tour guides thanked them profusely for taking the tour, visiting the city, and helping support the local economy. Their assurances that "every penny spent helps recovery" and that tourists "could not do more for us than [they're] doing just being here" had as much to do with their own livelihood as service industry workers as with the challenges still facing New Orleans.[79] The desire to resuscitate the hospitality industry and the tens of thousands of jobs associated with it nonetheless reestablished business as usual and relieved visitors of any political, social, or moral responsibility beyond being tourists. For example, one guide used humor to downplay the residual effects of the storm and praised tourists for simply visiting the city irrespective of discouraging media reports: "Thank God you all are coming. Like you're taking a chance because if you believe what's on TV, you still think we're flooded, got alligators jumping at your behind, and you have to wear masks and all that, but that's old footage. That's old stuff."[80] The "old stuff"—media coverage, pictorial representations, and tourist scenes of post-Katrina destruction and suffering—might be best understood as kitsch, "a[n] image or object [that] not only embodies a particular kind of prepackaged sentiment, but conveys the message that this sentiment is universally shared, that it is appropriate, and, importantly, that *it is enough*. When this takes place in the context of politically charged sites of violence, the effect is inevitably one that reduces political complexity to simplified notions of tragedy" (emphasis in original).[81] Tellingly, the tour guide's insistence that Katrina and its legacy are "old stuff" paves the way for a continued reliance on tourism and maintenance of the very policies that created

Katrina's man-made disaster.[82] Kevin Gotham and Miriam Greenberg, in their comparative study of recovery efforts after 9/11 and Katrina, suggest that efforts to promote tourism may, in fact, supersede efforts to rebuild and revitalize communities. They conclude that "in the present context, urban recovery and rebuilding in New York and New Orleans should be seen as a contradictory process of market-driven, socio-spatial transformation that is aggravating inequalities and impeding community recovery efforts."[83] Undoubtedly, the reliance on tourism mitigates against an overhaul of the city's predominant racialized narrative or other challenges to the status quo.

What resulted from the post-Katrina tourism narrative was an uneven, inconsistent construction of black New Orleans. By foregrounding disaster, most post-Katrina bus tours have been forced to acknowledge another New Orleans—one outside the tourist boundaries, primarily black, often poor, and still largely neglected by the city and government. Tourist brochures and advertisements, in contrast, have failed to relinquish (and encourage tourists to recall) the myths of racial exoticism and white supremacist desire for a construction of blacks as artistically talented but socially inferior. In the midst of this tension was the constant exuberant reassurance that the city that tourists love—that is, the white-dominated, "historic," and exotic New Orleans—had not been damaged and was even better than ever. In scripted and unscripted ways, New Orleans's emerging post-Katrina tourism vacillated between conventional narratives of white southern mythology and more recent narratives of black history and agency, between a tourist-sanctioned fantasy of a slavocracy and a post-Katrina vision of democracy. Even the post-Katrina bus tours, which physically leave behind the "Disney-fied" stability of tourist New Orleans, exhibited this uncertainty.[84] Mimicking their movement between the revitalized French Quarter and the ruins of the Ninth Ward, these tours ambivalently expressed both the view that the city had recovered from the storm intact and was ready to do business as usual and the belief that New Orleans and its residents, particularly its black population, continued to languish from neglect and abandonment (see figure 5.4). In most tours, the pre-Katrina narrative of racial desire rested uneasily alongside an emergent post-Katrina counternarrative of racial disaster.

Within three years, most of these post-Katrina tours had shifted their focus to rebirth and recovery, leaving one to wonder if the incipient moment of an alternative tourism narrative had passed.[85] The space—however limited—for African American stories and histories of resistance to vie with, or perhaps overtake, mainstream constructions of blackness had al-

FIGURE 5.4 • The meticulously landscaped grounds in the French Quarter's Jackson Square offer a stark contrast to the devastation in the Lower Ninth Ward (July 2008). Photograph by author.

ready diminished. One need only compare Tours by Isabelle's 2007 and 2008 brochures to see the tenacity of pre-Katrina narratives. The 2007 brochure cover presents a split image of New Orleans, exemplified by the juxtaposition of two unrelated images depicting two of the company's tours. The top half of the cover features a photograph of Isabelle Cossart, the company's owner, costumed as a southern belle against the backdrop of the palatial Oak Alley plantation. The caption for her photograph is the company's motto: "We'll make you fall in love with Louisiana!"[86] This visual introduction to the company's plantation tours clearly links the appeal of Louisiana for white tourists to the staging of antebellum romance. Visitors are promised a "pilgrimage back in time" that will presumably transport them to an era in which the opulence and grandeur represented in the photograph were sustained by the subjugation and exploitation of black Louisianans.[87] The bottom half of the cover, however, promotes the company's "Post-Katrina and City Tour." A meteorological representation of the eye of the storm as it made landfall in Louisiana directs the eye to the photograph below of an actual dilapidated house, seemingly imploded by the storm surge. Above the photograph, the imperative "witness post-Katrina devastation" demands that potential tourists face the harsh realities of contemporary Louisiana, thereby offering an unintended rejoinder to the antebellum mythology depicted by the costumed Cossart.[88]

These competing images visually replicated the competing narratives that tour companies and tourists negotiated in the first two years following Hurricane Katrina. Though eluding an easy resolution, their opposition pointed to the possibility of a tourism narrative in flux. The fact that the two photographs vied for the same tourists suggested that there may have been an opening—even in the mainstream tourism narrative—for alternative voices and visions of the region. Although Tours by Isabelle continued to offer its "Post-Katrina City Tour," the 2008 cover reverted to the exclusive use of the plantation imagery. The photograph of the costumed Cossart beneath a canopy of oak trees that frame the Big House fills the entire cover of the 2008 brochure, a sign perhaps that the post-Katrina narrative of disaster had already been subsumed by the pre-Katrina narrative of desire (see figures 5.5–5.6).[89] If so, an opportunity was lost to understand who black New Orleanians are, what we have contributed to the city, and what we might need to recover and rebuild.

Post-Katrina Black Heritage Tourism

Although mainstream tour companies reverted to pre-Katrina tourism images and practices, the city's African American tourism industry took a severe blow. The historically understaffed and underfunded New Orleans Multicultural Tourism Network (NOMTN) was hit harder than the city's other destination marketing organizations, all of which had been affected by Katrina, and was forced to operate with a staff of two, down from its high of six employees before the hurricane.[90] In an interview four years after Katrina, Toni Rice—the fifth president of the NOMTN (formerly known as the Greater New Orleans Black Tourism Network), all of whom were African American women—tempered the truism that with "smaller revenues, the blacks gonna get cut first" with an acknowledgment that the cuts had been a direct result of the loss of the African American tourist market. She explained:

> I don't think it was a specific "Let's just cut out the black programs."
> You have to put your monies in the general market because the general market is what's coming back. The African American market had

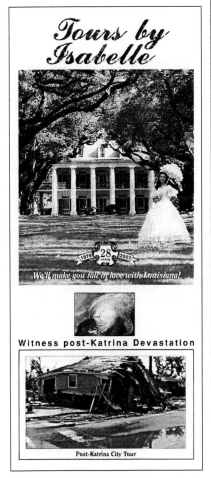

FIGURES 5.5–5.6 • *Left*: The 2007
Tours by Isabelle's brochure features
plantation and Hurricane Katrina
imagery, highlighting the tension
between pre-Katrina and emerging
post-Katrina tourism narratives.
Above: Tours by Isabelle's 2008 brochure
illustrates a retreat from post-Katrina
narratives of disaster and a return to a
pre-Katrina narrative of desire.

not started to come back yet. There are a couple different reasons. Some of the research show[s] that they love New Orleans, but they felt guilty about coming back. "How can I come back to New Orleans when people didn't have a place to live?" So that really is the last segment to start coming back. That's just now happening four years after. They always came for Essence; they always came for Bayou Classic, but outside of that, they didn't.[91]

While awaiting the return of African American visitors, Rice was forced to find new ways to meet the NOMTN's mission. She offered the following reflections on the changes the organization implemented after the storm:

> I almost have to break it down, pre-Katrina and post-Katrina, because pre-Katrina, we had a very well-defined, very clear mission and it was twofold: to promote New Orleans as a multicultural destination and to provide economic opportunities for small businesses in the tourism and hospitality industry. So we've been at the forefront of that since 1990.
>
> Post-Katrina, we still have the same mission, but we have to go about it in a very different way, mainly because so many of the small and emerging businesses are no longer here. They never came back after the storm. It's been very difficult to get up and running, so our primary focus has been just promoting New Orleans as a multicultural destination to people that have visited, thinking about visiting, used to visit every year but now they don't visit anymore. So that's more our mission.
>
> Also post-Katrina, there was a serious funding issue, as [there] was with every other organization in the city. Everybody relied on the hotel-motel tax. Post-Katrina there was no hotel-motel tax, so you're very limited in what you can accomplish with no money. So it's been hard, but we're gradually coming back. Some of the research tells us that we're on the right track, so we're getting back.[92]

Clearly, the road back was difficult for the NOMTN. The organization's three hundred members, whose dues had supported a range of services for members before the hurricane, "were just not able to pay post-Katrina," according to Rice. Four years after the storm, the NOMTN still had no paid membership and instead maintained a free database of minority businesses and disseminated information about conventions, tour groups, and family reunions. With its reduced staff and budget, the NOMTN had to discontinue its networking functions, training seminars, member-initiated programming, and even informal brokering between member businesses. As Rice described the situation, "we did a lot of hand-holding, and a lot of networking, and a lot of matchmaking. I'd like to get back to that again, but right now that's just not a possibility."[93]

The absence of this type of institutional support had broader implications for the persistence of counternarratives to the city's racialized tourism narratives. The fledgling, itinerant black heritage bus tours that had provided rare instances of performative resistance before Katrina seemed to disappear altogether in the hurricane's wake. Despite the inability of the NOMTN to provide the type of training and networking opportunities that might have sustained these companies in the past, Rice put much of the blame for these failures on the black-owned tour companies, which often floundered in "putting together a good tour that would appeal to African Americans." Dismissing criticisms that black heritage tours have been discriminated against by the white-dominated tourism industry, Rice held African American business owners accountable for learning how to navigate the tourism industry and adapt to its competitive, bottom-line philosophy:

> The hotels—it's strictly about money. If you're a large tourism operator, they are paying bellmen, the front desk people to promote their tours. That's the way it is in every city, every hotel. It doesn't matter; that's not going to change. They are going to promote the people that they're getting incentives from, and that's just that.
>
> The second thing is, I don't think we understand the value of marketing and networking because just this morning, [there was] a call about someone that wants a list of conventions coming to the city. I don't have a list of every convention that comes to the city. That is the Convention and Visitors Bureau. Invest in a membership, and you will have access to it. We don't want to do that. We want to go around the system. "Just give me the list." You have to invest in your business. You have to market. You have to go to every network function. When you get that list of conventions that are coming in, you just send them something in the mail. No one is going to promote your business. That is the thing that infuriates me most about African American businesses in general. They want somebody to promote them, and nobody's going to promote you. *You* have to promote you.[94]

Rice's frustration, although directed at African American businesses, might have also been a result of her sense that she was powerless to effectively serve her constituents or to be fully accepted by all facets of the white-dominated tourism industry, despite her organization's twenty-year track record at the forefront of cultural tourism.

Rice admitted to tiring of the constant need to prove herself and justify the existence of the NOMTN to tourism industry insiders: "This is a hard [pause]. It's hard to constantly have to validate and explain why you need to exist. It doesn't matter how much success, how much you can show the numbers. Every year you have to say, 'this is why you need to fund this.' I mean, not that I have to go back to ask for the funding. So it kind of wears you down to constantly have to explain yourself. But it's getting better. It's getting better. But as you get a new crop of people into the industry, you have to explain it again."[95]

When she did explain the NOMTN's contribution to building and sustaining New Orleans's tourism economy, she pointed to the organization's pivotal role in developing the niche markets of African American and multicultural tourism and the economic boons they have produced for the city. For instance, Rice estimated that family travel to New Orleans reached record highs in 2004. As the NOMTN's 2004 annual report affirms, "Those successes were partly attributed to the efforts of the NOMTN and its leadership role in the family reunion market, as multicultural tourists, particularly African-Americans, represented 19% of visitors to New Orleans."[96] In Rice's view, the number of visitors booking family reunions before Katrina "was crazy," perhaps even more astounding given that fifteen years before, the mainstream tourism industry had refused to market to, or in some cases even serve, African American visitors. Rice recollected: "I can remember not so long ago, all of the Brennan Restaurants would shut down over Fourth of July [during Essence Festival weekend]. That doesn't happen anymore. You're catering to everybody. I do see things changing. I don't think they would ever go back to that. That was just ignorance."[97] Since the days of the Brennan closures, Rice claimed that industry attitudes had changed because of the impact of African American spending power and the exponential growth of the African American travel market in the past two decades.[98] Her reiteration — "It's all about money" — is a legacy of the post–civil rights push for economic equality.[99]

Although the NOMTN had profited by making New Orleans a preferred destination for African Americans, the organization had not had success attracting Latinos—among other ethnic minorities—to the city, despite the fact that New Orleans was home to the largest Honduran population outside of Honduras.[100] The NOMTN's perennial frustration in trying to reach new niche markets was compounded by its post-Katrina struggle to recruit new or bring back old businesses. In this climate of scarcity, the organization developed new marketing strategies, such as its promotion of "quickie weddings" to non-Louisiana residents who were permitted to marry in New Orleans without the waiting period required in the rest of the state. According to Rice, the campaign worked better than expected. She elaborated on the rationale behind the promotion: "We are marketing in the hopes that when you market, people will use the businesses. They're gonna go to your website to register, but they're gonna look through the website. They're gonna see all these black restaurants, all these black places to go and, in turn, that'll generate revenue and business for the members." Rice's hopefulness drew on the NOMTN's twenty-year history of political agitation and social and economic advocacy. She reflected on the organization's accomplishments as she prepared for the challenges that lay ahead: "What these businesspeople and just regular folks were able to do is pretty phenomenal. They went up against the machine and ended up getting funding. And not only did they get funding, they have been very successful with what they've been able to do on very, very, very limited resources."[101] Over twenty years ago, the NOMTN and a contingency of small, often fledgling black businesses, civic, and political groups appropriated the tourism industry to fight for economic, political, and representational inclusion. Hurricane Katrina revealed just how uneven, fleeting, and tenuous those gains were and again called into question the efficacy of tourism as an economic or social remedy for systemic inequalities. Nevertheless, at a time when the tourism industry was being reconceptualized, those incisive acts of performative resistance that characterized pre-Katrina black heritage tourism were again being invoked to criticize and revise mainstream post-Katrina tourism narratives and their ambivalent construction of black New Orleans as both desirous and disastrous.

Epilogue

When the Saints won, we saw the blacks and whites and the browns and the yellows in this city, that are often apart, come together. And I think it made us realize that our recovery is just about done. And, on top of that, the things we thought we couldn't cure, we can. — *Garland Robinette, "Hope, Healing for New Orleans after Super Bowl," PBS*

Katrina made [the problems affecting many urban and suburban areas of the U.S.] more visible five years ago and continues to make a great illustration of the U.S. failures to treat all citizens with dignity and our failure to achieve our promise of liberty and justice for all. — *Bill Quigley, Davida Finger, and Lance Hill, "Five Years Later"*

In the five years after Hurricane Katrina ravaged New Orleans, the proliferation of music, literature, television shows, film, journalism, popular histories, and academic scholarship commenting on the storm, documenting the city's progress, and representing its inhabitants generated and reflected a renewed national interest in New Orleans's history and culture. The controversy over the inequalities exposed by the storm triggered national discussions about race, class, gender, and age disparities; the role of government; the viability of local cultures; and the potential of grassroots activism to effect change. Viewed alongside the decimation of once-thriving metropolises throughout the country due to disinvestment, racial polarization, and unequal access to resources, New Orleans's recovery became a litmus test for urban revitalization.[1] Not surprisingly, as has been the case for many U.S. urban centers seeking a reprieve from the economic malaise and racial polarization of the post–civil rights era, New Orleans pursued its revitalization through redefining and promoting its tourist image. During a time of racial, environmental, political, social, and economic rupture, mass-mediated representations of the city both resuscitated and revised dominant popular narratives that had long defined its tourist identity. New

Orleans's evolving post-Katrina identity and recovery reassembled popular images and tropes of the city in new and familiar ways, creating new tourism narratives that responded to and profited from shifting understandings of New Orleans's people and culture. This book has demonstrated how the tourism industry in New Orleans paved the road to Katrina through its paradoxical construction and dissemination of blackness: the cultivation and promotion of a desire for black culture alongside the symbolic and actual designation of black residents and neighborhoods as sources and sites of political, economic, social, and natural disaster. New Orleans's road to Katrina epitomizes how racialized tourism narratives have helped define the post–civil rights public sphere by altering racial geographies, economic policies, and political priorities.

In the aftermath of the hurricane, the road taken by New Orleans's tourism industry, in many respects, has mirrored the city's irregular recovery process, with some roads repaved, others still crumbling and impassable, and still others being constructed, leading in different—though often parallel—directions. Yet on the eve of the fifth anniversary of the storm, the tensions inherent in the emerging post-Katrina narrative were displaced by a blitz of favorable media coverage that competed with news of the city's slow, uneven, and inequitable recovery by refashioning a tale of national disaster into a more desirable fable of American resilience and rebirth. The election of the city's first white mayor in over thirty years, the New Orleans Saints' victory in the National Football League (NFL) Super Bowl, the critical acclaim and local fandom surrounding the launch of the HBO television series *Treme*, the tourism promotional campaign following the BP oil spill, and the positive national attention generated by the city's neoliberal solutions to public education and affordable housing relied on and reclaimed the tourist tropes of desire and disaster. In this construction, the desired post-Katrina recovery—manifested in a robust economy, a smaller urban footprint, higher-performing public schools, well-maintained housing stock, safe neighborhoods, and an apolitical gumbo-pot multiculturalism—remained perpetually threatened by the looming disaster posed by the overreliance on a vulnerable tourism industry, the displacement of the city's poorest residents, the educational abandonment of students with disabilities and other special needs, inadequate affordable housing, blighted neighborhoods, increasing rates of violent crime, class disparities, and racial inequities.[2]

As the script of New Orleans's recovery was still being written, the city was poised to emerge as a national symbol either of the desire for rebirth, renewal, and racial unity or of the need for remedies for and reparation of systemic social, economic, and ecological disasters. The New Orleans journalist and radio host Garland Robinette exemplified the former sentiment when he commented:

> We're doing great in the digital industry. We're doing great in attracting young people here like we never have before. Cost of living here is better than most of the places in the United States. So, innovators and inventors want to come here. And our educational system, which has almost been—always been the laughingstock, now is thought to be one of the better prototypes in the country.
>
> And we hear it, but I don't think we assimilated it. But, most importantly, when the Saints won, we saw the blacks and whites and the browns and the yellows in this city, that are often apart, come together. And I think it made us realize that our recovery is just about done. And, on top of that, the things we thought we couldn't cure, we can. So, I think they, kind of accidentally, awakened us to our own recovery.[3]

In contrast, in their assessment of New Orleans five years after Katrina, Bill Quigley, Davida Finger, and Lance Hill expresed the latter view of the symbolism of New Orleans's recovery:

> The challenges of post-Katrina New Orleans reflect the problems of many urban and suburban areas of the U.S.—insufficient affordable rents, racially segregated schools with falling populations, great disparities in income by color of households, serious pollution from remote uncaring corporations, and reductions in public services like transportation. Katrina made these more visible five years ago and continues to make a great illustration of the U.S. failures to treat all citizens with dignity and our failure to achieve our promise of liberty and justice for all.[4]

The nation—indeed, the world—was watching (and touring) to see which symbol would win out. After all, New Orleans's recovery was being marketed as an international tourist attraction by tourism promoters, politicians, journalists, academics, and grassroots activists who invited various niche markets to aid in the city's recovery by witnessing firsthand the effects of Katrina (disaster tourists), spending money on entertainment (leisure tourists), appreciating the city's historic and cultural richness (cultural and heritage tourists), rebuilding houses and communities (voluntourists), or even watching television programs portraying the city and its recovery (televisual tourists).[5] Just as it had framed the debates surrounding Hurricane Katrina, New Orleans's racialized tourism narrative continued to dictate the terms of the city's post-Katrina recovery.

"Richer, Whiter, Emptier"

Former Lieutenant Governor Mitch Landrieu's decisive victory in New Orleans's mayoral election on February 6, 2010, brought a white politician to the city's highest office for the first time since 1978, when the new mayor's father, Maurice "Moon" Landrieu, had finished serving two terms. Following Mitch Landrieu's election, in which he garnered a majority of the black vote, much was made of his family's political affinity with the city's black community.[6] Troy Henry, the African American runner-up in the mayoral election, went so far as to attribute the result to his belief that Landrieu "was the leading black candidate."[7] Though clearly a tongue-in-cheek acknowledgment of Landrieu's crossover appeal, Henry's misinterpretation of Toni Morrison's criticism of U.S. racialized political culture illustrates the degree to which the election results were used to promote an idea of post-Katrina racial solidarity.[8]

The newly elected mayor further perpetuated this idea in his postelection public addresses that hammered home the theme of "one team, one fight, one voice, one city."[9] In his acceptance speech, Landrieu suggested that his election signaled a new era of racial reconciliation for New Orleanians who had "decided that we were going to stick the pole in the ground and strike a blow for unity, strike a blow for a city that decided to be unified rather than divided," and who had concurred "that we are ready to move beyond and into the next generation."[10] Landrieu's inauguration speech even more explicitly acknowledged the city's painful racial legacy and invited those displaced because of Katrina—as well as previous racial injustices—to return to New Orleans and help bridge racial, class, and geographic divides. Emphatically, he challenged his constituents: "TODAY, THIS DAY, WE MUST LAY DOWN THE OPPRESSIVE BURDEN AND DYSFUNCTION OF RACE AND LIFT UP, FOR THE WHOLE WORLD TO SEE, THE POWER, THE ELEGANCE AND THE RICHNESS OF DIVERSITY" (emphasis in original).[11] Given Landrieu's past tenure as Louisiana's lieutenant governor, whose primary function since 1986 had been to head the state's Department of Culture, Recreation, and Tourism, it's not surprising that his notion of diversity is firmly grounded in the city's tourism identity.[12] Employing the rhetoric of the city's tourism narrative of the post–civil rights era, Landrieu defines New Orleans diversity as "a beautiful mosaic that only we in New Orleans have been able to create. Our music, our food, our joy of life; our clear understanding of the simple fact that culture means jobs, livelihood and just sheer fun separates us from the rest of the world and makes us the soul of America."[13] Drawing on its spiritual and black vernacular connotations, Landrieu's invocation of "soul" metaphorically ties the tourist conception of blackness—as rhythm, improvisation, authenticity, cultural creativity, and spirituality—to the city's (and nation's) economic health and social vibrancy. As a result, Landrieu's challenge to his audience, urging them to confront and ameliorate the racial injustices of the past, is reduced to the commodification of "sheer fun," the hallmark of the tourism economy and New Orleans's road to recovery.

Furthermore, Landrieu's celebration of racial unity must be viewed in light of 2010 census data that heralded the new reality of the city's post-Katrina demographics. A widely circulated headline announcing a "richer, whiter, emptier" New Orleans encapsulated the social, political, and economic implications of the displacement of over a hundred thousand African Americans and the accompanying disproportionate loss of low-income and nonwhite households; dilution of black voting power through redistricting; attrition of affordable housing due to gentrification, demolition, and neglect; and return of whites to political power in city government. Though New Orleans remained a majority-black city, its leadership was decidedly no longer black. Former Mayor Ray Nagin's infamous promise—or threat, depending on one's perspective—of New Orleans's return to a "chocolate" city remained unfulfilled.[14] The new mayor took the lead in enshrining the rememory of Katrina's racial legacy. In a stirring address to a multiracial audience on the fifth anniversary of the hurricane, Landrieu announced that "differences and divisions were washed away" with Katrina's floodwaters, revealing the "beautiful truth" that "we are all the same."[15] Landrieu's vision of diversity, like the touristic notion of gumbo-pot multiculturalism on which it draws for inspiration, substitutes the reality of racial divisions that persisted after Katrina with the rhetoric of racial harmony that prevailed in the post–civil rights era.

If Landrieu's road to City Hall was paved with the civil rights promise of racial unity, the New Orleans Saints' road to the Super Bowl XLIV championship presumably led down a path of postracial equality where all differences were subsumed in the Who Dat Nation, a diverse community of fans bound together in their support of the football team. Landrieu appealed directly to the Who Dat Nation and their enthusiasm for the Saints during his mayoral campaign. It is likely, in fact, that the city's obsession with the long-beleaguered football franchise's first-ever Super Bowl berth contributed to the low voter turnout—which may have been as decisive a factor in Landrieu's definitive victory as any crossracial political alliance. Occurring the day after Landrieu's election and two days before Mardi Gras, the Saints' championship victory catapulted the city into a fever-pitch state of excitement and euphoria that allegorically marked the culmination of a tainted history of losing football seasons, political ineptitude, post-Katrina fatigue, and racial polarization.[16] Given the NFL's history of "provid[ing] a stage on which a sort of racial theater has been performed," it is useful to explore how, more than any other symbol in the first five years after Hurricane Katrina, the Saints became a metaphor for post-Katrina postracialism.[17]

The racialization of the Saints is intimately tied to the team's pivotal early role in advancing a national image of the city as racially tolerant—to help tourism promotion—even as New Orleans politicians and business owners flouted national civil rights legislation. New Orleans's acquisition of a professional football franchise was a reflection and product of this post–civil rights era racial paradox. The city's bid for a professional football team was delayed—though not ultimately denied—during the first half of the 1960s after persistent episodes of racial discrimination and harassment of black athletes in the French Quarter sullied the city's tourist image and deterred collegiate and professional teams from competing in the city. Despite the persistence of racial discrimination, however, the NFL and Louisiana politicians brokered a deal that paved the way for the city's acquisition of a professional team without censuring its racist practices. Although the New Orleans Saints played its first game as an integrated franchise in 1967, it was not until 1970—years after passage of the 1964 Civil Rights Act—that New Orleans legislators finally acquiesced to pressures by civil rights activists for a public accommodations ordinance that enforced desegregation in bars and other venues that had not voluntarily acceded to integration.[18]

The Louisiana Superdome—the Saints' home stadium, whose massive domed structure serves as an obtrusive icon of the city's tourism industry— likewise exemplifies the racial paradox of New Orleans's tourist identity. Completed in 1975, the modernist architectural structure symbolically ushered in a modern era of race relations through racial patronage, a bounty of service-industry jobs, and the promise of a revitalized tourism economy expected to remedy widespread poverty and urban blight. However, the construction of the Superdome signaled the demise of black neighborhoods previously leveled by eminent domain and stripped of economic resources, which were used instead to finance the construction and maintenance of the Superdome and to subsidize the football team.[19] The political scientist Paul Passavant aptly places the Superdome within a post–civil rights neoliberal landscape that has promoted "the reorientation of New Orleans infrastructure away from its residents and toward tourists."[20] Ultimately, instead of serving as a panacea for racial turmoil and economic inequalities, the construction of and financial commitment to the Superdome accelerated the touristification of New Orleans and exacerbated racial segregation, economic polarization, and urban decline.

These disparities became even more stark following Hurricane Katrina, when the Superdome came to personify New Orleans's post-Katrina transformation from disaster to desire. Metamorphosing from a shelter of last resort in the immediate aftermath of Katrina to a symbol of rebirth during the 2006 nationally televised broadcast of the Saints' first home game following the hurricane, the Superdome became a pivotal metaphor in a national narrative of New Orleans's physical and spiritual recovery. A central tenet of this post-Katrina narrative was the dissociation of New Orleans's place identity from the rumors and images of squalor, violence, and lawlessness that stigmatized African Americans trapped in the Superdome in the days after Katrina. Yet, while government subsidies and political will went into accelerating the reconstruction of the Superdome, signaling that the city was again viable and ready to accommodate tourists, far less attention and resources were directed at the tens of thousands of New Orleans residents—primarily black and poor—who could not return home.[21]

On the contrary, the rebuilding of the Saints' franchise—marked by a new stadium, a new coach, a new quarterback, and a new winning attitude— metonymically provided all the elements for a feel-good story of New Orleans's recovery and resilience necessary to shift national attention away from post-Katrina inequities and indignities. Ultimately, the Saints' road to the Super Bowl helped replace the memory of black abandonment and despair with the trademark erasure of race in New Orleans's tourism narrative of the post–civil rights era. A broad cross section of observers—including national media, city boosters, public officials, fans, and players—used the Saints' victory and the crossracial camaraderie it generated to represent and promote racial harmony and meritocracy as the legacies of New Orleans's unique history.[22] This post-Katrina narrative and the neoliberal "colorblindness" on which it relies mask the structural inequalities responsible for the creation and subsequent neglect of the city's most vulnerable populations. Indeed, as Phillip Hutchison persuasively argues in "The Political Economy of Colorblindness: Neoliberalism and the Reproduction of Inequality in the United States," the post–civil rights notion of race-neutrality "*conceals, displaces, and misidentifies the roots of contemporary racial inequality* [by] disconnect[ing] the racial past from the racial present—more specifically, it foments a situation where the racial policies of the past are construed as having no effect on the racial patterns of the present" (emphasis in original).[23] In this context, the Saints-inspired adage that "there is no black and white in the black and gold" links the team's colors with a vision of color blindness based on the historical fiction of New Orleans's racial exceptionalism. The vision of the Saints as an emblem of New Orleans's physical and racial recovery animated post-Katrina tourism narratives and reinvigorated the city's tourism industry.[24] Mayor Landrieu capitalized on this postracial romanticism during his speech on the fifth anniversary of Katrina when he reminded the members of his audience of their commonalities: "We sing the same songs, we root for the same Saints, and we share the same dreams."[25] Yet, like the touristic desire for black expressive culture, the dream of postracialism demands a corollary of black disaster by which those who are not encompassed by the collective "we" intoned by Landrieu can be identified, judged, and disciplined.[26]

Tourist Sites and Sounds in Treme

The April 11, 2010, debut of David Simon and Eric Overmyer's HBO series *Treme* offered one of the most compelling explorations of the collective experiences of post-Katrina New Orleans. In dramatizing the challenges faced by New Orleanians three months after Katrina, the first season of *Treme* provides a powerful criticism of the city's tourism-dominated recovery and disregard for the nation's democratic promise. Critics and fans praised the series for dispensing with the most banal tourist tropes in favor of capturing the real lives and struggles of New Orleanians from all walks of life.[27] In attending to issues of violent crime, police corruption, a lack of affordable housing, political malfeasance, and bureaucratic inefficiency, the first season highlights the tension between the city's tourist identity and the reality for those who live there. The final scene of the third episode, "Right Place, Wrong Time," poignantly captures this tension, but it also reveals the racial tension undergirding the series itself.

Set in a devastated neighborhood in the Lower Ninth Ward three months after Katrina, the scene follows Mardi Gras Indian chief Albert Lambreaux (Clarke Peters) as he leads a memorial service for a fellow tribesman who drowned during the flood. As the group sings the traditional Mardi Gras Indian anthem "Indian Red," a tour bus loaded with camera-flashing passengers approaches to witness and document this "authentic" display of black culture. Much of the scene's power rests in its unsettling soundscape. The Mardi Gras Indians' robust chant-singing, accompanied by the percussive rhythm of drums, tambourines, and hand clapping, fills the silence of the deserted neighborhood and attests to the resilience of the city's black community.[28] However, the raw emotional tribute is abruptly silenced by the approaching tour bus, with its squealing brakes and respiring exhaust. The ensuing terse exchange between the white bus driver and the black Mardi Gras Indians offers its own cadence:

> TOUR BUS DRIVER [*surveying the assemblage of Mardi Gras Indians*]: How you doing, sir? What's this about?
>
> BIG CHIEF LAMBREAUX [*signaling toward the tour bus*]: You tell me what this here's about.
>
> TOUR BUS DRIVER: Well, people want to see what happened. [*Pointing toward the house in the background*] Hey, is that your house?
>
> TRIBE MEMBER 1: Drive away from here, sir.
>
> TOUR BUS DRIVER [*signaling behind him toward the tour bus passengers*]: No, we was just coming around—
>
> TRIBE MEMBER 2 [*interrupting loudly*]: Just drive away!
>
> *A tense, uncomfortable pause as the bus driver gazes on the indignant faces of the Mardi Gras Indians. In the background can be heard the sound of muffled voices from inside the tour bus.*

TOUR BUS DRIVER [*raising hand, as if in surrender*]: I'm sorry. You're right. I'm sorry.

The scene concludes with the sounds of the bus's engine restarting, the crunch of footsteps on the barren dirt road as the tribe members mill into the street to watch the departing bus, and the diminuendo of the exhaust as the bus drives away. The sounds and silences of the scene reflect the contradictory impulses of desire and disaster in post-Katrina New Orleans: evidence of black survival and resilience juxtaposed against signs of African American death and displacement; the embrace and celebration of black expressive culture threatened by its spectacularization and commodification; the veneration of heritage music and traditional black folk customs accompanied by the erasure or vilification of the more rageful, irreverent bounce music and other contemporary artistic expressions; the possibility of interracial understanding and healing set against entrenched histories of paternalism and structural racism; the touristic desire to see, understand, and learn from catastrophe opposed to the exploitative potential of disaster tourism.

Though the bus driver apologizes and departs with the tourists, the camera fixes the viewers' gaze on the disrupted memorial and deserted neighborhood and thus validates for *Treme* viewers the bus driver's contention that "people want to see what happened." David Simon, co-creator of the series, has said that it "should not be a tourism slide show. If we do it right, it (will be) about why New Orleans matters."[29] Yet *Treme* takes up where the disaster tour leaves off, giving viewers—televisual tourists—access to purportedly authentic places, people, events, and experiences beyond the tourist landscape. Like the post-Katrina disaster tour, the series maps out a new racial geography of tourist New Orleans but does so by resuscitating the old tourist tropes of racial harmony, racial exceptionalism, and racial respectability. In advancing particular story lines, histories, and cultural productions—to the exclusion of others—the first season of *Treme* often disregards or glosses over New Orleans's history of racial conflict and injustice in favor of new narratives of crossracial unity among Katrina survivors and paternalistic actions by white characters uniquely positioned to speak on behalf of all New Orleanians. The HBO *Treme*-inspired tourist revival of the actual Tremé neighborhood has taken place in tandem with the demolition of public housing, longtime residents' resistance to the enforcement of vendor permits and music ordinances, racial and class tensions over increased gentrification and preservation efforts, and the exclusion of poor and black residents from the recovery process.[30]

The post-Katrina restoration of Louis Armstrong Park, located in Tremé, is a case in point. Park repairs and improvements were initiated by Mayor Ray Nagin, whose administration oversaw the completion of the first of three phases of renovations in early 2009. Planning for the next two phases of the park's redesign continued without input from Tremé's poor and working-class black residents, who expressed feelings of resentment and disaffection toward the exclusionary process. At community meetings, residents and neighborhood activists opposed the use of federal recovery money for the development of tourist spaces in the park, such as a sculpture garden, and agitated instead for the development of community spaces, such as recreational facilities and green spaces, as a partial remedy to the racist urban renewal policies that had devastated the neighborhood throughout the twentieth century. Despite residents' protests, the sculpture garden and tourist-oriented renovations were hastily and shoddily completed in the waning days of Nagin's administration, as the mayor's swan song to the city. Within days, however, crumbling and cracked concrete forced the park to be closed to the public, and it remained closed for most of the following eighteen months because of further damage to existing structures, poor workmanship on repairs, and negotiations between the city and insurers.[31] Yet, it would be a mistake to view the Armstrong Park debacle solely as an example of the Nagin administration's incompetence or—as Nagin's successor, Mitch Landrieu, put it—"complete and utter dysfunction at every level."[32] The lack of foresight, poor planning, exclusionary practices, and prioritization of tourists' interests over residents' needs that characterized the post-Katrina renovation of Armstrong Park were not an aberration but a continuation of the site's contentious racial history that pitted white elites and poor and working-class black residents against one another in dealing with the uses, meanings, and memories of Louis Armstrong, the Tremé neighborhood, and the racial and cultural legacy of New Orleans's civil rights movement.[33]

BP Will Make This Right?

Despite the public embarrassment of the Armstrong Park fiasco, no single event in the five years after Katrina threatened New Orleans's mythical recovery as much as the April 20, 2010, Deepwater Horizon explosion that killed eleven workers and spewed 210 million gallons of crude oil into the Gulf of Mexico over the course of eighty-seven days.[34] Just as city boosters stood poised to commemorate Hurricane Katrina's fifth anniversary with proclamations of an economic and cultural renaissance—fueled largely by a revived tourism economy and tourist identity—another man-made disaster threatened to upend the carefully crafted image of rebirth and resilience. As it had in the wake of Katrina, public scrutiny and debate turned to issues of perverse structural economic inequality and the impact of neoliberal corporate and government policies on the nation's most vulnerable communities. Like Hurricane Katrina, the BP oil spill laid bare the incongruence between the touristic image of desire promoted to visitors and the stark reality of disaster experienced by many of those who sustained the tourist economy. Yet BP harnessed the region's tourist identity in a shrewd public relations campaign that simultaneously redeemed both the company's and the affected cities' popular images.

BP initiated the campaign following former CEO Tony Hayward's highly publicized gaffes, most notably his complaint that he would "like to have [his] life back."[35] Newspaper and television ads reiterated the campaign slogan "We Will Make This Right," which slyly capitalized on the name recognition and political activist cachet of Brad Pitt's Make It Right Foundation, which was committed to rebuilding the Lower Ninth Ward with sustainable, affordable housing. At a cost of over $93 million in its first four months, the BP ad campaign attempted to alter the company's image of corporate greed and put forward a face of social responsibility, caring, and community engagement.[36]

In a move that typifies the racial paradox of neoliberal color blindness, BP made the face of this campaign—and the face of the company—two African American executives, both New Orleans natives. In several television and print ads, Darryl Willis and Iris Cross each earnestly faced the camera and told a national audience that they would be in the Gulf "for as long as it takes to get it right." At the same time that the NAACP was investigating the impact of the oil spill on the region's most vulnerable communities— whose members suffered financial woes, loss of livelihood, increased physical and mental health problems, concerns over seafood safety, and intensified pressure on families and community networks—BP was reassuring the American people that the region would recover completely and that all of those affected by the spill would be made whole.[37] Through its African American surrogates, who symbolized the company's race and class neutrality even as they implicitly invoked and responded to the company's exploitation of the region's most marginalized communities, BP deflected a resurgent environmental activism.

Yet it was through its investments in Louisiana's tourism industry that BP most effectively shored up the state's historic dependence on the oil and gas industry and largely silenced local government criticism. New Orleans was granted the largest share, $6 million of the $30 million that BP committed to help restore Louisiana's tourism industry.[38] The city's Convention and Visitor's Bureau used the money to initiate a marketing campaign reminiscent of its post-Katrina efforts that compelled potential visitors to replace memories of human suffering, social injustice, and environmental disaster with tourist images of festive, carefree, and apolitical scenes untarnished by racial, environmental, or social problems. Steve Perry, president of the bureau, emphasized the dual message of the campaign to tourism promoters: "You've got to be deeply honest about this, saying this breaks our hearts; it's literally a gut-wrenching, horrible catastrophe . . . that's the same distance away from us that Philadelphia is from New York."[39] Perry's duplicitous message was evidently successful. Due in large part to BP's contribution, New Orleans reached a tourism milestone in 2010 by attracting more than eight million visitors for the first time since Hurricane Katrina. With increased sales tax revenues and higher hotel occupancy rates, the city experienced an economic boom and a revival as a top international tourist destination that extended into the next decade.[40]

"Some Wounds . . . Have Not Yet Healed"

Of course, beyond the refurbished and newly created tourist zones, many neighborhoods continued to languish from an incomplete and uneven recovery that was reflected in the challenges of persistent environmental vulnerability, a dearth of affordable housing, a controversial corporatized charter school system, a corrupt and ineffective police department, and inadequate access to health care. Although many post-Katrina practices and policies excluded or marginalized the largely black and poor New Orleanians who inhabited these neighborhoods, a burgeoning—or, in many cases, resurgence—of organizations, movements, performances, and cultural productions attempted to highlight and ameliorate persistent disparities and emerging injustices throughout the city.[41] Yet, although much post-Katrina activism brought needed attention and resources to previously neglected communities, other interventions were mediated through—and constrained by—popular narratives that define New Orleans's tourist identity. What often resulted was a politics of inactivism that has many of the same shortcomings as its contemporary cousins "slacktivism," "clicktivism," and "activism 2.0"—the assortment of "feel good" actions such as signing online petitions, "liking" a cause on Facebook, or purchasing merchandise with a charity's slogan that critics contend give the illusion of effecting real social change without actually challenging the status quo. President Barack Obama's remarks on the fifth anniversary of Hurricane Katrina illuminate how the federal approach to New Orleans's post-Katrina recovery promotes this type of tourist-inflected inactivism.

Addressing a packed auditorium at the historically black Xavier University in New Orleans, the president acknowledged that the storm's devastation was as much a man-made disaster as it was a natural disaster. "The truth is," the president admitted, "there are some wounds that have not yet healed. And there are some losses that can't be repaid. And for many who lived through those harrowing days five years ago, there's searing memories that time may not erase." Obama's statement was a powerful—and rare—recognition by a U.S. president that the American democratic promise of human equality and justice for all remained unfulfilled. Yet almost immediately—and without proposing how U.S. citizens might create, or perfect, a democracy that prevents future Hurricane Katrinas and that does away with the racial, regional, class, and gender inequalities that Hurricane Katrina exposed—the president turned to a familiar tourist trope of New Orleans with which his local and national audiences would have been familiar. He continued: "But even amid so much tragedy, we saw stirrings of a brighter day.... And we saw music and Mardi Gras and the vibrancy, the fun of this town undiminished."[42] Obama's evocation of New Orleans as a place of fun, frivolity, escape, and good times draws on a much longer history, one that juxtaposes the New Orleans of disaster (natural, environmental, political, economic, or racial) with the New Orleans of desire (sensual, exotic, carefree, decadent, or taboo). In assimilating this tension, the president's speech—and, more important, the proposals for remedy outlined in it—advanced the "neoliberal restructuring" of the previous administration.[43] Despite Obama's rhetorical shift, the national response to Katrina continued to promote the private sector at the expense of the public good.

In his remarks, President Obama held up post-Katrina New Orleans as "a symbol of resilience and of community and of the fundamental responsibility that we have to one another," extolling examples of individual heroes, voluntary associations, corporate-private partnerships, and non-profit organizations for their "innovative approaches to fight poverty and improve health care, reduce crime, and create opportunities for young people."[44] In so doing, Obama espoused what the political scientist Cedric Johnson has called a "notion of public works suited to neoliberal times, an approach to infrastructure improvement and maintenance that is publicly financed but executed by private contractors."[45] New Orleans's post–civil rights tourism industry is a model of this type of public-private partnership aimed at stimulating economic growth and development through economic neoliberalism.[46]

Not surprisingly, Obama's speech appealed directly to New Orleans's tourist identity by reiterating the central themes of history, music, and food.[47] The selection of Xavier University, the nation's only historically black Roman Catholic university, highlighted New Orleans's racial distinctiveness and paid tribute to the historic and contemporary contributions of the city's black professional class and educated elite. Obama's designation of New Orleans's "culture of music and art" as "part of the soul of this city—and the soul of this country" linked the spiritual and artistic health of the nation to the cultural productions rooted in the black community. His enthusiastic endorsement of New Orleans food—"shrimp po'boy and some of the gumbo," "bread pudding," "30-foot po'boy made with shrimps and oysters from the Gulf"—promoted the local cuisine and echoed the reassurances of the Louisiana Restaurant Association, the Louisiana Seafood Promotion and Marketing Board, and government agencies that attempted to assuage concerns about the safety of seafood after the BP oil spill.[48] As these examples illustrate, New Orleans's post-Katrina recovery had become conflated with the recovery of the city's tourism industry, thereby deemphasizing the responsibility of government to alleviate social injustice and minimizing the role of structural inequalities that sustain that injustice.[49]

Hurricane Katrina was not the end of the road for New Orleans tourism or the tropes of desire and disaster that it bolstered. By the fifth anniversary of the storm, the city's post–civil rights tourism narrative had been adapted to a postracial era. The election of a white mayor, the Saints' NFL championship, the debut of the HBO series *Treme*, BP's "We Will Make This Right" campaign, and an African American president's endorsement of private-sector initiatives for the city's reconstruction ultimately reflected the ambivalence of the city's neoliberal tourism initiatives by substituting postracial romanticism for political, economic, and social recovery in the city. Citizens were invited to take action—touring, cheering, purchasing, volunteering, and even watching television—but were rarely called to activism. New Orleans, like other regions in the global south, had turned to tourism to capitalize on local disaster and cultivate outsiders' desire for indigenous cultures and locales. Although the goals of economic development, infrastructure improvement, and poverty alleviation are certainly commendable, the benefits for the most vulnerable and marginalized communities have been more dubious. By offering the promise of ethical engagement and social responsibility without requiring a sustained commitment to social justice work or redistributive public policy, New Orleans's post-Katrina tourism has promoted the type of political inactivism common with other forms of "do-good capitalism" and "grassroots privatization" that undermine democratic processes, perpetuate social hierarchies and inequalities, and reinforce the status quo.[50]

As the city prepares to commemorate the tenth anniversary of Hurricane Katrina, New Orleans may have already joined Oklahoma City and Ground Zero as another site on the national tour of history.[51] Post-Katrina tours, neoliberal policies that prioritize the tourism industry, and new racialized tourism narratives about the city's rebirth underscore the contradictions inherent in a recovery that is based on meeting the desire for black cultural products while it creates disaster (ecological, social, economic, and political) for the communities that originate and disseminate those products. Of course, these communities have drawn on a long history of cultural and political resistance to systemic injustice and will continue to do so. What remains to be seen in New Orleans—and elsewhere—is if social entrepreneurship has replaced social movements as the linchpin of democratic participation and political engagement.[52]

Notes

One. "The City I Used to Come to Visit"

1 In his study of competing claims for authenticity in the New Orleans tourism industry, Kevin Gotham defines racialization as "a range of historically changing ways in which structures and ideas become endowed with racial meanings and significations" (*Authentic New Orleans*, 186). He traces the racialization of New Orleans tourism to the 1920s, when it became characterized by "a set of racial relations, segregationist ideology, and institutional tourism practices based on racial meanings and distinctions" that were intended "to build and legitimate an image of New Orleans as a racially exclusive destination for white tourists and conventioneers" (84–85). I use the term *tourism narrative* to refer to the constellation of language, images, and motifs repeatedly used to construct a particular story and experience of a place for visitors. Such narratives are often crystallized in tourist guidebooks and other promotional materials. For a history of the use of prescriptive tourist literature to create and market certain national narratives of identity and citizenship, to the exclusion of others, see Shaffer, *See America First*, 169–220.

2 For an example of media coverage in the aftermath of the hurricane, see "Official." The historian Anthony Stanonis makes similar observations about the Katrina media coverage (*Creating the Big Easy*, 25).

3 Greenspan, *Creating Colonial Williamsburg*, 15.

4 For examinations of New Orleans's construction as an image and idea in travel, literary, and other popular accounts, see Bryan, *The Myth of New Orleans in Literature*; De Caro and Jordan, *Louisiana Sojourns*; Hearn, *Inventing New Orleans*; Kennedy, *Literary New Orleans*; Stanonis, *Creating the Big Easy*, 1–21.

5 For a fuller discussion of these elements, see Barber, *Reno's Big Gamble*, 1–11.

6 Starr, "Introduction: The Man Who Invented New Orleans," xxiv.

7 Long, *The Great Southern Babylon*; Dawdy, *Building the Devil's Empire*, 3 and 23; De Caro and Jordan, *Louisiana Sojourns*, 69–70; Pittman, "New Orleans in the 1760s"; Stanonis, *Creating the Big Easy*, 18–19; Gotham, *Authentic New Orleans*, 33–44, 55–60, and 65–68. For a discussion of how nineteenth-century writers employed race and gender in their constructs of New Orleans, see Bryan, *The Myth of New Orleans in Literature*, 12–78.

8 J. Weeks, *Gettysburg*, 83 and 98. For more on the particular trends and developments that facilitated the rise of urban tourism at the beginning of the twentieth century, see Cocks, *Doing the Town*, 5–7.

9 Gotham, *Authentic New Orleans*, 69–94; Shaffer, *See America First*, 160–68; Sta-nonis, *Creating the Big Easy*, 195–234; Starnes, introduction, 5–6; Yuhl, *A Golden Haze of Memory*, 127–56.

10 Souther, *New Orleans on Parade*, 1–10; Stanonis, *Creating the Big Easy*, 1–31; Starnes, introduction, 6–7. New Orleans tourism epitomized the premise of the cultural critic Dean MacCannell that "the best indication of the final victory of modernity over other sociocultural arrangements is not the disappearance of the nonmodern world, but its artificial preservation and reconstruction in modern society" (*The Tourist*, 8).

11 Gotham, *Authentic New Orleans*, 120–21.

12 Souther, *New Orleans on Parade*, 185–220; Souther, "The Disneyfication of New Orleans."

13 Herman Gray suggests that major transformations in the structure and config-urations of global media; black self-representation; and political, social, and economic systems had dramatically reshaped the creation and dissemination of black cultural production by the dawn of the twenty-first century (*Cultural Moves*). See also Gilroy, *Against Race*; C. Horton, *Race and the Making of Amer-ican Liberalism*; Hutchison, "The Political Economy of Colorblindness"; Wise, *Colorblind*.

14 C. Horton, *Race and the Making of American Liberalism*, 228. Horton offers a compelling example of how racial contradictions operate in the post–civil rights era: "Even more problematically, any memory that the movement was in fact dedicated to building an interracial coalition committed to the joint pursuit of racial and class equity seems to have been completely erased from public consciousness" (228). For similar critiques of the modern liberal state and narra-tives of colorblindness, see Chong, "'Look, an Asian!'"; Giroux, "Playing in the Dark"; J. Hall, "The Long Civil Rights Movement and the Political Uses of the Past."

15 The cultural studies scholar Ellis Cashmore refers to this inversion of civil rights goals as "America's paradox." He explains: "In black culture, we can find a history of American perfidy, American violence, American oppression and American racism, all captured for our delectation in a way that provokes reflection without spurring us to action . . . black culture provides more comfort than challenge" (*The Black Culture Industry*, 181). See also Giroux, "Playing in the Dark," 103–4; Goldberg, *The Racial State*.

16 Bonilla-Silva, *Racism without Racists*; Kristof, "Racism without Racists." See also Lum, "The Obama Era."

17 Regis, "'Keeping Jazz Funerals Alive'"; Regis, "Second Lines, Minstrelsy, and the Contested Landscapes of New Orleans Afro-Creole Festivals"; Souther, *New Orleans on Parade*, 126–27; Thomas, "'The City I Used to . . . Visit,'" 256. In his seminal study of tourist practices, MacCannell contends that "the worker is integrated into modern society as tourist and tourist attraction (work display), as actor and spectator in the 'universal drama of work'" (*The Tourist*, 63). In New Orleans, African American service workers who form and perform the city's

premodern tourist experience are similar to MacCannell's tapestry workers, who "seem almost museumized . . . outside of industrial time" (68–69).

18 For influential historiographical examples, see G. King, *New Orleans*; Rankin, "The Impact of the Civil War on the Free Colored Community of New Orleans"; Rankin, "The Politics of Caste." Similar arguments that minimize the divisions within the community of Creoles of color are found in Foner, "The Free People of Color in Louisiana and St. Domingue" and Hanger, *Bounded Lives, Bounded Places.* For more recent scholarship that argues for Creole radicalism and alliances between enslaved and free blacks, see Bell, *Revolution, Romanticism, and the Afro-Creole Protest Tradition in Louisiana*; G. Hall, *Africans in Colonial Louisiana*, 237–74; Hirsch and Logsdon, *Creole New Orleans.*

19 It is important to note that in the New World, this black-white binary was a peculiarly American phenomenon that differed in important ways from the views and practices of the French and Spanish during the colonial period. From the eighteenth through the early nineteenth centuries, racial designations in colonial Louisiana derived from the complicated relationships among multiple factors, including class status, ethnicity, and skin color. For recent studies that shrewdly demonstrate the racial complexity of the colonial period, see Dawdy, *Building the Devil's Empire*; Spear, *Race, Sex, and Social Order in Early New Orleans.*

20 Fairclough, *Race and Democracy*, 336.

21 Souther, *New Orleans on Parade*, 73–101.

22 Souther, *New Orleans on Parade*, 208. For a range of publications documenting the rise of black heritage tourism, see Cantor, *Historic Landmarks of Black America*; Chase, *In Their Footsteps*; Eichstedt and Small, *Representations of Slavery*; Ferris, "Around the South in Search of the Past"; Hayden, *The Power of Place*, 44–80; Hodder, "Savannah's Changing Past."

23 Yuhl, *A Golden Haze of Memory*, 131. See also Starnes, *Southern Journeys.*

24 See Regis, "Blackness and the Politics of Memory in the New Orleans Second Line"; Regis, "Second Lines, Minstrelsy, and the Contested Landscapes of New Orleans Afro-Creole Festivals"; and Souther, *New Orleans on Parade*, 102–31.

25 Lipsitz, "Mardi Gras Indians"; Roach, *Cities of the Dead*; Souther, *New Orleans on Parade*; Thomas, "Kissing Ass and Other Performative Acts of Resistance."

26 Campbell-Rock, "Black Tourists Pump Millions into the New Orleans Economy"; Osbey, "Tourism in New Orleans"; R. King, "Blowing Life Back into the Birthplace of Jazz."

27 Long, *The Great Southern Babylon*, 5–6. See also Long, "'A Notorious Attraction,'" 24. Alicia Barber argues that Nevada serves a similar function for U.S. visitors (*Reno's Big Gamble*, 1).

28 In *Slavery and Public History*, Edward Linenthal similarly argues that both whites' and blacks' "enduring hunger for redemptive narratives smooths any rough edges in these indigestible stories" (Epilogue, 215).

29 Thevenot and Russell, "Rumors of Deaths Greatly Exaggerated."

30 For reports that corroborate this type of community effort, see Penner and Ferdinand, *Overcoming Katrina*; "Update #3"; "St. Mike's Hardware."

31 Babington, "Some GOP Legislators Hit Jarring Notes in Addressing Katrina"; Barrett, "A Right to Rebuild"; Cass, "Notable Mardi Gras Absences Reflect Loss of Black Middle Class"; Dao, "Study Says 80% of New Orleans Blacks May Not Return"; Davis, "Who Is Killing New Orleans?"; Howell and Vinturella, "Forgotten in New Orleans."

32 "President Participates in Roundtable with Small Business Owners and Community Leaders in New Orleans." See also Newman, "Bush Notes Progress in New Orleans Cleanup." President Bush's first visit to New Orleans likewise avoided a walkthrough of the most devastated sections of the city, which the president toured by helicopter. In remarks during that visit, the president similarly drew on his tourist nostalgia for the city: "I believe the town where I used to come—from Houston, Texas, to enjoy myself, occasionally too much . . . [laughter] . . . will be that very same town, that it will be a better place to come to" ("Bush's Remarks in New Orleans"). See also Bumiller, "Promises by Bush amid the Tears."

33 Hammer, "Citizens in Road Home Purgatory"; Herczog, "Tourist Areas in New Orleans Rebound While Other Parts Remain Far Behind"; Krupa, "Road Home Isn't Easy Street"; Moran, "Without Charity Hospital, the Poor and Uninsured Struggle to Find Health Care"; "New Orleans Update"; *Public School Performance in New Orleans*; Simon, "Report Critical of Charter Schools"; Jacquetta White, "Ad Campaign Fights Katrina Myths" and "If You Sell It, Will They Come?"; Finn, "Two Years after BP Oil Spill, Tourists Back in U.S. Gulf."

34 Campanella, *Bienville's Dilemma*, 179–85; Campanella, *Geographies of New Orleans*, 297–314; Campanella and Campanella, *New Orleans Then and Now*, 26 and 28; Lewis, *New Orleans*, 37–100 and 144–47; Hair, *Carnival of Fury*, 73–74.

35 Campanella, *Bienville's Dilemma*, 153 and 185–87; Campanella, "An Ethnic Geography of New Orleans," 710–11; Campanella and Campanella, *New Orleans Then and Now*, 26; Lewis, *New Orleans*, 102, 128, 138–53.

36 Lewis, *New Orleans*, 95.

37 Campanella and Campanella, *New Orleans Then and Now*, 28; Hirsch, "Simply a Matter of Black and White," 304–19; Lewis, *New Orleans*, 125.

38 Campanella, *Bienville's Dilemma*, 183, 185–87; Lewis, *New Orleans*, 121–37; Campanella and Campanella, *New Orleans Then and Now*, 26 and 28; Souther, *New Orleans on Parade*, 185–86, 191.

39 Lewis, *New Orleans*, 160–61; Souther, *New Orleans on Parade*, 206–7, 226, and 228–29. The political scientist Paul Passavant identifies a confluence of local, state, and federal policies that increased racial segregation, economic polarization, and urban decline, leading to "the reorientation of New Orleans infrastructure away from its residents and toward tourists" ("Mega-Events, the Superdome, and the Return of the Repressed in New Orleans," 98).

40 Campanella, *Bienville's Dilemma*, 152–53. The urban geographer Richard Campanella surmises that "isolated from public view, dismissed by the historical and architectural community, and plagued by the same social ills found throughout inner-city America, the rear sections of the Lower Ninth Ward seemed

like a world unto itself—cherished by its residents, avoided by everyone else" (153).

41 Campanella, *Bienville's Dilemma*, 165; Campanella, "An Ethnic Geography of New Orleans"; Campanella, "Greater Gentilly," 3–4, 6–9; Campanella and Campanella, *New Orleans Then and Now*, 26, 28; "Dillard Neighborhood Snapshot"; Lewis, *New Orleans*, 80, 82, 137; "Pines Village Neighborhood Snapshot"; "Plum Orchard Neighborhood Snapshot"; "Read Blvd West Neighborhood Snapshot"; Sothern, *Down in New Orleans*, 214–20; Souther, "Suburban Swamp"; "Village de l'Est Neighborhood Snapshot"; "West Lake Forest Neighborhood Snapshot."

42 Campanella and Campanella, *New Orleans Then and Now*, 147; Crutcher, "Historical Geographies of Race in a New Orleans Afro-Creole Landscape," 30–33; Scott, "The Atlantic World and the Road to Plessy v. Ferguson"; "Tremé / Lafitte Neighborhood Snapshot."

43 Campanella and Campanella, *New Orleans Then and Now*, 28.

44 Campanella and Campanella, *New Orleans Then and Now*, 147; Crutcher, "Historical Geographies of Race in a New Orleans Afro-Creole Landscape," 32–35; Sakakeeny, "'Under the Bridge,'" 13–16, 21–24. The HBO series *Treme*, which began airing in 2010, depicts some of these tensions.

45 Associated Press, "Census Shows New Orleans Losing Many Blacks"; Campanella, *Bienville's Dilemma*, 153 and 184; Campanella, "An Ethnic Geography of New Orleans," 714–15; Campanella, "Greater Gentilly," 9; Clarke, "Katrina Leaves New Orleans Political Landscape Looking Whiter"; Crutcher, "Historical Geographies of Race in a New Orleans Afro-Creole Landscape," 36; DeBerry, "For Black Road Homers, a Hollow Victory"; DuBos, "Redistricting Free-For-All"; Flaherty, "A New Day for New Orleans?"; Fussell, Sastry, and Van Landingham, *Race, Socioeconomic Status, and Return Migration to New Orleans after Hurricane Katrina*; Hammer, "Road Home's Grant Calculations Discriminate against Black Homeowners"; Krupa, "Census Shows Katrina Effects"; Krupa, "Fewer Than Half of the Census Questionnaires Sent Out in Orleans and St. Bernard Were Returned"; Krupa, "Minority Populations Still Growing in New Orleans Area"; Mildenberg, "Census Data Show a Far Less Populous New Orleans"; Perry, "New Orleans Residents Still Struggling to Get Back Home"; Quigley, Finger, and Hill, "Five Years Later"; Robertson, "Smaller New Orleans after Katrina, Census Shows"; Sothern, *Down in New Orleans*, 215; Tilove, "Five Years after Hurricane Katrina."

46 I rely on the definition of "racial project" proffered by Michael Omi and Howard Winant: "*A racial project is simultaneously an interpretation, representation, or explanation of racial dynamics, and an effort to reorganize and redistribute resources along particular racial lines.* Racial projects connect what race *means* in a particular discursive practice and the ways in which both social structures and everyday experiences are racially *organized*, based upon that meaning" (*Racial Formation in the United States*, 56; emphasis in original).

47 As Herman Gray posits, such an analysis must move beyond simply critiquing stereotypical representations and also attend to "the frameworks and social con-

ditions out of which they are generated and the *desires* to which they respond. Together, these conditions structure the assumptions through which such desires are made legible and culturally meaningful" (*Cultural Moves*, 28–29).

48 Lewis, *New Orleans*, 170.

49 Certeau, *The Practice of Everyday Life*, xi–xii.

50 Gill, *Lords of Misrule*; Gotham, *Authentic New Orleans*; Souther, *New Orleans on Parade*; K. Williams, "A Comparison of Travel Behaviors of African American and White Travelers to an Urban Destination."

Two. "Life the Way It Used to Be in the Old South"

1 C. V. Gambina Inc. was a small business owned by a white family and based in New Orleans. I purchased the dolls from a New Orleans department store in 1996.

2 In August 2009, I found several of the black Gambina dolls for sale on Ebay, including, "Gambina Doll Vintage Odelia Praline Lady" and "Scarlett, Southern Belle." "Kay and Lyn." 2000–2007. http://texaswatertowers.com/kayandlyn /gambina.html.

3 Nickel, "New Tourism Philosophy: Eat, Drink, Be Merry,—and Learn."

4 I am extending David Blight's formulation in *Race and Reunion* of a reconciliationist memory of the Civil War that prioritized national healing over racial justice. For other studies that advance the idea that national unity came at the expense of African Americans, see Cox, "Branding Dixie: The Selling of the American South, 1890–1930"; Silber, *The Romance of Reunion*.

5 Gotham, *Authentic New Orleans*; Long, *The Great Southern Babylon*; Souther, *New Orleans on Parade*; Stanonis, *Creating the Big Easy*; Thomas, "Race and Erasure in New Orleans Tourism."

6 R. King, "Blowing Life Back into the Birthplace of Jazz." See also Souther, *New Orleans on Parade*, 209.

7 Quoted in M. E. Crutcher, *Treme*, 87.

8 Souther, "The Disneyfication of New Orleans." See also Long, *The Great Southern Babylon*; Souther, *New Orleans on Parade*; Stanonis, *Creating the Big Easy*.

9 "New Orleans: America's European Masterpiece, Self-Guided Walking and Driving Tours," November 1982, n.p. "Greater New Orleans Tourist and Convention Commission, 1985 and before" vertical file, Louisiana and Special Collections Department, Earl K. Long Library, University of New Orleans, Louisiana (hereafter Louisiana and Special Collections).

10 For an example of national media coverage of violent crime in the city, see "NOPD Blues." For the historical context of media portrayals of black lawlessness, see Stabile, *White Victims, Black Villains*; Souther, *New Orleans on Parade*, 226–27. For examples of local media attention to crime's impact on tourism, see Alexander, "Tourism Execs Seek New Ways to Get Safety Message out to Visitors"; Parent, "Hit on Tourism Only a Flesh Wound, So Far"; Pennington, "Welcome to New Orleans"; Slaton, "Hoteliers Say Crime Is Partly to Blame for

Sluggish Bookings"; Slaton, "Tourism Holding Up under Weight of Crime—So Far"; "Tourism in Louisiana Could Suffer from a Violent Image." Although the popular tourism website NewOrleans.com does include a fairly extensive section on neighborhoods, the site provides a warning for only predominantly black New Orleans East: "Neighborhoods vary in this area, so be aware. Take taxis at night" ("Areas of the City: New Orleans East"). This warning seems appropriate to most, if not all, neighborhoods in the city, yet—ironically—it is applied to only one. Furthermore, the only areas of New Orleans East that are highlighted in the section include the white neighborhoods of the Holy Cross community and the suburb of St. Bernard Parish, neither of which are truly part of New Orleans East. Another website joins the prevailing demarcation of the French Quarter as safe, with the warning: "The area along the **N. Rampart St.** side of the Quarter, and some parts near **Esplanade** are probably *not safe any time.*" The site lists the "*iffy-to-dangerous*" areas of the city as "**anywhere across Esplanade Avenue into Elysian Fields**" and "**any place approaching N. Rampart Street, from Canal to Esplanade,**" with an additional note that the public housing development at the former site of the historic Storyville neighborhood "look[s] rough to me" ("Safety Tips"; emphasis in original).

11 Kevin Gotham traces the roots of New Orleans's tourist iconography to the 1884 World's Industrial and Cotton Exposition (*Authentic New Orleans,* 55–60).

12 Easterlin, "Our Attitudes about Tourism Have Changed."

13 The rhetoric of New Orleans's uniqueness is not limited to local tourism marketing efforts. The idea has also been adopted by print and web resources that present themselves as objective purveyors of reliable tourist information, such as Lonely Planet, Fodor's, and Rough Guides Travel, which publish both web and print resources. SoulofAmerica.com, a black travel website, underscores this idea: "The word 'unique' is an overused descriptor for cities, but it really applies to New Orleans" ("Historical Context, Cities").

14 Taggart, "The Music, Culture and Food of New Orleans."

15 "Laissez Les Bon Temps Rouler!," 8.

16 For the genesis of this argument, see Tannenbaum, *Slave and Citizen.* For online portrayals of New Orleans's distinctiveness, see Crouere, "History of New Orleans"; "Facts and History"; "French Quarter Guide"; Greenberg, "History"; "Historical Context, Cities"; "Laissez Les Bon Temps Rouler!"; Leavitt, "Melting Pot"; "Locals' Dictionary"; Morial, "Dear Friends"; "New Orleans" (2002); Pipes, "Spirit"; Taggart, "A Lexicon of New Orleans Terminology and Speech"; Taggart, "The Music, Culture and Food of New Orleans"; "Welcome to New Orleans, Louisiana"; "Yatspeak."

17 Greenberg, "History."

18 Nina Silber's analysis of the postbellum South's appeal to northern travelers offers a useful framework for contextualizing New Orleans's distinctiveness (*The Romance of Reunion,* 66–92).

19 In the past forty years, historiography has been influenced by the civil rights and Black Power movements and their impact on academia—particularly the es-

tablishment of African American studies programs, beginning in the late 1960s. The legacy of this academic development has been a challenge to and revision of dominant narratives that focused almost exclusively on white subjects and authors.

20 For more extensive studies of particular shifts in historical narratives and the resulting effects on tourism, museum, and other popular culture practices, see Fabre and O'Meally, *History and Memory in African-American Culture*; Handler and Gable, *The New History in an Old Museum*; Karp, Kreamer, and Levine, *Museums and Communities*; Kirshenblatt-Gimblett, *Destination Culture*; Molyneaux and Stone, *The Presented Past*; Samuel, *Theatres of Memory*; Walsh, *The Representation of the Past*.

21 Gotham, *Authentic New Orleans*, 6.

22 "Welcome."

23 Branley, "New Orleans History."

24 For examples, see Fricker, "Uncommon Character"; "Historic Homes"; "Historical Facts about New Orleans"; "Historically Speaking"; "Welcome to the New Orleans French Quarter." Most major tour companies offered history tours of the city. Although the city's jazz heritage was also promoted in the second half of the twentieth century, the tourist packaging of jazz was often presented ahistorically, with little attention to the social and political contexts that shaped the genre (see Souther, *New Orleans on Parade*, 102–31).

25 Fricker, "Uncommon Character."

26 "Historically Speaking": Coviello, "Style Points," 10; G. Hall, "The Formation of Afro-Creole Culture," 59.

27 "Historical Facts about New Orleans."

28 "New Orleans," 1991, n.p., "Greater New Orleans Tourist and Convention Commission, 1994" vertical file, Louisiana and Special Collections.

29 Honey Naylor, "New Orleans: America's European Masterpiece," 1988, "Greater New Orleans Tourist and Convention Commission, 1986–88" vertical file, Louisiana and Special Collections.

30 Other areas of the city are also portrayed as European. For instance, NOMCVB's visitor's guide includes a section on the Garden District that notes: "Primarily a residential area, the Garden District attracts both history buffs and lovers of European architecture; many of the majestic Greek-, Italian- and Spanish-style colonials here date back to the mid-1800s" ("Introduction to New Orleans," 18).

31 "French Quarter Guide."

32 "Introduction to New Orleans," 12–14.

33 Osbey, "Tourism in New Orleans."

34 "Louisiana."

35 "French Quarter Guide." Although most historians agree that New Orleans developed separately and distinctly from other U.S. cities, the early colony was plagued by epidemics, an inhospitable climate and locale, and wanton violence. As a result, the colony suffered greatly from underpopulation. From 1717 to 1720, the French government sent prisoners and other questionable characters to

the colony to increase its population, with little success. Because of widespread poverty, only the small group of the colony's elite could probably afford to send their children to school in France. See G. Hall, *Africans in Colonial Louisiana*, 1–27.

36 P. Johnson, "Thank God the French Got Here First." See also "Phil Johnson at the Table."

37 For detailed arguments about how Africans' language, customs, political traditions, labor, and technology influenced and sustained the new colony, as well as how Africans, Native Americans, and Europeans interacted, see Cassimere, *African Americans in New Orleans before the Civil War*; Dawdy, *Building the Devil's Empire*; G. Hall, *Africans in Colonial Louisiana*; Hanger, *Bounded Lives, Bounded Places*; Hirsch and Logsdon, *Creole New Orleans*; Usner, *Indians, Settlers and Slaves in a Frontier Exchange Economy*; Vincent, *The African American Experience in Louisiana*.

38 "New Orleans—A WorldWeb Review."

39 "Louisiana Basics."

40 Ingersoll, "Free Blacks in a Slave Society," 176.

41 See, for example, Bell, *Revolution, Romanticism, and the Afro-Creole Protest Tradition in Louisiana, 1718–1868*; G. Hall, *Africans in Colonial Louisiana*; Hanger, *Bounded Lives, Bounded Places*.

42 See Ingersoll, *Mammon and Manon in Early New Orleans*; W. Johnson, *Soul by Soul*.

43 "Family Pages."

44 Most New Orleans tourist guides and websites feature plantations located on River Road, also known as "plantation alley." River Road stretches for about seventy miles between New Orleans and Baton Rouge, running on both sides of the Mississippi River. The road is noted for the elaborate plantations that were constructed by exorbitantly wealthy sugarcane planters in the years preceding the Civil War. See "The River Road." In addition to charter companies that customize tours, Cajun Pride Swamp Tours, Charlie's Tours, Good Old Days, Gray Line Tours, Machu Picchu, Tours by Isabelle, Old River Road Plantation Adventure, Steppin' Out Tours, and New Orleans Tours all offered tours from New Orleans to River Road plantations prior to Hurricane Katrina.

45 "Tours."

46 "Evergreen Plantation—New Orleans Tours," 116; "Houmas House Plantation and Garden," 116; "San Francisco Plantation," 107; "Tezcuco Plantation," 107; "Romance, History and Beauty on the Great River Road," 131; "Les Grande Dames of the River Road," 127.

47 "Things to Do in New Orleans."

48 San Francisco Plantation has even moved slave cabins and a school room onto the property to lend more verisimilitude to the plantation ("San Francisco Plantation").

49 "Nottoway Plantation Restaurant and Inn," 42.

50 "What Makes New Orleans Special?," 1990, n.p., "Greater New Orleans Tourist

and Convention Commission, 1989–90" vertical file, Louisiana and Special Collections.

51 Films such as *Hush, Hush, Sweet Charlotte*, *Interview with a Vampire*, *Primary Colors*, *North and South*, and *Gone with the Wind* were either filmed at or inspired by Louisiana plantations, including Houmas House, Oak Alley, Chretien Point, and Greenwood Plantations. See "Chretien Point Plantation B and B"; "Greenwood Plantation B and B"; "Houmas House Plantation and Gardens"; "Media."

52 "Oak Alley Plantation."

53 Eichstedt and Small, *Representations of Slavery*, 2.

54 Eichstedt and Small, *Representations of Slavery*, 3. For examples of proslavery ideology, see Faust, *The Ideology of Slavery*. For a similar argument about the erasure of slavery on Louisiana plantation tours, see Adams, *Wounds of Returning*, 54–85.

55 The website includes the Hermann-Grima Home, Williams Residence, Beauregard-Keyes House, Longue Vue House and Gardens, and Women's Opera Guild Home ("Historic Homes").

56 Bouchon, "Big Easy Dining: Feelings Café"; "New Orleans Real Estate: Elegant Victorian Home"; "Past Perfect Reservations"; Crawford, "Maison De Ville."

57 Crawford, "Maison De Ville."

58 Examples include the Original Pierre Maspero's Restaurant, which is advertised as the site of the Old Slave Exchange, and Feelings Café which once served as the slave quarters for D'Aunoy Plantation.

59 The Omni Royal Orleans is on the site of the former St. Louis Hotel, which held slave auctions in the nineteenth century. This account is given on several New Orleans multicultural or black heritage walking tours, including Le Monde Créole French Quarter Courtyards Tour, the "African American Legacy Heritage Tour" offered in association with the Tennessee Williams Festival, and Eclectic Tours' "Freedom's Journey: An African American Perspective." For details about the St. Louis Hotel, see Works Progress Administration, *New Orleans City Guide*, 245–46.

60 Osbey, "Tourism in New Orleans."

61 Dubin, "Symbolic Slavery." See also Cox, "Branding Dixie"; Goings, *Mammy and Uncle Mose*; Hale, *Making Whiteness*, 121–98; Kern-Foxworth, *Aunt Jemima, Uncle Ben, and Rastus*, 43–114; Turner, *Ceramic Uncles and Celluloid Mammies*, 3–61. Ted Ownby's reflection that postbellum sectional differences "might have had as much to do with desire or even fascination as with conflict or a sense of superiority" is also applicable to racial and class differences ("Thoughtful Souvenirs," 20). For specific studies of how the mammy and Aunt Jemima iconography reinforced racial hierarchies, see Manring, *Slave in a Box*; McElya, *Clinging to Mammy*; Stanonis, "Just Like Mammy Used to Make"; Wallace-Sanders, *Mammy*.

62 Stanonis, "Just Like Mammy Used to Make," 224.

63 For example, see Greenberg, "History."

64 W. Johnson, *Soul by Soul*.

65 Quoted in Hirsch and Logsdon, introduction to Part I, *Creole New Orleans*, 9.

New Orleans functions literally and symbolically in nineteenth-century slave narratives as "down river" or the epitome of the slaveholding Deep South. The city figures prominently in nineteenth-century slave narratives as the ultimate punishment for bondsmen and -women. In these narratives, New Orleans is equated to its slave market, the center of slave trading in the United States. In turn, the market is associated with the lowest elements of slave society— namely, unscrupulous slave traders and harsh or negligent slave masters. Runaways, unwilling concubines, and other recalcitrant bondsmen and -women were constantly being threatened with being sent to New Orleans for sale. The city and its slave market embodied for bondsmen and -women the evils of the slave system—the heart-wrenching separation of family members, the moral undermining and abuse of black womanhood, and inhumane conditions, including unrelenting labor and inadequate provisions. Although numerous nineteenth-century narratives include references to New Orleans and its feared slave market, three narratives in particular give sustained accounts: Bibb, *Narrative of the Life and Adventures of Henry Bibb*; W. Brown, *Narrative of William W. Brown*; Northrup, *Twelve Years a Slave*. For a brief discussion of New Orleans's association with the evils of slavery, see Cleman, *George Washington Cable Revisited*, 5–6.

66 Souther, *New Orleans on Parade*, 224.

67 Crouere, "History of New Orleans: Post WWII to Present."

68 Baker, *The Second Battle of New Orleans*; Bridges, *Through My Eyes*; Fairclough, *Race and Democracy*; Germany, *New Orleans after the Promises*, 31–37; Manning and Rogers, "Desegregation of the New Orleans Parochial Schools." Although New Orleans's tourism narrative has largely ignored Bridges's brave stand, the vitriolic local resistance to desegregation was poignantly captured for a national audience in John Steinbeck's best-selling 1962 *Travels with Charley: In Search of America* and Norman Rockwell's 1963 painting "The Problem We All Live With," which was reproduced in the January 14, 1964, issue of *Look* magazine.

69 Brannon, "Tourism Drives Local Economy as White-Collar Jobs Slip Away, Report Says"; Easterlin, "Our Attitudes about Tourism Have Changed"; Esolen, "Developing Tourism in New Orleans"; Greater New Orleans Tourist and Convention Commission, "GNOTCC Mission Statement," n.d., and "Keeping Up with the Visiting Joneses: The GNOTCC Researches Non-Convention New Orleans Visitors," April 14, 1993, "Greater New Orleans Tourist and Convention Commission, 1992–93" vertical file, Louisiana and Special Collections; Edward McNeill, "To All GNOTCC Members," April 14, 1993, "Greater New Orleans Tourist and Convention Commission, 1992–93" vertical file, Louisiana and Special Collections; Nickel, "New Tourism Philosophy"; "Promoting Tourism"; Ridenhour, "Can Tourism Halt Boom, Bust Cycle?"; Slaton, "New Orleans Seen as a Good Fit with Changing Vacation Trends"; "Tourism with Culture."

70 Roddewig, "What *Is* Cultural Tourism?," 5 and 8.

71 Richard O. Baumbach, "Issues and Opportunities in Cultural Tourism," National Trust for Historic Preservation, June 1, 1988, "WLAE TV" vertical file, Louisiana

and Special Collections; Brooks and Lacho, "Developing Coalitions in a Tourist-Based Economy," conference paper, (Charlotte, NC: Urban Affairs Association, April 18–21, 1990): 1–22, "New Orleans Joint Center for Tourism" vertical file, Louisiana and Special Collections; Eggler, "City Will Market Arts to Tourists"; Louise S. Glickman and Associates, "Client/Project Synopsis," n.d.; "Arts and Tourism Partnership, Midlo Center for New Orleans Studies" vertical file, University of New Orleans, Louisiana; "Going after Arts-Minded Visitors"; "Selling the City . . . without Selling Out: The Challenge of Tourism Management," 1988, "WLAE TV" vertical file, Louisiana and Special Collections.

72 "Selling the City," n.p. See also Roddewig, "What *Is* Cultural Tourism?"

73 Brenda Thornton, quoted in Campbell-Rock, "Black Tourists Pump Millions into the New Orleans Economy."

74 For instance, in 1995 the Louisiana Department of Culture, Recreation, and Tourism published its first multicultural guide, "Our Culture Abounds: A Pictorial Directory of Louisiana's African-American Attractions."

75 Gotham, *Authentic New Orleans*, 208.

76 "New Orleans Official Tourism Web Site"; Pipes, "History"; "Explore the City of Mystery," 14; "New Orleans Multicultural Tourism Network." For other references to New Orleans's gumbo of cultures, see "French Quarter Guide"; "New Orleans Cuisine"; "Laissez Les Bon Temps Rouler!," 20; "Louisiana—A Brief History"; "Welcome to New Orleans!"

77 "Welcome," 1.

78 Morial, "Dear Friends," 3.

79 Nagin, "Welcome to New Orleans," 5.

80 Handler and Gable, *The New History in an Old Museum*, 116.

81 Crouere, "History of New Orleans: Post WWII to Present."

82 Greenberg, "History."

83 "Laissez Le Bon Temps Rouler."

84 Pipes, "History."

85 In 1782, J. Hector St. John de Crèvecoeur famously wrote that in America "individuals of all nations are melted into a new race of men" (*Letters from an American Farmer*, 44).

86 See Dominguez, *White by Definition*; G. Hall, *Africans in Colonial Louisiana*; Hirsch and Logsdon, *Creole New Orleans*.

87 Gotham, *Authentic New Orleans*, 84.

88 "Creoles." The bibliography appended to the article does not contain a single reference dated after 1977. Some references date to the late nineteenth century, and one is a fictional account. Included in the bibliography are George W. Cable, *The Creoles of Louisiana* (first published in 1884), and *The Grandissimes* (first published in 1880); Rodolphe L. Desdunes, *Our People and Our History*, translated by Dorothea O. McCants (first published in 1911); Clement Eaton, *The Growth of Southern Civilization* (1961); Gary B. Mills, *The Forgotten People* (1977); and Frances J. Woods, *Marginality and Identity* (1972).

89 Leavitt, "Common Blood, Different Cultures."

90 "Social Traditions and Cemeteries."

91 Leavitt, "Common Blood, Different Cultures."

92 Pipes, "History."

93 Branley, "On Being Creole."

94 Pipes, "Events and Festivals."

95 Branley, "On Being Creole."

96 Most notably, the historians Grace King (*New Orleans*), Charles Gayarré
    (*History of Louisiana: The American Domination*), and David C. Rankin ("The
    Forgotten People," "The Impact of of the Civil War on the Free Colored Com-
    munity of New Orleans," and "The Politics of Caste") have argued that Creoles
    of color unwaveringly upheld elite, white interests through slave ownership,
    endogamy, and their insistence on a cultural, political, and social divide between
    themselves and enslaved blacks. For similar arguments, see Foner, "The Free
    People of Color in Louisiana and St. Domingue"; Hanger, *Bounded Lives,
    Bounded Places*. For recent scholarship that argues for Creole radicalism and
    alliances between enslaved and free blacks, see Bell, *Revolution, Romanticism,
    and the Afro-Creole Protest Tradition*; G. Hall, *Africans in Colonial Louisiana*,
    especially chapter 8; Hirsch and Logsdon, *Creole New Orleans*.

97 G. King, *New Orleans*, 333.

98 The historian Arnold Hirsch explains how this complex history has been dis-
    torted and oversimplified: "The coinciding demographic and social fault lines
    involving issues of color, class, language, religion, and geography facilitated the
    emergence of popular images that were rooted in fact although stereotypical
    and overdrawn. The downtown Creole of color (fair-skinned, French-speaking,
    Catholic, free or freed prior to abolition, often well-to-do and educated, con-
    servative by nature and aloof from the masses) stood in stark contrast to the
    uptown African American (darker, English-speaking, Protestant, the descendant
    of slaves, relatively bereft of material resources and skills). It made little differ-
    ence that literally thousands of exceptions undermined those gross descriptions;
    they reflected just enough of the visible reality of New Orleans to ring true"
    ("Fade to Black," 754).

99 J. Johnson, "Colonial New Orleans: A Fragment of the Eighteenth-Century
    French Ethos," 53.

Three. "Urbane, Educated, and Well-To-Do Free Blacks"

1 The title "Le Monde Créole French Quarter Courtyards Tour" is the name used
   on the tour company's brochure at the time of my research. Variations of this
   name, including "Le Monde Créole French Quarter Courtyards and Cemetery
   Tour" and "Le Monde Créole Secret Courtyards of the French Quarter and
   Cemetery Tour" appear in tourist guidebooks and on the company website.

2 Nevski interview.

3 Coble interview.

4 Jay (pseud.) interview.

5 Nevksi interview.

6 A growing body of scholarship locates these incongruences in racial neoliberalism. See, for instance, Goldberg, *The Threat of Race.*

7 Laura Locoul's memoirs were edited and published in 2000 by the operators
of Laura Plantation as Gore, *Memories of the Old Plantation Home.*

8 Laura Plantation distinguishes itself from other plantations in the area,
whose tours focus on replicating antebellum southern grandeur with antique
and replica furnishings, Civil War reenactments, and detailed descriptions
of nineteenth-century architecture and ornamentation—all limited, of course,
to the Big House and its wealthy, white former occupants. Tours of Laura, a re-
stored 1805 Creole-style sugarcane plantation, do venture beyond the Big House
and some of its attendant mythologies about white southern honor and splen-
dor. On the grounds are four of the forty-nine extant slave cabins. These cabins
mark the original site of the "Compair Lapin" stories, told by former bondsmen
and -women and recorded by the folklorist Alcee Fortier in the 1870s and later
recorded in English as the tales of "Br'er Rabbit" by Fortier's Georgia colleague
Joel Chandler Harris. These stories and the histories of those who told them are
part of Laura Plantation's sixty-minute interpretive tour, which focuses on the
stories of the four generations of women who operated the plantation; some
of the bondsmen and -women who lived and worked there; and the contributions of bondsmen, bondswomen, and free people of color to the plantation and
Louisiana. For a critique of Laura Plantation and its claims of inclusiveness, see
Adams, *Wounds of Returning,* 62–63.

9 Nevski interview.

10 Nevski interview.

11 I am indebted to my colleague Catherine Michna for highlighting the assumptions undergirding this theory of social change.

12 Coble interview.

13 Nevski interview.

14 Coble interview.

15 Coble interview.

16 Nevski interview.

17 At the time of this writing, LMC charges twenty-four dollars for the tour and,
like most New Orleans tours in the wake of Hurricane Katrina, has likely ad-
justed the script to reference the storm, its antecedents, and its aftermath
(see "'Le Monde Creole Tours' Present").

18 Nevski interview.

19 Nevski interview.

20 Coble interview.

21 Wallace, *Mickey Mouse History and Other Essays on American Memory,* 171. A
number of other public histories productively explore the challenge of presenting difficult histories to audiences expecting entertainment. See, for instance,
Abram, "Kitchen Conversations"; Greenspan, *Creating Colonial Williamsburg;*

J. Horton and L. Horton, *Slavery and Public History*; Stanton, *The Lowell Experiment*; J. Weeks, *Gettysburg*.

22 Robin (pseud.) interview.

23 Coble interview.

24 Coble interview.

25 See, for example, Eric Lott's argument in *Love and Theft* that minstrelsy reflected both whites' racism and their love for black culture.

26 For a discussion of the influential neoconservative challenge to the social liberal vision of the civil rights movement, see C. Horton, *Race and the Making of American Liberalism*, 191–222.

27 *Le Monde Créole: French Quarter Courtyards Tour* brochure, acquired by author in 2002.

28 "Le Monde Creole" in *The Soul of New Orleans* (1998), 68. See also "Le Monde Creole" in *The Soul of New Orleans* (2002), 56.

29 "One of the French Quarter's 'Best Kept Secrets'," 5. An ad for LMC in the same issue says that the French Quarter tour "focuses on hidden courtyards and forgotten people: Creole men and women, Free People of Color and slaves" ("Le Monde Créole" advertisement). Various versions of this description appeared in other tourist guidebooks and websites before Hurricane Katrina.

30 Coble interview.

31 Several instances of New Orleans's preoccupation with rules regulating racial mixing and defining racial identity come to mind. Of particular interest are the quadroon balls and system of *plaçage*, described below, which established a particular convention according to which racial mixing was socially acceptable; the large population of free people of color that developed in colonial and antebellum New Orleans with a distinct, yet tenuous, position in the city; the 1896 *Plessy v. Ferguson* Supreme Court case in which Homer Plessy, the octoroon plaintiff, argued that racial indeterminacy was grounds to invalidate racial segregation, and that resulted in the entrenchment of Jim Crow segregation; and the 1983 *Jane Doe v. State of Louisiana* case in which Susie Phipps lost her suit against the State of Louisiana to change her birth certificate classification from colored to white, ultimately upholding Louisiana's 1970 1/32 blood law that classified as black anyone with at least 1/32nd "Negro blood," irrespective of how that person identifies him- or herself.

32 Before Hurricane Katrina, LMC provided three French Quarter tours each day, two in English and one in French.

33 "Le Monde Creole French Quarter Courtyards and Cemetery Tour," 2001, 142. See also "LeMonde Creole, French Quarter Courtyards and Cemetery Tour," 2002–3, 142 and "LeMonde Creole, French Quarter Courtyards and Cemetery Tour," 2003–4, 143.

34 Turner, *Ceramic Uncles and Celluloid Mammies*.

35 Turner, *Ceramic Uncles and Celluloid Mammies*, and Greenwood, "Collecting Black Memorabilia with Althea Burton." For a more extensive discussion

of these cultural practices, see G. Alexander, "Collecting Our History"; Bogle, *Toms, Coons, Mulattoes, Mammies, and Bucks*; Hernandez, "Black Memorabilia Find Big Demand"; "New Racist Forms"; Reno, *Collecting Black Americana*.

36 "La Cuisine Créole," *Le Monde Créole*, newsletter, 2, in the author's possession.

37 The Creole reads, "Si nouri lémond de li Louisiane, kimoun selman blan, piti bôl di ri se ase pouo tou pay!" Unsigned, untitled drawing, *Le Monde Créole* newsletter, 3, in the author's possession.

38 Listed second through sixth of the twenty-one "Bestselling Books: Non-fiction" are: Gary B. Mills, *The Forgotten People: Cane River's Creoles of Color*; Linda Brent, *Incidents in the Life of a Slave Girl*, William F. Allen, Charles P. Ware, and Lucy McKim Garrison, *Slave Songs of the United States*; Mary Gehman, *Free People of Color of New Orleans*; and Sybil Kein, *Creole: The Legacy of Free People of Color*. Other titles of note include Joel Williamson, *New People: Miscegenation and Mulattos in the United States*; F. James Davis, *Who Is Black?*; Velma M. Thomas, *Lest We Forget: The Passage from Africa to Slavery and Emancipation*; and W. E. B. Du Bois, *The Souls of Black Folk*. On the "Bestselling Fiction" list, titles of note include Barbara Hambly, *Free Man of Color* and *Sold Down the River*; Anne Rice, *Feast of All Saints*; and Jewell Rhodes, *Voodoo Dreams*. The quotation from Du Bois reads: "This is the tragedy of our age . . . not that men are poor; for all men will know poverty sometime in their lives. Not that men are evil; for who is truly good? And not that men are ignorant; for what is truth? Nay, it is that men do not know men," "Bestselling Books: Non-Fiction," *Le Monde Créole* newsletter, 2; "Bestselling Fiction," *Le Monde Créole* newsletter, 3, in the author's possession.

39 "Welcome!," *Le Monde Créole* newsletter, 1, 2, in the author's possession.

40 "Welcome!," *Le Monde Créole* newsletter, 1, in the author's possession.

41 Gehman, "Free People of Color," *Le Monde Créole* newsletter, 2, in the author's possession.

42 "Welcome!" *Le Monde Créole* newsletter, 3, in the author's possession.

43 Nevski interview.

44 Bennett, *The Birth of the Museum*, 109; Samuel, *Theatres of Memory*, 25–27, 158–202.

45 Quote from the visitor survey I conducted on March 25, 2002.

46 Robin (pseud.) interview. .

47 Jay (pseud.) interview; Robin (pseud.) interview; Coble interview.

48 Coble interview.

49 Pat (pseud.), during a tour on March 25, 2002.

50 Robin (pseud.) interview.

51 Drew Gilpin Faust examines the development of a unified proslavery argument in the antebellum South. She argues that by advocating both interdependence and inequality among masters and slaves, "the proslavery argument asserted its opposition to the growing materialism of the age and offered the model of evangelical stewardship as the best representation of its labor system. The master was God's surrogate on earth; the southern system institutionalized the Chris-

tian duties of charity in the master and humility in the slave" (*The Ideology of Slavery*, 13).

52 Coble interview.

53 Coble interview. During the tour I took led by Coble on October 27, 2002, he did not include this explanation of slavery.

54 Although some tour guides stated during the tour that Toussaint was not freed by his father, they did not attempt to reconcile this fact with their portrayals of Emile as a would-be abolitionist. Only during our interview did Coble come close to underscoring this irony. He told me that Emile never indicated "that he was open-minded enough that they should have a plantation with hired help. So, again, a complex character" (Coble interview).

55 Coble interview.

56 Robin (pseud.) interview.

57 For a theoretical discussion of this construct, see Berzon, *Neither White nor Black*; S. Brown, *Negro Poetry and Drama, and the Negro in American Fiction*; Gillman, "The Mulatto, Tragic or Triumphant?"; Hiraldo, *Segregated Miscegenation*; Sollors, *Neither Black nor White yet Both*.

58 Coble interview.

59 Coble interview. Guides do not inform visitors during the tour that the images of characters are not authentic representations.

60 Williams, *Playing the Race Card*, xiv.

61 Jay (pseud.) carefully avoids giving a sympathetic portrayal of Emile by refraining from the sentimental elements of his storyline. In Jay's version, the pivotal scene of Emile's departure is not marked by his former slaves' tearful tribute out of respect to their benevolent employer. Instead, Jay told visitors that the black workers were lined up as Emile departed, but there was no handkerchief waving, and only Emile—not the black workers—was crying. This distinction is a significant one for Jay, who explained during our interview: "[The slaves] just came out. They wasn't [*sic*] sure why [Emile] was crying." Jay suggested several reasons why Emile might have cried—such as his deteriorating health or his departure from his childhood home—that have nothing to do with his affection for his bondsmen and -women. Jay's resistance to New Orleans's tourism narrative is explored in chapter 4.

62 Although excused in the script by Laura's loyalty to the family, we are told later in the tour that she did, in fact, run the plantation for ten years to work off the family's debts. These types of inconsistencies are easily glossed over or explained away in the tour in order to keep particular character types intact.

63 A considerable body of literature exists on whites' portrayals of African American characters. For examples, see Ellison, *Going to the Territory* and *Shadow and Act*; T. Lott, *The Invention of Race*; Morrison, *Playing in the Dark*; D. Nelson, *The Word in Black and White*; Nielsen, *Writing between the Lines*; L. Williams, *Playing the Race Card*; Wonham, *Criticism and the Color Line*.

64 For discussions of the impact of the Haitian revolution on the United States and colonial New Orleans, see Berlin, *Many Thousands Gone*, 219–27; Fordham,

"Nineteenth-Century Black Thought in the United States"; G. Hall, *Africans in Colonial Louisiana*, especially 345–74; Lachance, "The 1809 Immigration of Saint-Domingue Refugees to New Orleans"; J. Logsdon, "Americans and Creoles in New Orleans"; J. Logsdon and Bell, "The Americanization of Black New Orleans," 205; Williams-Myers, "Slavery, Rebellion, and Revolution in the Americas."

65 Coble interview.

66 Chris (pseud.), during a tour on October 22, 2002 ; Coble, during a tour on October 27, 2002.

67 Guillory, "Some Enchanted Evening on the Auction Block."

68 Coble interview.

69 See Clark and Gould, "The Feminine Face of Afro-Catholicism in New Orleans"; Copeland, *The Subversive Power of Love*. Delille's life was portrayed in the 2000 film *The Courage to Love*, directed by Kari Skogland. In 2010 the Roman Catholic Church declared Delille venerable, an important milestone in the Vatican's consideration of her for canonization. See Nolan, "Henriette Delille Moves Closer to Sainthood for Work with New Orleans Slaves."

70 Coble interview.

71 Pat (pseud.), during a tour on March 25, 2002.

72 Despite this distinction between conceptions of race before and after the Louisiana Purchase, tour guides regularly collapsed historical periods and practices, creating an ahistorical and often contradictory narrative.

73 Shawn (pseud.), during a tour on August 9, 2000.

74 For a summary of the shift in historiography, see Williams-Myers, "Slavery, Rebellion, and Revolution in the Americas." For histories of slave resistance, see Aptheker, *American Negro Slave Revolts*; Genovese, *From Rebellion to Revolution*. For histories of resistance among blacks in New Orleans in particular, see Bell, *Revolution, Romanticism, and the Afro-Creole Protest Tradition in Louisiana*; Blassingame, *Black New Orleans*; G. Hall, *Africans in Colonial Louisiana*, 237–74; Rasmussen, *American Uprising*; Sublette, *The World That Made New Orleans*; Thrasher, *On to New Orleans!*; Daniel Walker, *No More, No More*.

75 Gould, "'A Chaos of Iniquity and Discord,'" 237–38.

76 Only Jay (pseud.), the renegade tour guide, offered a different interpretation of the FPC's slave ownership by claiming that although FPC did purchase slaves, they did not do so on the auction block. Instead, they purchased their relatives (Jay, during a tour on September 5, 2002).

77 G. Hall, *Africans in Colonial Louisiana*, 304–5. See also Dawdy, *Building the Devil's Empire*; Spear, *Race, Sex, and Social Order in Early New Orleans*.

78 Coble interview.

79 This critique has been repeated in scholarship on whiteness that demystifies white identity by revealing it as a social construct with real structural and institutional causes and consequences. For examples of this scholarship, see Babb, *Whiteness Visible*; Delgado, *Critical White Studies*; Dyer, *White*; Jacobson, *Whiteness of a Different Color*; E. Lott, *Love and Theft*; Morrison, *Playing in the*

Dark; Omi and Winant, *Racial Formation in the United States*; Roediger, *The Wages of Whiteness*.

80 In December 2004, however, I went on a tour that included the controversial ending.

81 Coble interview.

82 During the tour, guides did offer a basic overview of voodoo as an African religion focused on ancestral worship and practiced under the guise of Catholicism in the New World. Some guides also linked voodoo's proliferation in New Orleans to the arrival of Haitian émigrés following that country's 1790 slave revolt. Although acknowledging that voodoo provided a means for bondsmen and -women to gain independence from their slave masters, guides seemed only to suggest a type of spiritual or psychological independence, not a physical or political one.

83 Tour guides did not acknowledge the contributions of enslaved blacks, whose craftsmanship and labor were used to construct many of these structures. See Blassingame, *Black New Orleans*, 2.

84 The Iberville public housing development was built as a whites-only complex in the early 1940s with funds from the 1937 United States Housing Act, also known as the Wagner Bill. After suffering minimal damage, it was one of the few public housing developments that reopened following Hurricane Katrina. Because of its central location near the French Quarter, the Iberville development for years has been at the center of debate regarding redevelopment. Business and tourism interests have lobbied the city to demolish or redevelop the site, citing aesthetics and high crime rates. In 2011, the Housing Authority of New Orleans was awarded $30.5 million by the U.S. Department of Housing and Urban Development's Choice Neighborhoods Initiative to demolish the housing development and rebuild a mixed-income community in its place. Demolition began in September 2013. See Edwards, "Upgrades in Store for Blighted Iberville Housing Development"; "Iberville Development Neighborhood Snapshot"; Reckdahl, "HANO Gets $30.5 Million to Re-Do Iberville Public-Housing Complex"; Shaban, "In Address, Nagin Announces Several Big Plans"; Webster, "Demolition of Ibervile Housing Development Begins."

85 See Long, *The Great Southern Babylon*.

86 One guide did point out Plessy's tomb and the significance of the Supreme Court's decision in *Plessy v. Ferguson* for the systemization of Jim Crow laws throughout the South (Pat [pseud.], during a tour on March 25, 2002).

87 Stanonis, "Dead but Delightful," 257–60; Hanger, *Bounded Lives, Bounded Places*; Schafer, *Becoming Free, Remaining Free*.

88 Coble, during a tour on October 27, 2002.

89 LMC's failure to acknowledge such challenges to New Orleans mythology affirms the historian Edward Linenthal's observation about concerted resistance to memorializing painful national histories, such as slavery and Jim Crow: "If there is a past that may be, in fact, subversive of such cherished identities, erasure, denial, transformation, and intentional consignment to oblivion are called for" ("Epilogue," 215–16).

1   In his study of the linkages between popular culture and collective memory, George Lipsitz argues that through complex and uneven ways, people use avenues available in popular culture to revise and reenvision American myths, thereby attempting to confront, if not combat, the hegemonic discourses that pervade and pervert their lives. In a chapter on popular novels and their revisions of dominant historical narratives, Lipsitz explains that "women, Afro-Americans, and other groups relegated to the margins of dominant discourse learn that the 'truths' of society obscure unconscionable lies, while the lies of myth and folklore offer opportunities for voicing long suppressed truths" ("History, Myth, and Counter-Memory," 212). I employ Lipsitz's definition of countermemory as "a way of remembering and forgetting that starts with the local, the immediate, and the personal . . . then builds outward toward a total story" (ibid., 213), a tool that relies on "the past for the hidden histories excluded from dominant narratives" (ibid., 213). These rejoinders to dominant narratives point to the possibility of revising historical memory. As the author Melvin Dixon has argued, such revisions "enlarge the frame of cultural reference for the depiction of black experiences by anchoring that experience in memory—a memory that ultimately rewrites history" ("The Black Writer's Use of Memory," 20).

2   For my use of "performative resistance," I rely on Frantz Fanon's conception of resistance in the chapter "Algeria Unveiled" in *Studies of a Dying Colonialism* (1965). As I argued in greater detail in "Kissing Ass and Other Performative Acts of Resistance," Fanon's portrayal of Algerian women's use of the veil and their own bodily performance to deceive the French colonialists provides an important reconceptualization of J. L. Austin's theory of the performative (Austin, *How to Do Things with Words*). Unlike Austin—whose discussion of the performative assumes equal, if not harmonious, relationships—Fanon, writing in the postcolonial era, attends to the performative in the case of incompatibility and extreme inequality. Fanon's "Algeria Unveiled" demonstrates how the powerless and seemingly voiceless use tacitly agreed-on conventions inappropriately to attain what they would not otherwise be able to have. Thus, this model is useful for exploring the performative possibilities for resistance by members of groups that are marginalized, disfranchised, or rendered invisible in popular narratives.

3   The merits of the heritage industry itself, particularly in the United States and Britain, have been debated by scholars in recent years. In practice, heritage encompasses many, often divergent, meanings and is embraced by both the political right and left to different ends. The heritage industry has drawn criticism from the academic community for trivializing cultures, commodifying and idealizing a fictitious past, and presenting a distorted sense of time and place that ultimately create a hegemonic form of discourse. Proponents of the heritage industry, on the other hand, say that it challenges intellectual elitism by authenticating the agency of heritage site visitors who are capable of historical reflection

and analysis. Furthermore, they argue that the heritage industry offers a new way of seeing history, one that is more accessible to common experience and popular memory; provides alternative modes of teaching; and acknowledges and sustains a multiethnic past and future. For some seminal analyses of the heritage industry, see Adorno, *The Culture Industry*; Handler and Gable, *The New History in an Old Museum*; Herbert, *Heritage, Tourism and Society*; Hewison, *The Heritage Industry*; Kirshenblatt-Gimblett, *Destination Culture*; Lowenthal, *The Past Is a Foreign Country* and *Possessed by the Past*; Molyneaux, "Introduction"; Rothman, *The Culture of Tourism, The Tourism of Culture*; Uzzell, *Heritage Interpretation*; Walsh, *The Representation of the Past*.

4 Ruffins, "Mythos, Memory, and History."

5 Black travel guides, such as *The Green Motorist Green Book* and *Travelguide*, were published during the Jim Crow era to provide information about businesses that accommodated African Americans. For discussions of African Americans' uses of these guides, see Onion, "A Midcentury Travel Guide for African-American Drivers Navigating Jim Crow"; Seiler, "'So That We as a Race Might Have Something Authentic to Travel By,'" 1099–109; Studies tracking the expansion of domestic tourism and changing African American travel and spending patterns at the end of the twentieth century are documented in "African-American Travelers"; Campbell-Rock, "Black Tourists Pump Millions into the New Orleans Economy"; "Travelers' Desire to Experience History and Culture Stronger Than Ever"; "White House Conference on Travel and Tourism Task Forces Completed Work" in *The Networker*, fall–winter 1995–96, "Greater New Orleans Black Tourism Network" vertical file, Louisiana and Special Collections Department, Earl K. Long Library, University of New Orleans, Louisiana (hereafter Louisiana and Special Collections); and K. Williams, "A Comparison of Travel Behaviors of African American and White Travelers to an Urban Destination."

6 Campbell-Rock, "Black Tourists Pump Millions into the New Orleans Economy"; Ferris, "Around the South in Search of the Past"; Owens, "Black Tourism Gained Respect via Essence."

7 For a more comprehensive view of how Pierre Nora's theory of lieux de mémoire applies to African American history and culture, see Fabre and O'Meally, *History and Memory in African-American Culture*.

8 Souther, *New Orleans on Parade*, 73–101, 160; Gotham, *Authentic New Orleans*, 98.

9 Osbey, "Tourism in New Orleans."

10 Osbey, "Tourism in New Orleans." See also Campbell-Rock, "Black Tourists Pump Millions into the New Orleans Economy"; "Network Profile," 18.

11 Grant, "Race, Place, and Memory: African American Tourism in the Postindustrial City," 411. See also Boyd, "Reconstructing Bronzeville"; A. Johnson, "Black Historical Sites." For a discussion of the dismantling of Great Society programs and its impact on New Orleans, see Germany, *New Orleans after the Promises*, 296–313.

12 "Amendment to the Working Agreement between the Greater New Orleans

Tourist and Convention Commission (GNOTCC) and the Greater New Orleans Black Tourism Network (GNOBTN)," November 6, 1990, private files, New Orleans Multicultural Tourism Network, New Orleans, Louisiana (hereafter private files, NOMTN); "Articles of Incorporation—GNOBTN," 1990, private files, NOMTN; Campbell-Rock, "Black Tourists Pump Millions into the New Orleans Economy"; Crabtree, "New Group Is Seen as a Vehicle to Boost Black Tourism Business"; "History of New Orleans Tourism Marketing Corporation," n.d., private files, NOMTN; "Network Profile," 18; Osbey, "Tourism in New Orleans"; "Working Agreement between the Greater New Orleans Tourist and Convention Commission ('GNOTCC') and the Greater New Orleans Black Tourism Network ('GNOBTN')," October 4, 1990, private files, NOMTN. On the primacy of the GNOTCC, see Gotham, *Authentic New Orleans*, 103–9; Souther, *New Orleans on Parade*, 172.

13 Phala Mire, letter to prospective members, January 30, 1996, "Greater New Orleans Black Tourism Network" vertical file, Louisiana and Special Collections.

14 Campbell-Rock, "Black Tourists Pump Millions into the New Orleans Economy"; Charles, "Morial Touts N.O. as Fair City in Bid to Keep Conventions"; Crabtree, "New Group Is Seen as a Vehicle to Boost Black Tourism Business"; Eggler, "For New Orleans, It Was the Best of Times"; Souther, *New Orleans on Parade*, 76.

15 Campbell-Rock, "Black Tourists Pump Millions into the New Orleans Economy." The conference was planned to rotate among other sites, beginning in 1999, when it was held in Washington, D.C. However, this was the conference's final year.

16 "Network Profile," 18.

17 Baldwin, "Black Tourism Network."

18 "Network Profile," 19.

19 "Welcome, Essence Fest."

20 "New Orleans Secures Essence Music Festival for 1996" in "The Networker," fall–winter 1995–96, "Greater New Orleans Black Tourism Network" vertical file, Louisiana and Special Collections; Yerton, "Essence Trying to Broaden Audience."

21 Campbell-Rock, "Black Tourists Pump Millions into the New Orleans Economy."

22 Quoted in Owens, "Black Tourism Gained Respect via Essence."

23 Yerton, "Celebration of Heritage, Music Will Aid Tourism," "Essence Festival a Jewel in N.O: Hospitality Crown," and "Essence Festival Back for Seconds."

24 Quoted in Charles, "Morial Touts N.O. as Fair City in Bid to Keep Conventions." See also Judice, "Group Polishes N.O. Image"; "Morial Keeps Heat on Foster"; Yerton, "Essence Festival a Jewel in N.O: Hospitality Crown" and "Essence Festival Back for Seconds." The city was threatened with a similar boycott in 1991 when former Klansman David Duke ran unsuccessfully for governor. See Owens, "Black Tourism Gained Respect via Essence."

25 Campbell-Rock, "Black Tourists Pump Millions into the New Orleans Econ-

omy"; Owens, "Black Tourism Gained Respect via Essence"; Salvail, "Efforts to Lure More Minority Events to City Are Paying Off"; Treadway, "Essence Music Festival to Return to N.O. in 1998"; Jaquetta White, "Multicultural Welcome"; Yerton, "Essence Festival a Jewel in N.O: Hospitality Crown" and "Essence Festival Back for Seconds."

26 Hopkins, "Essence Music Festival." 28.

27 Campbell-Rock, "Black Tourists Pump Millions into the New Orleans Economy"; Owens, "Black Tourism Gained Respect via Essence"; Salvail, "Efforts to Lure More Minority Events to City Are Paying Off"; Jaquetta White, "Multicultural Welcome"; Yerton, "Celebration of Heritage, Music Will Aid Tourism" and "Essence Festival a Jewel in N.O. Hospitality Crown."

28 Quoted in Salvail, "Efforts to Lure More Minority Events to City Are Paying Off."

29 Salvail, "Efforts to Lure More Minority Events to City Are Paying Off."

30 Campbell-Rock, "Black Tourists Pump Millions into the New Orleans Economy"; Owens, "Black Tourism Gained Respect via Essence."

31 Quoted in Osbey, "Tourism in New Orleans."

32 Campbell-Rock, "Tourism."

33 Campbell-Rock, "Tourism."

34 Quoted in Osbey, "Tourism in New Orleans."

35 Quoted in Osbey, "Tourism in New Orleans."

36 Osbey, "Tourism in New Orleans."

37 Pecot-Hebert, "UNO Metropolitan College Leads Effort to Diversify Tourism Industry."

38 Quoted in Owens, "Black Tourism Gained Respect via Essence." It should be noted that New Orleans developed concentrated black business districts in the twentieth century as institutionalized segregation created more racially polarized neighborhoods. North Rampart Street, Dryades Avenue, and Claiborne Avenue were notable centers of black enterprise until the end of the century, when discriminatory urban renewal projects, desegregation, and the exodus of the middle class left a more racially and economically polarized city and signaled the demise of these business districts. See M. E. Crutcher, *Treme*, 50–65; Ingham, "Building Businesses, Creating Communities," 650; Medley, "Dryades Street/ Oretha Castle Haley Boulevard: Remembrance and Reclamation"; Simmons, "Black Girls Coming of Age," 81–86; Spain, "Race Relations and Residential Segregation in New Orleans."

39 Campbell-Rock, "Black Tourists Pump Millions into the New Orleans Economy."

40 Quoted in Pecot-Hebert, "UNO Metropolitan College Leads Effort to Diversify Tourism Industry."

41 Mire interview.

42 Osbey, "Tourism in New Orleans." For examples, see "Historical Map and Points of Interest"; "New Orleans Map and Points of Interest"; "New Orleans: America's European Masterpiece, Self-Guided Walking and Driving Tours," November

1982, and "New Orleans Self-Guided Walking and Driving Tours," September 1984, both "Greater New Orleans Tourist and Convention Commission, 1985 and before" vertical file, Louisiana and Special Collections; "New Orleans Self-Guided Walking and Driving Tours," May 1987, and "New Orleans Self-Guided Walking and Driving Tours," 1988, both "Greater New Orleans Tourist and Convention Commission, 1986–88" vertical file, Louisiana and Special Collections; "'Soul of New Orleans': African American Heritage Map."

43 Osbey, "Tourism in New Orleans."

44 "New Orleans" (New Orleans: GNOTCC, 1991), n.p., "Greater New Orleans Tourist and Convention Commission, 1994" vertical file, Louisiana and Special Collections. See also "Working Agreement between the Greater New Orleans Tourist and Convention Commission ('GNOTCC') and the Greater New Orleans Black Tourism Network ('GNOBTN')," October 4, 1990, private files, NOMTN; "New Orleans Travel Resource Guide," 1988–89, "Greater New Orleans Tourist and Convention Commission, 1989–90" vertical file, Louisiana and Special Collections; "Mardi Gras," August 1988, "Greater New Orleans Tourist and Convention Commission, 1986–88" vertical file, Louisiana and Special Collections. It should be noted, however, that before the inauguration of *The Soul of New Orleans*, the GNOTCC did publish at least two editions of "Black Heritage of New Orleans" that featured points of interest divergent from its "New Orleans Self-Guided Walking and Driving Tours." The brochure claimed to introduce tourists to "the wealth of Black American culture in New Orleans" and encouraged visitors "to view [sites that no longer existed or with no accompanying physical markers] with imagination and awareness of their historical significance" ("Black Heritage of New Orleans," February 1988, "Greater New Orleans Tourist and Convention Commission, 1986–88" vertical file, Louisiana and Special Collections).

45 Owens, "Black Tourism Gained Respect via Essence."

46 Powell, "Visitor's Welcome," 4. See also Barthelemy, "Welcome to New Orleans." For a discussion of the differences in leadership between Barthelemy and his predecessor, Ernest "Dutch" Morial, see Hirsch, "Simply a Matter of Black and White," 290, and "Fade to Black," 759–60.

47 For example, see Marc Morial, "Greetings." For an analysis of the two administrations' different approaches to the question of race in New Orleans, see Hirsch, "Simply a Matter of Black and White."

48 "A Message from GNOBTN," 4.

49 Hodge, "New Orleans Culture," 26.

50 "About New Orleans," 5.

51 Gotham, *Authentic New Orleans*, 116–41.

52 Hodge, "New Orleans Culture," 26.

53 "NORD: New Orleans Recreation Department," 24.

54 This focus on youth and families is a legacy of black New Orleanians' vision of the Great Society. Recreation became a pivotal battleground for post–civil rights activism in New Orleans in 1966, when black women activists successfully

used War on Poverty funds to circumvent the New Orleans Recreation Department's discriminatory policies and develop a recreation program that shifted power to local neighborhoods. See Germany, *New Orleans After the Promises*, 83–86.

55 "About New Orleans," 5. See also Gotham, *Authentic New Orleans*, 116–41.

56 "A Message from GNOBTN," 4.

57 "About NOMTN." Articles from *The Soul of New Orleans* were also reproduced on the New Orleans Marketing Corporation's website, NewOrleansOnline.com.

58 M. Crutcher, "Historical Geographies of Race in a New Orleans Afro-Creole Landscape"; "History"; Logsdon and Elie, *Faubourg Tremé*; Sumpter, "Segregation of the Free People of Color and the Construction of Race in Antebellum New Orleans"; "Welcome to New Orleans, Louisiana." Although the New Orleans Convention and Visitors Bureau's website and NewOrleans.com included detailed information on New Orleans's neighborhoods, neither mentioned Faubourg Tremé. See "Areas of the City in New Orleans"; Greenberg, "Lay of the Land."

59 "Faubourg Tremé: America's Oldest Black Neighborhood," 72.

60 For a discussion of some of the post-Katrina attention to the neighborhood, see Thomas, "'People Want to See What Happened.'"

61 "Faubourg Tremé."

62 "Faubourg Tremé."

63 Since its beginnings in 1996, the New Orleans African American Museum of Art, Culture, and History, which specializes in African art and culture, has struggled to keep its doors open because of financial and logistical constraints. After being audited, the museum closed because of improper use of funds in 2003. It was still closed at the time Hurricane Katrina hit and caused some wind damage to the structure. The museum reopened and began offering programming in 2007, and it was awarded a $3 million Community Development Block Grant in 2011 for improvements and enhancements. See Kinzer, "Arts in America"; Delehanty, "Waiting for the Resurrection"; Eggler, "New Orleans African American Museum to Undergo Renovations."

64 Osborn, "Free People of Color and Creoles," 63.

65 Osborn, "Free People of Color and Creoles," 63.

66 Osborn, "Free People of Color and Creoles," 63.

67 "What's Creole? What's Cajun?" 9. The article was reproduced online (see "What's a Creole?").

68 "Welcome to New Orleans, Louisiana."

69 "Famous Residents."

70 See Regis, "Blackness and the Politics of Memory in the New Orleans Second Line" and "Second Lines, Minstrelsy, and the Contested Landscapes of New Orleans Afro-Creole Festivals." Joseph Roach (*Cities of the Dead*) and George Lipsitz ("Mardi Gras Indians") also consider the ways that these black nontourist rituals function as part of and in contrast to the image of New Orleans.

71 Price et al., "Zulu Social Aid and Pleasure Club," 38. The article was reproduced

online (see Price et al., "Zulu Social Aid and Pleasure Club," NewOrleansOnline .com).

72 "Mardi Gras." Roach expounds on this performative critique in *Cities of the Dead.*

73 "Mardi Gras."

74 "Social Traditions and Cemeteries."

75 "The Jazz Funeral, a New Orleans Cultural Tradition Steeped in African Roots," 43. The article was reproduced online (see "The Jazz Funeral").

76 "Social Traditions and Cemeteries."

77 Quoted in "Second Linin'," in *The Soul of New Orleans,* 27. The article also appeared online (see "Second Linin'," New Orleans Online; "Second Linin'," SoulofNewOrleans.com).

78 "Naturally New Orleans"; "Food."

79 "Historical Context, Cities."

80 Bergeron, "Louisiana's Free Men of Color in Gray"; Hollandsworth, *The Louisiana Native Guards.*

81 "About NOMTN."

82 "History."

83 "Food."

84 "Historical Context, Cities."

85 "Historical Context, Cities."

86 The riot began when Robert Charles, a black emigrant from Mississippi, clashed with New Orleans police in a shoot-out and culminated days later with Charles's slaying and indiscriminate white mob violence instigated and condoned by the white press. According to William Hair, Robert Charles's biographer, these events highlighted "the hardening of racial attitudes" throughout the Jim Crow South in the wake of the *Plessy v. Ferguson* decision and state-sanctioned racial violence, while Charles's armed self-defense served "as a harbinger of the rising black assertiveness in future years" (*Carnival of Fury,* xxvi). See also Wells-Barnett, *Mob Rule in New Orleans: Robert Charles and His Fight to Death, the Story of His Life, Burning Human Beings Alive, Other Lynching Statistics.*

87 "Historical Context, Cities."

88 "Historical Context, Cities."

89 Hirsch, "Fade to Black," 755–56; "Historical Context, Cities." For a contrasting portrayal of New Orleans desegregation, see Crouere, "History of New Orleans: Post WWII to Present."

90 "Historical Context, Cities."

91 Although there were efforts by African Americans to create tours before the 1980s, these early attempts were largely not recognized or supported by the mainstream tourism industry. One example is a 1975 black history tour developed by a Dillard University professor and her history class. The tour was the brainchild of Clifton Johnson, who was then director of the Amistad Research Center. See Rose Kahn, "Black Historical Tour: Goal of Dillard's History Class,"

1975, "African-American Tourism," Amistad Research Center, Tulane University, New Orleans, Louisiana.

92 Quoted in Osbey, "Tourism in New Orleans."

93 Osbey, "Tourism in New Orleans"; "Roots of New Orleans."

94 Pecot-Hebert, "Le'Ob's Tours"; Wade, "Black Heritage City Tour."

95 Wade, "Black Heritage City Tour."

96 Advertisement for Le'Ob's Tours, MardiGrasDigest.com.

97 Handler and Gable, *The New History in an Old Museum*, 78–101.

98 "Heritage Tours: Africans in Louisiana Tours."

99 Home page, Africansinlouisiana.com.

100 "Slave Tour Itinerary."

101 "Slave Tour Itinerary."

102 "City Tour," LoewsExpress.com. In contrast, LeObsTours.com's city tour includes the same description but adds "Africans" to its list of contributing groups ("Welcome to New Orleans—the Past and Present").

103 "Black Heritage Tour."

104 As the sociologists Jennifer Eichstedt and Stephen Small demonstrate in their study of southern plantation museums, separate tours produce a "segregation and marginalization of knowledge" that often subordinates representations of African American history by "limit[ing] the exposure the public has to this knowledge and reinforc[ing] the importance and normalcy of learning only a white-centric history" (*Representations of Slavery*, 10, 170). For a comparable analysis of segregated tourism in twenty-first-century Charleston, see Kytle and Roberts, "'Is It Okay to Talk about Slaves?'"

105 "Black Heritage City Tour."

106 "'Soul of New Orleans': African American Heritage Map," n.p.

107 Jay (pseud.) interview; "New Orleans Area—Women to Watch in 1992"; Osborn interview; Pecot-Hebert, "Le'Ob's Tours."

108 G. Hall, *Databases for the Study of Afro-Louisiana History and Genealogy*; Osborn interview.

109 I took this tour with Osborn on March 23, 2002.

110 Jay (pseud.) interview.

111 Osborn interview; Pecot-Hebert, "UNO Metropolitan College Leads Effort to Diversify Tourism Industry"; Reidus interview.

112 Quoted in Pecot-Hebert, "Le'Ob's Tours."

113 Jay (pseud.) interview. Leander Perez (1891–1969) was a prominent Louisiana politician who led the White Citizens' Council's fight against desegregation in New Orleans. See Souther, *New Orleans on Parade*, 80–81.

114 Osborn interview.

115 Jay (pseud.) interview.

116 Jay (pseud.) interview.

117 Some mainstream tour companies offered black heritage tours, such as Hotard/Gray Line's "The Creole Connection," described as "a well seasoned blend

of African American and Creole cultural contributions to this great city we call 'the Big Easy'" ("Hotard Gray Line Tours," 57). See also Crabtree, "New Group Is Seen as a Vehicle to Boost Black Tourism Business"; McClain, "Black History Tour Proves Tough Sell."

118 Quoted in Llorens, "New Orleans' Finest." See also Coleman, "Black-Owned Businesses in the French Quarter"; Osborn interview; Owens, "Black Tourism Gained Respect via Essence"; "What Makes New Orleans Special?," 1990, "Greater New Orleans Tourist and Convention Commission, 1989–90" vertical file, Louisiana and Special Collections.

119 Weems, "African American Consumers since World War II"; Walker, "Black Dollar Power: Assessing African American Consumerism since 1945."

120 Grant, "Race, Place, and Memory," 406.

Five. "Starting All Over Again"

1 I analyzed the nascent post-Katrina tourism using participant-observation of six different post-Katrina bus or van tours and close readings of websites, tourist sites, and promotional materials following the storm. I took the following bus or van tours: Cajun Encounters Tours' "City Tour," Celebration Tours' "Katrina Recovery Tour," Dixie Tours' "Katrina Recovery Tour," Gray Line Tours' "Hurricane Katrina: 'America's Greatest Catastrophe,'" Louisiana Swamp Tours/ Louisiana Tour Company's "New Orleans City and Post-Katrina Tour," and Tours by Isabelle's "Post-Katrina City Tour." At the time of my field research in July and August 2007, Airboat Adventures' "Hurricane Katrina Tour" was not available due to mechanical problems, and the Old River Road Plantation Adventure's "Chronicles of Katrina" was not operating because business was slow during the month of August.

2 Blight, *Race and Reunion*, 19. Other studies arguing for the importance of collective memory in appropriating the past and shaping the future of the nation include Fabre and O'Meally, *History and Memory in African-American Culture*; Kammen, *Mystic Chords of Memory*; Yuhl, *A Golden Haze of Memory*.

3 Numerous news reports chronicling the slow progress of New Orleans recovery efforts and the multiple reasons for it appeared in the years following the storm. Examples include Associated Press, "Amnesty International Accuses Federal, State Governments of Katrina-Related Abuses"; Cass, "Notable Mardi Gras Absences Reflect Loss of Black Middle Class"; Davis, "Who Is Killing New Orleans?"; Eaton, "New Orleans Recovery Is Slowed by Closed Hospitals"; Flaherty, "The Second Looting of New Orleans"; Gidley, "Three Years after Katrina Swept through Town"; Nossiter, "After Fanfare, Hurricane Grants Leave Little Mark," "Largely Alone, Pioneers Reclaim New Orleans," and "With Regrets, New Orleans Is Left Behind"; Quigley, "The Right to Return to New Orleans."

4 *Celebrate Our History*; "New Orleans CVB Announces Aggressive Rebranding Campaign to Focus on Authentic and Dynamic Culture of New Orleans"; "New

Orleans CVB Encourages Locals to Be a Tourist in Your Own Hometown";
Stodghill, "Driving Back into Louisiana's History"; Webster, "New Orleans
Tourism Industry Still Plagued with Same Problems It Had in Late 2005";
Jaquetta White, "Ad Campaign Fights Katrina Myths," "If You Sell It, Will They
Come?," and "Multicultural Tourism Network Hit Hard by Storm." See also Go-
tham, *Authentic New Orleans*, 202; Gotham and Greenberg, "From 9/11 to 8/29."

5 Sturken, *Tourists of History*, 6.

6 Toussaint, Marsalis, Clarkson, and Lagasse, "Welcome to New Orleans," 3.

7 John White, "The Persistence of Race Politics and the Restraint of Recovery
in Katrina's Wake." The *Du Bois Review*'s special 2006 issue titled "Katrina: Un-
masking Race, Poverty, and Politics in the Twenty-First Century" included several articles addressing the class and racial divisions that the storm uncovered.

8 Handler and Gable, *The New History in an Old Museum*, 116.

9 Home page, New Orleans Convention and Visitors Bureau.

10 "New Orleans Ready for EXPO!"

11 Roach, *Cities of the Dead*, 3.

12 For a historical overview of the role of stereotypes in shaping U.S. popular
culture, see Dates and Barlow, *Split Image*; Verney, *African Americans and US
Popular Culture*.

13 "New Orleans Ready for EXPO!"

14 See, for instance, Hartnell, "Katrina Tourism and a Tale of Two Cities"; Pezzullo,
"'This Is the Only Tour That Sells.'"

15 Toni Morrison introduced the term *rememory* in her novel *Beloved* (1987). See
McKible, "'These Are the Facts of the Darky's History,'" 231.

16 For the range of media coverage surrounding Gray Line Tours, in particular, see
Auchmutey, "Katrina Tour Gives a Look at New Orleans Devastation"; Cald-
well, "New Orleans Company Plans a Tour of the Catastrophe"; Guidry, "New
Orleans Bus Tour Shows Ravages of Hurricane Katrina"; "Hurricane Katrina
Disaster Tours Still Popular"; McConnaughey, "Katrina Tours Get Mixed Re-
action"; Associated Press, "New Tour of Katrina-Devastated Area Is Sold Out";
Plaisance, "Demand High for Bus Tour of Katrina Devastation"; Vogel, "Hurri-
cane Katrina: This Bus for You?"; L. Weeks, "A Bus Tour of Hurricane Hell."

17 Tours by Isabelle claims to have begun tours in September 2005, whereas Gray
Line's tour began in January 2006. See McConnaughey, "Demand for Post-
Katrina Disaster Tours Remains High."

18 The exceptions are Gray Line Tours' "Hurricane Katrina: 'America's Greatest
Catastrophe'" and Tours by Isabelle's "Post-Katrina City Tour," which devote
their entire tours to post-Katrina metropolitan New Orleans.

19 The Army Corps of Engineers is replacing concrete I-wall levee supports that
failed during Hurricane Katrina with T-walls that are considered more stable
and more protective against soil erosion because of their inverted "T" shape.
MR-GO is the nickname of the Mississippi River Gulf Outlet, a channel constructed by the Corps of Engineers in 1965 to allow large ships to pass between
the Gulf of Mexico and New Orleans's Industrial Canal. Search-and-rescue

crews spraypainted a mark on each house they entered to indicate the date of the search, the name of the group searching the house, and the number of bodies or pets that were found inside. FEMA is the Federal Emergency Management Agency that supplied trailers to be used as temporary housing for residents whose homes were damaged or destroyed by Katrina.

20 Pezzullo, "'This Is the Only Tour That Sells,'" 105.

21 Tour guide, Tours by Isabelle, "Post-Katrina City Tour," during a tour on July 30, 2007.

22 Pezzullo, "'This Is the Only Tour That Sells,'" 105.

23 I made these presumptions about the tour guides based on their physical appearance and their comments about their neighborhoods, cultural heritage, and familial and social affiliations.

24 Tour guide, Tours by Isabelle, "Post-Katrina City Tour," during a tour on July 30, 2007.

25 For statistics on Lakeview, see "Lakeview Neighborhood Snapshot"; "Lakeview Neighborhood: People and Household Characteristics." For Metairie demographics, see "Metairie CDP, Louisiana."

26 Tour guide, Celebration Tours, "Katrina Recovery Tour," during a tour on August 1, 2007.

27 Tour guide, Tours by Isabelle, "Post-Katrina City Tour," during a tour on July 30, 2007. Honoré, a black Creole native of Louisiana, garnered national attention for his leadership coordinating military relief efforts in New Orleans as the commander of Joint Task Force Katrina.

28 Bondgraham, "Dollar Day for New Orleans"; Saulny, "5,000 Public Housing Units in New Orleans Are to Be Razed."

29 Tour guide, Tours by Isabelle, "Post-Katrina City Tour," during a tour on July 30, 2007. For a comparison, see "'The Deserving Poor' vs. Welfare Recipients."

30 Tour guide, Tours by Isabelle, "Post-Katrina City Tour," during a tour on July 30, 2007.

31 Tour guide, Celebration Tours, "Katrina Recovery Tour," during a tour on August 1, 2007.

32 Tour guide, Tours by Isabelle, "Post-Katrina City Tour," during a tour on July 30, 2007; tour guide, Dixie Tours, "Katrina Recovery Tour," during a tour on August 6, 2007.

33 Sturken, *Tourists of History*, 15.

34 Roach, *Cities of the Dead*, 20. The description by Roach of the 1991 encounter between the Zulu and Rex Mardi Gras parades is constructive here in proposing the possibility of an opposing black countermemory against performances of white supremacy.

35 For more on communities that were marginalized by Hurricane Katrina coverage, see Chiang, *A Village Called Versailles*; Kao, "Where Are the Asian and Hispanic Victims of Katrina?"; Ortega, "Othering the Other." Cajun Encounters Tours' "City Tour" and Gray Line Tour's "Hurricane Katrina: 'America's Greatest

Catastrophe'" remained on the periphery of the Ninth Ward and did not allow tourists to disembark into the neighborhoods. On the other hand, Dixie Tours's "Katrina Recovery Tour" permitted passengers to take photographs from the van, and Celebration Tours' "Katrina Recovery Tour" allowed passengers to leave the van to take photographs. On the online description of Louisiana Swamp Tours' "New Orleans City and Post-Katrina Tour," Milton Walker Jr., the company's owner, describes the Ninth Ward's role in his tour: "We kicked off a City/Katrina tour that included the good & bad. We tried to highlight the attractions, as they were restarted, and showed the 9th ward as the bad" ("New Orleans City and Post Katrina"). For discussions of the spectacularization of Hurricane Katrina, see Gotham, "Critical Theory and Katrina"; Kellner, "The Katrina Hurricane Spectacle and the Crisis of the Bush Presidency."

36 Gotham, "Critical Theory and Katrina."

37 Gotham, "Critical Theory and Katrina," 94.

38 Tour guide, Celebration Tours, "Katrina Recovery Tour," during a tour on August 1, 2007.

39 Tour guide, Celebration Tours, "Katrina Recovery Tour," during a tour on August 1, 2007.

40 Tour guide, Tours by Isabelle, "Post-Katrina City Tour," during a tour on July 30, 2007. The two guides were both evidently referring to housing stock built at different times during the development of the Lower Ninth Ward. The Greater New Orleans Community Data Center estimates that 59 percent of housing units in the Lower Ninth Ward were owner occupied, based on the 2000 census. This percentage was higher than the average rate of homeownership in the city of New Orleans.

41 Tour guide, Tours by Isabelle, "Post-Katrina City Tour," during a tour on July 30, 2007.

42 Tour guide, Celebration Tours, "Katrina Recovery Tour," during a tour on August 1, 2007.

43 Tour guide, Celebration Tours, "Katrina Recovery Tour," during a tour on August 1, 2007.

44 David, "Cultural Trauma, Memory, and Gendered Collective Action," 146.

45 David, "Cultural Trauma, Memory, and Gendered Collective Action," 155.

46 Tour guide, Celebration Tours, "Katrina Recovery Tour," August 1, 2007.

47 Tour guide, Tours by Isabelle, "Post-Katrina City Tour," during a tour on July 30, 2007.

48 David, "Cultural Trauma, Memory, and Gendered Collective Action," 155.

49 Barry, *Rising Tide*.

50 Tour guide, Tours by Isabelle, "Post-Katrina City Tour," during a tour on July 30, 2007.

51 Tour guide, Celebration Tours, "Katrina Recovery Tour," during a tour on August 1, 2007; tour guide, Tours by Isabelle, "Post-Katrina City Tour," during a tour on July 30, 2007.

52 Tour guide, Tours by Isabelle, "Post-Katrina City Tour," during a tour on July 30, 2007.

53 Tour guide, Dixie Tours, "Katrina Recovery Tour," during a tour on August 6, 2007.

54 Tour guide, Tours by Isabelle, "Post-Katrina City Tour," during a tour on July 30, 2007.

55 Tour guide, Tours by Isabelle, "Post-Katrina City Tour," during a tour on July 30, 2007.

56 Tour guide, Tours by Isabelle, "Post-Katrina City Tour," during a tour on July 30, 2007.

57 Howell and Vinturella, "Forgotten in New Orleans."

58 Lieberman, "'The Storm Didn't Discriminate,'" 8; See also Gotham, *Authentic New Orleans*, 207; J. Hall, "The Long Civil Rights Movement and the Political Uses of the Past"; Hutchison, "The Political Economy of Colorblindness."

59 Tour guide, Celebration Tours, "Katrina Recovery Tour," during a tour on August 1, 2007.

60 Woods, "Les Misérables of New Orleans," 773.

61 Dewan, "Resources Scarce, Homelessness Persists in New Orleans"; Gidley, "Three Years after Katrina Swept through Town"; Heath, "Katrina's Wrath Lingers for New Orleans' Poor"; Passavant, "Mega-Events, the Superdome, and the Return of the Repressed in New Orleans," 102–3; Reckdahl, "City May Move Homeless from Underpass to Shelter," "Homeless Camp Springs Up on Claiborne Avenue," "On the Streets," and "Staying at the Plaza."

62 For a list of a sample of such organizations, see "Some Grassroots Racial Justice Organizations." For an analysis of grassroots social movement organizations, see Luft, "Beyond Disaster Exceptionalism."

63 Tour guide, Dixie Tours, "Katrina Recovery Tour," during a tour on August 6, 2007.

64 Quoted in Sasser, "Our Town: Bush Visits Local Diner, Promises Help Is Coming." See also "President George W. Bush and Laura Bush Stop in at Stewart's Diner in the Ninth Ward of New Orleans."

65 Tour guide, Tours by Isabelle, "Post-Katrina City Tour," during a tour on July 30, 2007.

66 Tour guide, Celebration Tours, "Katrina Recovery Tour," during a tour on August 1, 2007.

67 Campanella, *Time and Place in New Orleans*, 103. See also Elie, "Planners Push to Tear out Elevated I-10 over Claiborne."

68 Baumbach and Borah, *The Second Battle of New Orleans*; Souther, *New Orleans on Parade*, 38–72.

69 Sakakeeny, "'Under the Bridge,'" 5–6.

70 Campanella, *Time and Place in New Orleans*, 103. In his study of New Orleans soundscapes, Matt Sakakeeny describes the space "under the bridge" as a "soundmark" for black New Orleanians who have reappropriated urban public spaces to sustain and reinvigorate a living music culture ("'Under the Bridge,'" 2–3).

71 Regis, "Blackness and the Politics of Memory in the New Orleans Second Line," 765.

72 Tour guide, Tours by Isabelle, "Post-Katrina City Tour," during a tour on July 30, 2007.

73 Tour guide, Gray Line Tours, "Hurricane Katrina: 'America's Greatest Catastrophe,'" during a tour on July 25, 2007.

74 Briggs, *Reproducing Empire*, 205.

75 Tour guide, Cajun Encounters Tours, "City Tour," during a tour on July 26, 2007. In contrast, the tour guide for Dixie Tours' "Katrina Recovery Tour" on August 6, 2007, polled passengers to see if they would prefer to see more Katrina-ravaged neighborhoods in St. Bernard Parish or to resume the traditional route to St. Charles Ave. The passengers voted to follow the traditional route. Only Gray Line's "Hurricane Katrina: 'America's Greatest Catastrophe'" and Tours by Isabelle's "Post-Katrina City Tour" did not travel to the Garden District and remained in the areas most affected by the storm.

76 "City Tour," Cajunencounters.com. By adopting the anachronistic term "the American Sector," introduced following the 1803 Louisiana Purchase to distinguish between French Creole and American New Orleans, the tour website symbolically "othered" black New Orleanians devastated by the storm, reinscribing them as un-American.

77 Tour guide, Celebration Tours, "Katrina Recovery Tour," during a tour on August 1, 2007.

78 Louisiana Swamp Tours, "New Orleans City and Post-Katrina Tour," during a tour on August 2, 2007; Dixie Tours, "Katrina Recovery Tour," during a tour on August 6, 2007.

79 Tour guide, Cajun Encounters Tours, "City Tour," during a tour on July 26, 2007; tour guide, Celebration Tours, "Katrina Recovery Tour," during a tour on August 1, 2007.

80 Tour guide, Tours by Isabelle, "Post-Katrina City Tour," during a tour on July 30, 2007.

81 Sturken, *Tourists of History*, 26.

82 Souther, "The Disneyfication of New Orleans," 811.

83 Gotham and Greenberg, "From 9/11 to 8/29," 1055; see also 1052.

84 Souther, "The Disneyfication of New Orleans"; Souther, *New Orleans on Parade*, 159–84.

85 As part of a week-long commemoration of the fifth anniversary of Hurricane Katrina, the New Orleans Redevelopment Authority offered a free tour called "New Orleans Journey: From Ruin to Renaissance" to highlight the city's progress since the storm. The fully booked twice-daily tour strategically bypassed sites that showed little sign of improvement since the storm. See Thompson, "Hurricane Katrina Recovery Highlighted in Bus Tour"; Ehrhardt, "New Orleans Journey Full to Capacity Re: Recovery Bus Tour."

86 "Tours by Isabelle," 2007.

87 "Tours by Isabelle," 2007.

88 "Tours by Isabelle," 2007.

89 "Tours by Isabelle," 2008.

90 Destination marketing organizations, such as convention and visitors' bureaus, are highly competitive agencies that attempt to attract visitors and grow their limited budgets through direct marketing campaigns, customized visitor surveys, and other strategic programs. See K. Williams, "A Comparison of Travel Behaviors of African American and White Travelers to an Urban Destination."

91 Rice interview. Rice has been president of the NOMTN since 2003, having been employed in a variety of capacities with the organization since 1996, when she began as a receptionist.

92 Rice interview.

93 Rice interview.

94 Rice interview.

95 Rice interview.

96 New Orleans Multicultural Tourism Network, 2004 Annual Report, 18. See also Gloria Herbert, "Family Reunions: Destinations That Specialize in Family Reunions," in Black Meetings and Tourism magazine (April 1996): 26+, "African-American Tourism," Amistad Research Center, Tulane University, New Orleans, Louisiana.

97 Rice interview.

98 See K. Williams, "A Comparison of Travel Behaviors of African American and White Travelers to an Urban Destination," 4–5.

99 Rice interview.

100 Aguiar, "Nuevo New Orleans: Latino Immigrants Remake the Crescent City"; Atlan, "After Katrina, Where Have All the Hondurans Gone?"; Rice interview; Walton, "Sabor Latino: Central American Folk Traditions in New Orleans."

101 Rice interview.

Epilogue

1 For examples, see Spirou, Urban Tourism and Urban Change; Sugrue, The Origins of the Urban Crisis.

2 Krupa, "Hurricane Katrina Recovery Assessed Five Years Out"; Liu and Plyer, New Orleans Index at Five; Quigley, Finger, and Hill, "Five Years Later."

3 "Hope, Healing for New Orleans after Super Bowl."

4 Quigley, Finger, and Hill, "Five Years Later."

5 For more on the different types of post-Katrina tourism, see Hartnell, "Katrina Tourism and a Tale of Two Cities"; Pezzullo, "'This Is the Only Tour That Sells'" and "Tourists and/as Disasters"; Thomas, "'Roots Run Deep Here'" and "'People Want to See What Happened.'"

6 The racial romanticism surrounding Mitch Landrieu's legacy highlighted his commendable record on civil rights but conveniently erased the limitations of his administration's willingness and ability to challenge the city's racial status

quo. See Hirsch, "Simply a Matter of Black and White," 295–304, and "Fade to Black," 753.

7 Quoted in Krupa and Donze, "Mitch Landrieu Claims New Orleans Mayor's Office in a Landslide." Although many people interpreted Landrieu's victory as a postracial triumph, it bears noting that low voter turnout, especially among African Americans; the absence of a veteran, well-known black candidate in the race; and the distraction of Carnival and the Saints' road to the Super Bowl also contributed to Landrieu's victory. See McGill, "Saints, Parades Overshadow New Orleans Mayor Race"; Vogt, "A Time against Race."

8 Drawing comparisons between the class- and region-based partisan attacks on President Bill Clinton during the Monica Lewinsky sex scandal and indiscriminate attacks on black men, Toni Morrison referred to President Clinton as "the first black president," which was later misinterpreted as a positive recognition of Clinton's racial politics. See Morrison, "The Talk of the Town: Comment" and "10 Questions for Toni Morrison."

9 Quoted in Carr, "Mayor-Elect Mitch Landrieu Addresses His Supporters at Victory Party." See also "New Orleans Mayor Mitch Landrieu's Hurricane Katrina Anniversary Remarks"; "Read the Text of Mayor Mitch Landrieu's Inauguration Speech."

10 Quoted in Carr, "Mayor-Elect Mitch Landrieu Addresses His Supporters at Victory Party."

11 "Read the Text of Mayor Mitch Landrieu's Inauguration Speech."

12 "Executive Branch." Landrieu served as lieutenant governor from 2004 to 2010. In 2005 he spearheaded "Louisiana Rebirth: Restoring the Soul of America," a public relations campaign to make tourism the centerpiece of post-Katrina recovery efforts. See C. Nelson, "Katrina's Lesson: Recreation Leading Re-Creation."

13 "Read the Text of Mayor Mitch Landrieu's Inauguration Speech."

14 Census data reflected a loss of 29 percent of New Orleans's total population, with an increase in the proportion of white residents and a decrease in the proportion of black residents. Compared to 2000, in 2010 the black share of the city's population had decreased from 67 percent to 60 percent, while the white share had increased from 28 to 33 percent. See Mildenberg, "Census Finds Hurricane Katrina Left New Orleans Richer, Whiter, Emptier." The political scientist Michael Dawson similarly characterizes post-Katrina New Orleans as "smaller, richer, whiter" (Not in Our Lifetimes, 24, 39, 40). See also Associated Press, "Black Segregation in U.S. Drops to Lowest in Century" and "Census Shows New Orleans Losing Many Blacks"; Blake, "The Decline of the Majority-Black District, and What It Means"; Burdeau, "New Orleans' Post-Katrina Gentrification Is Touchy"; J. Clarke, "New Orleans Black Diaspora: Will the Residents Come Back?"; K. Clarke, "Katrina Leaves New Orleans Political Landscape Looking Whiter"; Eggler, "New Orleans City Council a Mix of New, Familiar Faces"; Krupa, "Minority Populations Still Growing in New Orleans Area"; Liu and Plyer, New Orleans Index at Five; Pope, "Evoking King, Nagin Calls N.O.

'Chocolate' City"; Robertson, "Smaller New Orleans after Katrina, Census Shows"; Vogt, "A Time against Race."

15 "New Orleans Mayor Mitch Landrieu's Hurricane Katrina Anniversary Remarks."

16 Knoettgen, "We Are the 'Who Dat' Nation," 113–41; Marshall, "New Orleans Saints Have a Special Bond with Their Fans"; Moller, "Gov. Bobby Jindal Proclaims 'Who Dat Nation Week' in Louisiana"; McGill, "Saints, Parades Overshadow New Orleans Mayor Race"; "Mitch's Mandate"; Vogt, "A Time against Race"; Barrow, "Who Dat Nation Erupts with Joy as New Orleans Saints Win NFC Championship"; Cannon, "Drew Brees, Mitch Landrieu, and the Pre-Lenten Gift NOLA Gave Itself"; Hammer, "New Orleans Saints Fans Build Color-Blind Bonds in Who Dat Nation."

17 Oriard, Brand NFL, 211.

18 Bartley, The Rise of Massive Resistance, 134–35; Clement, "Civil Rights and Municipal Corporations"; Lomax, "The African American Experience in Professional Football," 170–72; Oriard, Brand NFL, 20–21, 212–13; Souther, New Orleans on Parade, 73–101.

19 Passavant, "Mega-Events, the Superdome, and the Return of the Repressed in New Orleans," 103–6; Souther, New Orleans on Parade, 163.

20 Passavant, "Mega-Events, the Superdome, and the Return of the Repressed in New Orleans," 98. See also Gotham and Greenberg, "From 9/11 to 8/29," 1050–56; Souther, New Orleans on Parade, 226, 228–29.

21 Hogan, "New Orleans Saints' Monday Night Football Game against Atlanta in the Dome Return Was Memorable for Broadcasters"; Konigsmark, "Superdome Reopens to First Post-Katrina NFL Game"; "The Louisiana Superdome—an Icon Transformed"; Passavant, "Mega-Events, the Superdome, and the Return of the Repressed in New Orleans," 113–17; Restrepo, "Five Years Later"; Varney, "Superdome Reopening Is Something New Orleans Saints Still Marvel at Performance vs. Atlanta Falcons." Although I am critical of the way that the narratives of renewal surrounding the Superdome and the Saints undermined actual renewal of many nontourist areas, I recognize the powerful role that these narratives played in the lives of New Orleanians. For an excellent analysis of the way that Saints fandom brought New Orleanians together, see Knoettgen, "We Are the 'Who Dat' Nation," especially chapters 5 and 6.

22 Izenberg, "New Orleans Saints Brought Salvation to Their City"; Sando, "Dungy's Prediction No Match for Destiny"; Knoettgen, "We Are the 'Who Dat' Nation," 131–41.

23 Hutchison, "The Political Economy of Colorblindness," 6–7. See also Gotham, Authentic New Orleans, 207–8; J. Hall, "The Long Civil Rights Movement and the Political Uses of the Past"; Ishiwata, "'We Are Seeing People We Didn't Know Exist'"; Omi and Winant, Racial Formation in the United States, 145–59; Perlman, "Rush Limbaugh and the Problem of the Color Line"; Wise, Colorblind.

24 Cannon, "Drew Brees, Mitch Landrieu, and the Pre-Lenten Gift NOLA Gave

Itself"; Jaquetta White, "New Orleans Tourism Officials Expect One of the Strongest Springs Ever."

25 "New Orleans Mayor Mitch Landrieu's Hurricane Katrina Anniversary Remarks."

26 Recent scholarship on neoliberalism and race has usefully identified this binary as a product of the neoliberal state. Passavant refers to the binary as the "consumer-criminal double" whereby "those who are not valuable as consumers are . . . either forgotten or repressed" ("Mega-Events, the Superdome, and the Return of the Repressed in New Orleans," 118). See also, Hutchison, "The Political Economy of Colorblindness," 6.

27 "David Simon's Treme Captures New Orleans"; Robertson, "New Orleanians Gather to Watch as the City Takes the Spotlight on HBO"; Dave Walker, "HBO's 'Treme' Finally Gets New Orleans Right."

28 For a brief discussion of how New Orleans's musical practices have historically been localized and racialized, see Sakakeeny, "'Under the Bridge,'" 4–5.

29 Quoted in Dave Walker, "HBO Sets Drama Series in Treme." (Walker's addition.)

30 Treme has generated a new genre of tourism, based on the musicians, locales, and sites featured on the show. See de Turk, "Bullet's Sports Bar"; Fensterstock, "Find Local Bars as Seen on HBO's 'Treme'"; Tan, "In Treme, Where Jazz Was Born, You Feel the Heartbeat of New Orleans."

31 M. E. Crutcher, Treme; Devlin, "Mayor Ray Nagin's Armstrong Park Statue Plan Draws Criticism"; Eggler, "Armstrong Park Sculpture Plans Criticized at Treme Meeting"; Elie, "Armstrong Park Planning Exclusionary, Treme Residents Complain"; Hammer, "New Orleans Mayor Ray Nagin's Grand Sculpture Plan Has Workers Scurrying in Armstrong Park"; Landrieu, "State of the City Address"; Reckdahl, "Armstrong Park Sculpture Garden Already Crumbling," "Spruced-Up Armstrong Park Reopens Friday with New Sculptures," and "Mayor Mitch Landrieu."

32 Landrieu, "State of the City Address."

33 M. E. Crutcher, Treme, 66–81.

34 Juhasz, "Investigation."

35 Quoted in Mouawad and Krauss, "Another Torrent BP Works to Stem."

36 Allen, "BP Spent $94M on Ads during Spill"; Anderson, "Ad Campaign Reassures Tourists That Louisiana 'Is Still a Great Place to Visit'"; "Gulf Oil Spill."

37 Juhasz, "Investigation"; Land, "BP Pushes Black Faces to Forefront of Mea Culpa Ad Campaign"; "My Name Is 6508799."

38 Cart, "Louisiana's Love-Hate Relationship with the Oil Industry"; Anderson, "Ad Campaign Reassures Tourists That Louisiana 'Is Still a Great Place to Visit'"; Moller, "First Installment of BP Money for Louisiana Tourism to Be Divided among All 64 Parishes"; Finn, "Two Years after BP Oil Spill, Tourists Back in U.S. Gulf."

39 Coviello, "New Orleans Tourism to Launch $5 Million Advertising Campaign."

40 Albright, "Though Many Tourism-Related Firms Are Barely Affected by Gulf Oil Spill, Fishing and Swamp Tours Are Taking a Hit"; Anderson, "Louisi-

ana Tourism Trending upward Despite Setbacks"; Finn, "Two Years after BP Oil Spill, Tourists Back in U.S. Gulf"; Hammer, "Gulf Oil Spill Creates Economic Boom for Some, Bust for Others"; Krupa, "New Orleans Tourism Breaks Record in 2011"; "N.O. Tourism Reaches a Milestone"; "New Orleans Achieves Major Tourism Milestone: 8.3 Million Visitors in 2010"; Rudawsky, "Five Years after Hurricane Katrina, New Orleans Tourism Rebounds"; Jaquetta White, "New Orleans Tourism Officials Expect One of the Strongest Springs Ever."

41 Luft, "Beyond Disaster Exceptionalism."

42 Obama, "Remarks by the President on the Fifth Anniversary of Hurricane Katrina in New Orleans, Louisiana."

43 C. Johnson, "Preface: 'Obama's Katrina,'" viii. See also Lipsitz, "Learning from New Orleans."

44 Obama, "Remarks by the President on the Fifth Anniversary of Hurricane Katrina in New Orleans, Louisiana."

45 C. Johnson, "Preface: 'Obama's Katrina,'" xi. Obama's praise for the Housing Authority of New Orleans's privatization of public housing; construction of a new, suburban-style medical complex to replace Charity Hospital; the city's controversial charter school experiment; and reform of the criminal justice system obscured critiques of these initiatives as racially and economically biased, exclusionary, and undemocratic. For examples, see Arena, "Black and White, Unite and Fight?"; "Public Housing Coming Down in New Orleans"; Eaton, "In New Orleans, Plan to Raze Low-Income Housing Draws Protest"; Gratz, "Why Was New Orleans's Charity Hospital Allowed to Die?"; Ott, "The Closure of New Orleans' Charity Hospital after Hurricane Katrina"; Dixson, "Whose Choice?"; Hill, "New Orleans"; Mock, "The Problem with New Orleans's Charter Schools"; Flaherty, "Seven Years after Katrina, A Divided City."

46 Gotham, *Authentic New Orleans*, 14.

47 Gotham, *Authentic New Orleans*, 137.

48 Obama, "Remarks by the President on the Fifth Anniversary of Hurricane Katrina in New Orleans, Louisiana." Huus, "Panel Challenges Gulf Seafood Safety All-Clear"; Muller, "Officials Try to Allay Fears of Oil-Spoiled Seafood."

49 Obama's message echoes the sentiments that Mayor Landrieu expressed in his acceptance and inauguration speeches when he told constituents that "we are thankful to the rest of America for everything that they have done for us. But what they have told us that the best way to continue to help us is for us to help ourselves" (quoted in Carr, "Mayor-Elect Mitch Landrieu Addresses His Supporters at Victory Party") and "we have asked for help. We will accept it if it comes. But we must also know that our survival begins and ends with us. We know that we are first and last personally responsible for ourselves, our homes, our families. If we want others to help us we must help ourselves first" ("Read the Text of Mayor Mitch Landrieu's Inauguration Speech").

50 C. Johnson, "Introduction: The Neoliberal Deluge," xxxii. See also, Flaherty, "Seven Years after Katrina, A Divided City"; C. Hall, *Pro-Poor Tourism*; C. Johnson, "Introduction: The Neoliberal Deluge," xxxi–xxxiii; Vrasti, *Volunteer*

Tourism in the Global South. Similarly, Catherine Michna has identified a post-Katrina missionary narrative embodied by a new class of young professionals arriving in New Orleans to "remake its troublesome culture" ("Theatre, Spiritual Healing, and Democracy in the City," 60).

51 Marita Sturken argues in *Tourists of History* that since the late twentieth century, U.S. culture has encouraged a tourist relationship to history that masks the country's complicity in global conflict, imperialism, and violence.

52 Flaherty, "Seven Years after Katrina, a Divided City"; Flanders, "After Sandy, Learning from New Orleans"; Luft, "Beyond Disaster Exceptionalism."

Bibliography

Manuscript Collections

African-American Tourism, Amistad Research Center at Tulane University, New
    Orleans, Louisiana.
Louisiana and Special Collections Department, Earl K. Long Library, University
    of New Orleans, Louisiana.
Midlo Center for New Orleans Studies, University of New Orleans, Louisiana.
Private files, New Orleans Multicultural Tourism Network, New Orleans, Louisiana.

Selected New Orleans Tours

Cajun Encounters Tours. "City Tour."
Celebration Tours. "Katrina Recovery Tour."
Dixie Tours. "Katrina Recovery Tour."
Eclectic Tours. "Freedom's Journey: An African American Perspective."
Gray Line Tours. "Hurricane Katrina: 'America's Greatest Catastrophe.'"
Le Monde Créole. "French Quarter Courtyards Tour."
Louisiana Swamp Tours/Louisiana Tour Company. "New Orleans City and Post-
    Katrina Tour."
Tennessee Williams Festival. "African American Legacy Heritage Tour."
Tours by Isabelle. "Post-Katrina City Tour."

Interviews in New Orleans by the Author

Coble, William. October 30, 2002.
Jay (pseud.). September 9, 2002.
Mire, Phala. May 2, 1997.
Nevksi, Paul. March 25, 2002.
Osborn, Gregory. February 22, 2002.
Reidus, Gwen. September 9, 2002.
Rice, Toni. August 10, 2009.
Robin (pseud.). October 30, 2002.

Primary and Secondary Sources

"About New Orleans." In *The Soul of New Orleans: The Official GNOBTN Visitor's
    Guide*, 5. New Orleans: Greater New Orleans Black Tourism Network, 1993.

"About NOMTN." SoulofNewOrleans.com. Accessed November 27, 2003. http://
www.soulofneworleans.com/about.htm.

Abram, Ruth J. "Kitchen Conversations: Democracy in Action at the Lower East Side
Tenement Museum." *Public Historian* 29, no. 1 (2007): 59–76.

Adams, Jessica. *Wounds of Returning: Race, Memory, and Property on the Postslavery
Plantation*. Chapel Hill: University of North Carolina Press, 2007.

Adorno, Theodor W. *The Culture Industry: Selected Essays on Mass Culture*. Edited by
J. M. Bernstein. 2nd ed. New York: Routledge, 2001.

Advertisement for Le'Ob's Tours, MardiGrasDigest.com, November 16, 2003. Accessed November 26, 2003. http://www.mardigrasdigest.com/travel/.

"African-American Travelers." In *The Minority Traveler*. 2000 edition, 13–25. Washington, DC: Travel Industry Association of America, 2000.

Aguiar, Rachel. "Nuevo New Orleans: Latino Immigrants Remake the Crescent City."
NowPublic, April 12, 2009. Accessed January 27, 2010. http://www.nowpublic
.com/world/nuevo-new-orleans-latino-immigrants-remake-crescent-city-0.

Albright, Matthew. "Though Many Tourism-Related Firms Are Barely Affected by
Gulf Oil Spill, Fishing and Swamp Tours Are Taking a Hit." *Times-Picayune*, June 13,
2010.

Alexander, Erin. "Tourism Execs Seek New Ways to Get Safety Message out to Visitors." *New Orleans CityBusiness*, April 19, 1993.

Alexander, George, and Monique R. Brown. "Collecting Our History." *Black Enterprise*, February 2000, 261.

Allen, Jonathan. "BP Spent $94M on Ads during Spill." *Politico*, September 1, 2010.
Accessed October 8, 2012. http://www.politico.com/news/stories/0910/41670
.html.

Anderson, Ed. "Ad Campaign Reassures Tourists That Louisiana 'Is Still a Great Place
to Visit.'" *Times-Picayune*, June 10, 2010.

Anderson, Ed. "Louisiana Tourism Trending Upward Despite Setbacks." *Times-
Picayune*, January 26, 2012.

Aptheker, Herbert. *American Negro Slave Revolts*. New York: International, 1963.

"Areas of the City in New Orleans." NewOrleans.com, 2003. Accessed April 2, 2003.
http://www.neworleans.com/?search=CAT&Category=AREAS&utm
_expid=43112794-0.

"Areas of the City: New Orleans East." NewOrleans.com, 2003. Accessed April 2, 2003.
http://www.neworleans.com/cgi-bin/oracle/hs.cgi?search=CAT&Category
=AREAS%3ANew%20Orleans%20East.

Arena, John. "Black and White, Unite and Fight? Identity Politics and New Orleans's
Post-Katrina Public Housing Movement." In *The Neoliberal Deluge: Hurricane Katrina, Late Capitalism, and the Remaking of New Orleans*, edited by Cedric Johnson,
152–83. Minneapolis: University of Minnesota Press, 2011.

Associated Press. "Amnesty International Accuses Federal, State Governments
of Katrina-Related Abuses." *Times-Picayune*, July 30, 2010.

Associated Press. "Black Segregation in U.S. Drops to Lowest in Century." *Washington
Times*, December 14, 2010.

Associated Press. "Census Shows New Orleans Losing Many Blacks." USA Today, February 4, 2011.

Associated Press. "New Tour of Katrina-Devastated Area Is Sold Out." USA Today, January 4, 2006.

Atlan, Daffodil. "After Katrina, Where Have All the Hondurans Gone?" IMDiversity. com, September 13, 2005. Accessed January 27, 2010. http://www.imdiversity.com /Villages/Hispanic/community_family/pns_katrina_hondurans_0905.asp.

Auchmutey, Jim. "Katrina Tour Gives a Look at New Orleans Devastation." Atlanta Journal-Constitution, February 26, 2007.

Austin, J. L. How to Do Things with Words. Edited by J. O. Urmson. Oxford: Oxford University Press, 1962.

Babb, Valerie M. Whiteness Visible: The Meaning of Whiteness in American Literature. New York: New York University Press, 1998.

Babington, Charles. "Some GOP Legislators Hit Jarring Notes in Addressing Katrina." Washington Post, September 10, 2005.

Baker, Liva. The Second Battle of New Orleans: The Hundred-Year Struggle to Integrate the Schools. New York: Harper Collins, 1996.

Baldwin, Troy. "Black Tourism Network: Impacting the Tourist Industry." New Orleans Tribune, November 1990.

Barber, Alicia. Reno's Big Gamble: Image and Reputation in the Biggest Little City. Lawrence: University Press of Kansas, 2008.

Barrett, Jennifer. "A Right to Rebuild." Newsweek, January 13, 2006. Accessed February 6, 2006. http://www.msnbc.msn.com/id/10841718/site/newsweek/.

Barrow, Bill. "Who Dat Nation Erupts with Joy as New Orleans Saints Win NFC Championship." NOLA.com, January 24, 2010. Accessed September 20, 2012. http://www.nola.com/saints/index.ssf/2010/01/who_dat_nation_erupts_with _joy.html.

Barry, John M. Rising Tide: The Great Mississippi Flood of 1927 and How It Changed America. New York: Simon and Schuster, 1997.

Barthelemy, Sidney. "Welcome to New Orleans." In The Soul of New Orleans: The Official GNOBTN Visitor's Guide, 2. New Orleans: Greater New Orleans Black Tourism Network, 1993.

Bartley, Numan V. The Rise of Massive Resistance: Race and Politics in the South during the 1950s. Baton Rouge: Louisiana State University Press, 1999.

Baumbach, Richard O., and William E. Borah. The Second Battle of New Orleans: A History of the Vieux Carre Riverfront Expressway Controversy. Tuscaloosa: University of Alabama Press, 1980.

Bell, Caryn Cosse. Revolution, Romanticism, and the Afro-Creole Protest Tradition in Louisiana, 1718–1868. Baton Rouge: Louisiana State University Press, 2004.

Bennett, Tony. The Birth of the Museum: History, Theory, Politics. New York: Routledge, 1995.

Bergeron, Arthur W., Jr. "Louisiana's Free Men of Color in Gray." In Louisianians in the Civil War, edited by Lawrence Lee Hewitt and Arthur W. Bergeron Jr., 100–119. Columbia: University of Missouri Press, 2002.

Berlin, Ira. *Many Thousands Gone: The First Two Centuries of Slavery in North America*. Cambridge, MA: Harvard University Press, 1998.

Berzon, Judith R. *Neither White nor Black: The Mulatto Character in American Fiction*. New York: New York University Press, 1979.

Bibb, Henry. *Narrative of the Life and Adventures of Henry Bibb: An American Slave*. New York: The author, 1849.

"Black Heritage City Tour." Williams Tours and Transportation. Accessed March 6, 2003. http://www.williamstoursandtransportation.com/blacktours.html.

"Black Heritage Tour." LoewsExpress.com. Accessed March 6, 2003. http://www.loewsexpress.com/tour.htm.

Blake, Aaron. "The Decline of the Majority-Black District, and What It Means." *Washington Post*, April 20, 2011. Accessed August 30, 2012. http://www.washingtonpost.com/blogs/the-fix/post/the-decline-of-the-majority-black-district-and-what-it-means/2011/04/19/AFTqqACE_blog.html.

Blassingame, John. *Black New Orleans*. Chicago: University of Chicago Press, 1973.

Blight, David W. *Race and Reunion: The Civil War in American Memory*. Cambridge, MA: Belknap Press of Harvard University Press, 2002.

Bogle, Donald. *Toms, Coons, Mulattoes, Mammies, and Bucks: An Interpretive History of Blacks in American Films*. 4th ed. New York: Bloomsbury Academic, 2001.

Bondgraham, Darwin. "Dollar Day for New Orleans." *ZMagazine*, February 2008. http://www.zcommunications.org/dollar-day-for-new-orleans-by-darwin-bondgraham.

Bonilla-Silva, Eduardo. *Racism without Racists: Color-Blind Racism and the Persistence of Racial Inequality in the United States*. Lanham, MD: Rowman and Littlefield, 2003.

Bouchon, Jolene. "Big Easy Dining: Feelings Café." Epicurious.com, 2003. Accessed October 7, 2003. http://www.epicurious.com/e_eating/e03_restaurants/neworleans/feelings.html.

Boyd, Michelle. "Reconstructing Bronzeville: Racial Nostalgia and Neighborhood Redevelopment." *Journal of Urban Affairs* 22, no. 2 (2000): 107–22.

Branley, Edward J. "New Orleans History." Yatcom.com, February 18, 1997. Accessed April 2, 2003. http://www.yatcom.com/neworl/history/hisstop.html.

Branley, Edward J. "On Being Creole." GumboPages.com, 1995. Accessed June 5, 2003. http://www.gumbopages.com/being-creole.html.

Brannon, Keith. "Tourism Drives Local Economy as White-Collar Jobs Slip Away, Report Says." *New Orleans CityBusiness*, November 8, 1999.

Bridges, Ruby. *Through My Eyes*. New York: Scholastic, 2000.

Briggs, Laura. *Reproducing Empire: Race, Sex, Science, and U.S. Imperialism in Puerto Rico*. Berkeley: University of California Press, 2002.

Brown, Sterling Allen. *Negro Poetry and Drama, and the Negro in American Fiction*. New York: Atheneum, 1969.

Brown, William Wells. *Narrative of William W. Brown, a Fugitive Slave*. Boston: Anti-Slavery Office, 1847.

Bryan, Violet Harrington. *The Myth of New Orleans in Literature: Dialogues of Race and Gender*. Knoxville: University of Tennessee Press, 1993.

Bumiller, Elisabeth. "Promises by Bush amid the Tears." *New York Times*, September 3, 2005.

Burdeau, Cain. "New Orleans' Post-Katrina Gentrification Is Touchy." Associated Press, August 28, 2012.

"Bush's Remarks in New Orleans." *New York Times*, September 2, 2005.

Caldwell, Dave. "New Orleans Company Plans a Tour of the Catastrophe." *New York Times*, December 25, 2005.

Campanella, Richard. *Bienville's Dilemma: A Historical Geography of New Orleans*. Lafayette: Center for Louisiana Studies, University of Louisiana at Lafayette, 2008.

Campanella, Richard. "An Ethnic Geography of New Orleans." *Journal of American History* 94, no. 3 (2007): 704–15.

Campanella, Richard. *Geographies of New Orleans: Urban Fabrics before the Storm*. Lafayette: Center for Louisiana Studies, University of Louisiana at Lafayette, 2006.

Campanella, Richard. *Greater Gentilly: An Introduction*. Neighborhood Market Area Report. New Orleans: Spark InSites, August 2010. Accessed December 2, 2010. http://sparkinsites.com/_downloads/_reports/Intro_GreaterGentilly _Campanella_Aug2010.pdf.

Campanella, Richard. *Time and Place in New Orleans: Past Geographies in the Present Day*. Gretna, LA: Pelican, 2002.

Campanella, Richard, and Marina Campanella. *New Orleans Then and Now*. Gretna, LA: Pelican, 1999.

Campbell-Rock, C. C. "Black Tourists Pump Millions into the New Orleans Economy . . . White Businesses Are Getting All the Bucks . . . What's Up?" *New Orleans Tribune*, July 1998.

Campbell-Rock, C. C. "Tourism: Boondoggle or Economic Stimulant." *New Orleans Tribune*, November 1987.

Cannon, Carl M. "Drew Brees, Mitch Landrieu, and the Pre-Lenten Gift NOLA Gave Itself." Politics Daily, February 11, 2010. Accessed September 11, 2012. http://www.politicsdaily.com/2010/02/11/drew-brees-mitch-landrieu-and-the -pre-lenten-gift-nola-gave-it/print/.

Cantor, George. *Historic Landmarks of Black America*. Detroit: Gale Research, 1991.

Carr, Martha. "Mayor-Elect Mitch Landrieu Addresses His Supporters at Victory Party." *Times-Picayune*, February 6, 2010.

Cart, Julie. "Louisiana's Love-Hate Relationship with the Oil Industry." *Los Angeles Times*, September 15, 2010.

Cashmore, Ellis. *The Black Culture Industry*. London: Routledge, 1997.

Cass, Julia. "Notable Mardi Gras Absences Reflect Loss of Black Middle Class." *Washington Post*, February 25, 2006.

Cassimere, Raphael. *African Americans in New Orleans before the Civil War*. New Orleans: University of New Orleans, College of Urban and Public Affairs, 1995.

Celebrate Our History, Invest in Our Future: Reinvigorating Tourism in New Orleans. New Orleans: New Orleans Strategic Hospitality Task Force, January 2010.

Certeau, Michel de. *The Practice of Everyday Life*. Translated by Steven Rendall. Berkeley: University of California Press, 2002.

Charles, Alfred. "Morial Touts N.O. as Fair City in Bid to Keep Conventions." *Times-Picayune*, February 7, 1996.

Chase, Henry. *In Their Footsteps: The American Visions Guide to African-American Heritage Sites*. New York: H. Holt, 1994.

Chiang, S. Leo. *A Village Called Versailles*. Arlington, VA: PBS, 2009. DVD.

Chong, Sylvia Shin Huey. "'Look, an Asian!': The Politics of Racial Interpellation in the Wake of the Virginia Tech Shootings." *Journal of Asian American Studies* 11, no. 1 (2008): 27–60.

"Chretien Point Plantation B and B." In *Official Louisiana Tour Guide*, 136. Baton Rouge: Louisiana Travel Promotion Association, 2003.

"City Tour." Cajunencounters.com. Accessed July 27, 2007. http://www.cajunenc ounters.com/citytour.html.

"City Tour." LoewsExpress.com. Accessed March 6, 2003. http://www.loewsexpress .com/tour.htm.

Clark, Emily, and Virginia Meacham Gould. "The Feminine Face of Afro-Catholicism in New Orleans, 1727–1852." *William and Mary Quarterly*, 3rd ser., 59, no. 2 (2002): 409–48.

Clarke, Jesse. "New Orleans Black Diaspora: Will the Residents Come Back?" *Race, Poverty, and the Environment* 15, no. 1 (2008): 22–25.

Clarke, Kristen. "Katrina Leaves New Orleans Political Landscape Looking Whiter." Grio, August 25, 2010. Accessed August 1, 2012. http://thegrio.com/2010/08/25 /hurricane-katrina-leaves-political-aftershocks-in-its-wake/.

Cleman, John. *George Washington Cable Revisited*. New York: Twayne, 1996.

Clement, Rutledge C., Jr. "Civil Rights and Municipal Corporations—The New Orleans Public Accommodations Ordinance: An Exercise of the Police Power under Home Rule." *Tulane Law Review*, 44 (1970): 805.

Cocks, Catherine. *Doing the Town: The Rise of Urban Tourism in the United States, 1850–1915*. Berkeley: University of California Press, 2001.

Coleman, Jan S. "Black-Owned Businesses in the French Quarter." *New Orleans Tribune*, July 1998.

Copeland, M. Shawn. *The Subversive Power of Love: The Vision of Henriette Delille*. Mahwah, NJ: Paulist, 2008.

Coviello, Will. "New Orleans Tourism to Launch $5 Million Advertising Campaign: 'This Isn't the First Time New Orleans Has Survived the British.'" *Gambit*, June 16, 2010.

Coviello, Will. "Style Points: French Quarter Architecture." *Visitor Magazine*, January 2003, 10–11.

Cox, Karen L. "Branding Dixie: The Selling of the American South, 1890–1930." In *Dixie Emporium: Tourism, Foodways, and Consumer Culture in the American South*, edited by Anthony J. Stanonis, 50–68. Athens: University of Georgia Press, 2008.

Crabtree, Penni. "New Group Is Seen as a Vehicle to Boost Black Tourism Business." *New Orleans CityBusiness*, January 14, 1991.

Crawford, Kate. "Maison de Ville, Vieux Carre, New Orleans, Louisiana." Ciao! Travel

with Attitude, September 2000. Accessed October 7, 2003. http://www.travelwith
attitude.com/MaisondeVille.htm.

"Creoles." Gateway New Orleans, 2000. Accessed June 5, 2003. http://www.gatewayno
.com/culture/Creoles.html.

Crèvecoeur, J. Hector St John de. *Letters from an American Farmer*. Edited by Susan
Manning. 1997. New York: Oxford University Press, 2009.

Crouere, Jeff. "History of New Orleans." NewOrleans.com, 2003. Accessed April 2,
2003. http://www.neworleans.com/cgi-bin/oracle/hs.cgi?search=CAT&Category
=HISTORY.

Crouere, Jeff. "History of New Orleans: Post WWII to Present." NewOrleans.com,
2003. Accessed April 2, 2003. http://www.neworleans.com/cgi-bin/oracle
/hs.cgi?search=CAT&Category=HISTORY_3.

Crutcher, Michael. "Historical Geographies of Race in a New Orleans Afro-Creole
Landscape." In *Landscape and Race in the United States*, edited by Richard H.
Schein, 23–38. New York: Routledge, 2006.

Crutcher, Michael E., Jr. *Treme: Race and Place in a New Orleans Neighborhood*. Athens: University of Georgia Press, 2010.

Dao, James. "Study Says 80% of New Orleans Blacks May Not Return." *New York
Times*, January 27, 2006.

Dates, Jannette L., and William Barlow, eds. *Split Image: African Americans in the Mass
Media*. Washington: Howard University Press, 1990.

David, Emmanuel. "Cultural Trauma, Memory, and Gendered Collective Action: The
Case of Women of the Storm Following Hurricane Katrina." *NWSA Journal* 20, no. 3
(2008): 138–62.

"David Simon's Treme Captures New Orleans." Bestofneworleans.com, April 5,
2010. Accessed August 4, 2011. http://www.bestofneworleans.com/gambit
/david-simons-treme-captures-new-orleans/Content?oid=1278312.

Davis, Mike. "Who Is Killing New Orleans?" Nation.com, March 23, 2006. Accessed
April 4, 2006. http://www.thenation.com/article/who-killing-new-orleans.

Dawdy, Shannon Lee. *Building the Devil's Empire: French Colonial New Orleans*. Chicago: University of Chicago Press, 2008.

Dawson, Michael C. *Not in Our Lifetimes: The Future of Black Politics*. Chicago: University of Chicago Press, 2011.

DeBerry, Jarvis. "For Black Road Homers, a Hollow Victory." *Times-Picayune*, August
20, 2010.

De Caro, Frank, and Rosan A. Jordan, eds. *Louisiana Sojourns: Travelers' Tales and
Literary Journeys*. Baton Rouge: Louisiana State University Press, 1998.

Delehanty, Randolph. "Waiting for the Resurrection: New Orleans in the Aftermath."
Museum News, June 2006, 54+.

Delgado, Richard. *Critical White Studies: Looking behind the Mirror*. Edited by Jean
Stefancic. Philadelphia: Temple University Press, 1997.

"'The Deserving Poor' vs. Welfare Recipients." PublicAgenda.org. Accessed
December 27, 2009. http://www.publicagenda.org/red-flags/deserving-poor
-vs-welfare-recipients.

De Turk, Bill. "Bullet's Sports Bar." NOLA.com, July 23, 2010. Accessed March 12, 2011. http://www.nola.com/bar-guide/index.ssf/2008/07/bullets_sports_bar.html.

Devlin, Paula. "Mayor Ray Nagin's Armstrong Park Statue Plan Draws Criticism." *Times-Picayune*, August 4, 2009.

Dewan, Shaila. "Resources Scarce, Homelessness Persists in New Orleans." *New York Times*, May 28, 2008.

"Dillard Neighborhood Snapshot." Greater New Orleans Community Data Center, October 5, 2002. http://www.gnocdc.org/orleans/6/27/snapshot.html.

Dixon, Melvin. "The Black Writer's Use of Memory." In *History and Memory in African-American Culture*, edited by Genevieve Fabre and Robert O'Meally, 18–27. New York: Oxford University Press, 1994.

Dixson, Adrienne. "Whose Choice? A Critical Race Perspective on Charter Schools." In *The Neoliberal Deluge: Hurricane Katrina, Late Capitalism, and the Remaking of New Orleans*, edited by Cedric Johnson, 130–51. Minneapolis: University of Minnesota Press, 2011.

Dominguez, Virginia. *White by Definition: Social Classification in Creole Louisiana*. New Brunswick, NJ: Rutgers University Press, 1986.

Dubin, Steven C. "Symbolic Slavery: Black Representations in Popular Culture." *Social Problems* 34, no. 2 (1987): 122–40.

Du Bois, W. E. B. *The Souls of Black Folk*. New York: Dover, 1994.

DuBos, Clancy. "Redistricting Free-For-All." *Gambit*, February 1, 2011.

Dyer, Richard. *White: Essays on Race and Culture*. New York: Routledge, 1997.

Easterlin, Linda. "Our Attitudes about Tourism Have Changed." *New Orleans City-Business*, February 12, 1990.

Eaton, Leslie. "In New Orleans, Plan to Raze Low-Income Housing Draws Protest." *New York Times*, December 14, 2007.

Eaton, Leslie. "New Orleans Recovery Is Slowed by Closed Hospitals." *New York Times*, July 24, 2007.

Edwards, Susan. "Upgrades in Store for Blighted Iberville Housing Development." WWLTV.com, May 21, 2009. Accessed June 29, 2009. http://www.wwltv.com /topstories/stories/wwl052109cbiberville.4145091.html.

Eggler, Bruce. "Armstrong Park Sculpture Plans Criticized at Treme Meeting." NOLA. com, last modified November 24, 2009. Accessed July 19, 2011. http://www.nola .com/politics/index.ssf/2009/09/armstrong_park_sculpture_plans.html.

Eggler, Bruce. "City Will Market Arts to Tourists." *Times-Picayune*, June 21, 1995.

Eggler, Bruce. "For New Orleans, It Was the Best of Times." *Times-Picayune*, December 20, 1992.

Eggler, Bruce. "New Orleans African American Museum to Undergo Renovations." *Times-Picayune*, January 10, 2011.

Eggler, Bruce. "New Orleans City Council a Mix of New, Familiar Faces." *Times-Picayune*, February 6, 2010.

Ehrhardt, Andrew. "New Orleans Journey Full to Capacity Re: Recovery Bus Tour." Email to author. August 26, 2010.

Eichstedt, Jennifer L., and Stephen Small. *Representations of Slavery: Race and Ideology* in *Southern Plantation Museums*. Washington: Smithsonian Institution Press, 2002.

Elie, Lolis Eric. "Armstrong Park Planning Exclusionary, Treme Residents Complain." NOLA.com, last modified October 14, 2009. Accessed July 19, 2011. http://www .nola.com/politics/index.ssf/2009/08/armstrong_park_planning_exclus.html.

Elie, Lolis Eric. "Planners Push to Tear out Elevated I-10 over Claiborne." NOLA .com, July 22, 2010. Accessed March 25, 2013. http://www.nola.com/news/index .ssf/2009/07/photos_for_iten.html.

Ellison, Ralph. *Going to the Territory*. New York: Random House, 1986.

Ellison, Ralph. *Shadow and Act*. New York: Random House, 1964.

Esolen, Gary. "Developing Tourism in New Orleans." *Gambit*, October 20, 1984.

"Evergreen Plantation—New Orleans Tours." In *New Orleans Official Visitors Guide*, 116. New Orleans: New Orleans Metropolitan Convention and Visitors Bureau, 2000.

"Executive Branch." Louisiana.gov. Accessed August 28, 2012. http://louisiana.gov /Government/Executive_Branch/.

"Explore the City of Mystery." In *New Orleans Official Visitors Guide*, 8+. New Orleans: New Orleans Metropolitan Convention and Visitors Bureau, 2002–3.

Fabre, Genevieve, and Robert O'Meally, eds. *History and Memory in African-American Culture*. New York: Oxford University Press, 1994.

"Facts and History: Pronunciation Guide." NewOrleans.com, 2003. Accessed April 2, 2003. http://www.neworleans.com/cgi-bin/oracle/hs.cgi?search=CAT&Category =FACTS%3Apronunciation%20Guide.

Fairclough, Adam. *Race and Democracy: The Civil Rights Struggle in Louisiana, 1915– 1972*. Athens: University of Georgia Press, 1995.

"Family Pages." New Orleans Metropolitan Convention and Visitors Bureau. Accessed March 1, 2003. http://www.neworleanscvb.com/new_site?visitor/visfaminfo.cfm.

"Famous Residents." SoulofAmerica.com. Accessed June 5, 2003. http://www.soulof america.com/cityfldr/orleans13.html.

Fanon, Frantz. "Algeria Unveiled." In *Studies in a Dying Colonialism*, 35–67. Translated by Haakon Chevalier. New York: Monthly Review Press, 1965.

"Faubourg Tremé." SoulofAmerica.com. Accessed June 5, 2003. http://www.soulof america.com/cityfldr/orleans17.html.

"Faubourg Tremé: America's Oldest Black Neighborhood." In *The Soul of New Orleans*, 72–73. New Orleans: Greater New Orleans Black Tourism Network, 1994–95.

Faust, Drew Gilpin. *The Ideology of Slavery: Proslavery Thought in the Antebellum South, 1830–1860*. Baton Rouge: Louisiana State University Press, 1981.

Fensterstock, Alison. "Find Local Bars as Seen on HBO's 'Treme.'" NOLA.com, July 21, 2010. Accessed July 27, 2011. http://www.nola.com/bar-guide/index.ssf/2010/07 /bars_as_seen_on_hbos_treme.html.

Ferris, Gerrie. "Around the South in Search of the Past: Black Tourism Industry Thrives in 90s Search for Black Heritage South." *Atlanta Journal Constitution*, June 30, 1996.

Finn, Kathy. "Two Years after BP Oil Spill, Tourists Back in U.S. Gulf." Reuters, May 27, 2012.

Flaherty, Jordan. "A New Day for New Orleans?" *Huffington Post*, February 9, 2010.

Accessed February 10, 2011. http://www.huffingtonpost.com/jordan-flaherty
/a-new-day-for-new-orleans_b_454604.html.

Flaherty, Jordan. "The Second Looting of New Orleans." AlterNet, January 17, 2007.
Accessed January 22, 2007. http://www.alternet.org/story/45953/the_second
_looting_of_new_orleans.

Flaherty, Jordan. "Seven Years after Katrina, a Divided City." Justice Roars, August 30,
2012. Accessed October 21, 2012. http://louisianajusticeinstitute.blogspot
.com/2012/08/seven-years-after-katrina-divided-city.html.

Flanders, Laura. "After Sandy, Learning from New Orleans: D6 and Beyond." *Nation*,
December 7, 2012. Accessed January 26, 2013. http://www.thenation.com
/blog/171649/after-sandy-learning-new-orleans-d6-and-beyond.

Foner, Laura. "The Free People of Color in Louisiana and St. Domingue: A Comparative Portrait of Two Three-Caste Slave Societies." *Journal of Social History* 3, no. 4
(1970): 406–30.

"Food." SoulofNewOrleans.com, March 17, 2003. Accessed June 5, 2003. http://
www.soulofneworleans.com/naturally%20New%20Orleans.htm#Food.

Fordham, Monroe. "Nineteenth-Century Black Thought in the United States: Some
Influences of the Santo Domingo Revolution." *Journal of Black Studies* 6, no. 2
(1975): 115–26.

"French Quarter Guide." DiscoverNewOrleans.com, 2003. Accessed April 2, 2003.
http://www.discoverneworleans.com/frenchquarter.html.

Fricker, Jonathan. "Uncommon Character." New Orleans Metropolitan Convention
and Visitors Bureau, June 2000. Accessed March 1, 2003. http://www.neworleans
cvb.com/new_site/visitor/visart_archit.cfm.

Fussell, Elizabeth, Narayan Sastry, and Mark Van Landingham. *Race, Socioeconomic
Status, and Return Migration to New Orleans after Hurricane Katrina*. Ann Arbor:
University of Michigan Population Studies Center, January 2009.

Gayarré, Charles. *History of Louisiana: The American Domination*. New York: William
J. Widdleton, 1866.

Genovese, Eugene D. *From Rebellion to Revolution: Afro-American Slave Revolts in the
Making of the Modern World*. Baton Rouge: Louisiana State University, 1979.

Germany, Kent B. *New Orleans after the Promises: Poverty, Citizenship, and the Search
for the Great Society*. Athens: University of Georgia Press, 2007.

Gidley, Ruth. "Three Years after Katrina Swept through Town." AlertNet, August 27,
2008. Accessed October 3, 2008. http://www.alertnet.org/db/blogs/1264/2008
/07/27-162945-1.htm.

Gill, James. *Lords of Misrule: Mardi Gras and the Politics of Race in New Orleans*. Jackson: University Press of Mississippi, 1997.

Gillman, Susan. "The Mulatto, Tragic or Triumphant? The Nineteenth-Century
American Race Melodrama." In *The Culture of Sentiment: Race, Gender, and Senti-
mentality in 19th-Century America*, edited by Shirley Samuels, 221–43. New York:
Oxford University Press, 1992.

Gilroy, Paul. *Against Race: Imagining Political Culture beyond the Color Line*. Cambridge, MA: Harvard University Press, 2000.

Giroux, Susan Searls. "Playing in the Dark: Racial Repression and the New Campus Crusade for Diversity." *College Literature* 33, no. 4 (2006): 93–112.

"Going after Arts-Minded Visitors." *Times-Picayune*, June 22, 1995.

Goings, Kenneth. *Mammy and Uncle Mose: Black Collectibles and American Stereotyping.* Bloomington: Indiana University Press, 1994.

Goldberg, David Theo. *The Racial State.* Malden, MA: Wiley-Blackwell, 2002.

Goldberg, David Theo. *The Threat of Race: Reflections on Racial Neoliberalism.* Malden, MA: Wiley-Blackwell, 2008.

Gore, Laura Locoul. *Memories of the Old Plantation Home: A Creole Family Album.* Edited by Norman Marmillion and Sand Marmillion. Vacherie, LA: Zoe Company, 2000.

Gotham, Kevin Fox. *Authentic New Orleans: Tourism, Culture, and Race in the Big Easy.* New York: New York University Press, 2007.

Gotham, Kevin Fox. "Critical Theory and Katrina: Disaster, Spectacle and Immanent Critique." *City* 11, no. 1 (2007): 81–99.

Gotham, Kevin Fox, and Miriam Greenberg. "From 9/11 to 8/29: Post-Disaster Recovery and Rebuilding in New York and New Orleans." *Social Forces* 87, no. 2 (2008): 1039–62.

Gould, Virginia Meacham. "'A Chaos of Iniquity and Discord': Slave and Free Women of Color in the Spanish Ports of New Orleans, Mobile, and Pensacola." In *The Devil's Lane: Sex and Race in the Early South*, edited by Catherine Clinton and Michele Gillespie, 232–46. New York: Oxford University Press, 1997.

Grant, Elizabeth. "Race, Place, and Memory: African American Tourism in the Postindustrial City." In *African American Urban History since World War II*, edited by Kenneth L. Kusmer and Joe W. Trotter, 404–23. Chicago: University of Chicago Press, 2009.

Gratz, Roberta Brandes. "Why Was New Orleans's Charity Hospital Allowed to Die?" *Nation*, April 27, 2011. Accessed January 11, 2013. http://www.thenation.com /article/160241/why-was-new-orleanss-charity-hospital-allowed-die.

Gray, Herman. *Cultural Moves: African Americans and the Politics of Representation.* Berkeley: University of California Press, 2005.

Greenberg, Paul A. "History: Origins of New Orleans." New Orleans Metropolitan Convention and Visitors Bureau, June 2000. Accessed March 1, 2003. http://www .neworleanscvb.com/new_site/visitor/vishistory_cont.cfm.

Greenberg, Paul A. "Lay of the Land." New Orleans Metropolitan Convention and Visitors Bureau, June 2000. http://www.neworleanscvb.com/new_site/visitor /visland.cfm.

Greenspan, Anders. *Creating Colonial Williamsburg: The Restoration of Virginia's Eighteenth-Century Capital.* 2nd ed. Chapel Hill: University of North Carolina Press, 2009.

Greenwood, Monique. "Collecting Black Memorabilia with Althea Burton." *Essence*, February 1997, 116.

"Greenwood Plantation B and B." In *Official Louisiana Tour Guide*, 185. Baton Rouge: Louisiana Travel Promotion Association, 2003.

Guidry, Nate. "New Orleans Bus Tour Shows Ravages of Hurricane Katrina." *Pittsburgh Post-Gazette*, February 20, 2006.

Guillory, Monique. "Some Enchanted Evening on the Auction Block: The Cultural Legacy of the New Orleans Quadroon Balls." PhD diss., New York University, 1999.

"Gulf Oil Spill: BP's Ad Spending Climbs." *Los Angeles Times*, September 1, 2010.

Hair, William Ivy. *Carnival of Fury: Robert Charles and the New Orleans Race Riot of 1900*. Baton Rouge: Louisiana State University Press, 2008.

Hale, Grace Elizabeth. *Making Whiteness: The Culture of Segregation in the South, 1890–1940*. New York: Vintage, 1999.

Hall, C. Michael, ed. *Pro-Poor Tourism: Who Benefits? Perspectives on Tourism and Poverty Reduction*. Clevedon, UK: Channel View, 2007.

Hall, Gwendolyn Midlo. *Africans in Colonial Louisiana: The Development of Afro-Creole Culture in the Eighteenth Century*. Baton Rouge: Louisiana State University Press, 1995.

Hall, Gwendolyn Midlo, ed. *Databases for the Study of Afro-Louisiana History and Genealogy: 1699–1860*. CD-ROM. Baton Rouge: Louisiana State University Press, 1999.

Hall, Gwendolyn Midlo. "The Formation of Afro-Creole Culture." In *Creole New Orleans: Race and Americanization*, edited by Arnold R. Hirsch and Joseph Logsdon, 58–87. Baton Rouge: Louisiana State University Press, 1992.

Hall, Jacquelyn Dowd. "The Long Civil Rights Movement and the Political Uses of the Past." *Journal of American History* 91, no. 4 (2005): 1233–63.

Hammer, David. "Citizens in Road Home Purgatory." NOLA.com, May 7, 2008. Accessed July 13, 2009. http://blog.nola.com/updates/2008/05/road_home _purgatory.html.

Hammer, David. "Gulf Oil Spill Creates Economic Boom for Some, Bust for Others." NOLA.com, last modified January 18, 2011. Accessed July 3, 2012. http://www.nola .com/news/gulf-oil-spill/index.ssf/2011/01/gulf_oil_spill_creates_economi.html.

Hammer, David. "New Orleans Mayor Ray Nagin's Grand Sculpture Plan Has Workers Scurrying in Armstrong Park." *Times-Picayune*, April 28, 2010.

Hammer, David. "New Orleans Saints Fans Build Color-Blind Bonds in Who Dat Nation." *Times-Picayune*, February 1, 2010.

Hammer, David. "Road Home's Grant Calculations Discriminate against Black Homeowners, Federal Judge Rules." *Times-Picayune*, August 16, 2010.

Handler, Richard, and Eric Gable. *The New History in an Old Museum: Creating the Past at Colonial Williamsburg*. Durham, NC: Duke University Press, 1997.

Hanger, Kimberly S. *Bounded Lives, Bounded Places: Free Black Society in Colonial New Orleans, 1769–1803*. Durham, NC: Duke University Press, 1997.

Hartnell, Anna. "Katrina Tourism and a Tale of Two Cities: Visualizing Race and Class in New Orleans." *American Quarterly* 61, no. 3 (2009): 723–47.

Hayden, Dolores. *The Power of Place: Urban Landscapes as Public History*. Cambridge, MA: MIT Press, 1995.

Hearn, Lafcadio. *Inventing New Orleans: Writings of Lafcadio Hearn*. Edited by S. Frederick Starr. Jackson: University Press of Mississippi, 2001.

Heath, Brad. "Katrina's Wrath Lingers for New Orleans' Poor." *USA Today*, December 13, 2007.

Herbert, David T., ed. *Heritage, Tourism and Society*. London: Mansell, 1995.

Herczog, Mary. "Tourist Areas in New Orleans Rebound While Other Parts Remain Far Behind." *Frommers*, February 14, 2006. Accessed July 15, 2009. http://www.frommers.com/articles/3419.html.

"Heritage Tours: Africans in Louisiana Tours." New Orleans Online. Accessed March 6, 2003. http://www.neworleansonline.com/tours-attractions/tours/heritagetours.html.

Hernandez, Carol. "Black Memorabilia Find Big Demand." *Wall Street Journal*, August 10, 1992.

Hewison, Robert. *The Heritage Industry*. London: Methuen, 1987.

Hill, Lance. "New Orleans: Beachhead for Corporate Takeover of Public Schools." Education Talk New Orleans, October 28, 2011. Accessed January 13, 2013. http://edutalknola.com/2011/10/28/new-orleans-beachhead-for-corporate-takeover-of-public-schools/.

Hiraldo, Carlos. *Segregated Miscegenation: On the Treatment of Racial Hybridity in the North American and Latin American Literary Traditions*. New York: Routledge, 2003.

Hirsch, Arnold R. "Fade to Black: Hurricane Katrina and the Disappearance of Creole New Orleans." *Journal of American History* 94, no. 3 (2007): 752–61.

Hirsch, Arnold R. "Simply a Matter of Black and White: The Transformation of Race and Politics in Twentieth-Century New Orleans." In *Creole New Orleans: Race and Americanization*, edited by Arnold R. Hirsch and Joseph Logsdon, 262–319. Baton Rouge: Louisiana State University Press, 1992.

Hirsch, Arnold R., and Joseph Logsdon, eds. *Creole New Orleans: Race and Americanization*. Baton Rouge: Louisiana State University Press, 1992.

Hirsch, Arnold R. and Joseph Logsdon. Introduction to Part I. In *Creole New Orleans: Race and Americanization*, edited by Arnold R. Hirsch and Joseph Logsdon, 3–11. Baton Rouge: Louisiana State University Press, 1992.

"Historic Homes: Step into the Past." New Orleans Online. Accessed March 6, 2003. http://www.neworleansonline.com/neworleans/history/hisho.html.

"Historical Context, Cities: New Orleans." SoulofAmerica.com. Accessed June 5, 2003. http://www.soulofamerica.com/cityfldr/orleans1.html.

"Historical Facts about New Orleans." New Orleans Online. Accessed March 6, 2003. http://www.neworleansonline.com/neworleans/history/facts.html.

"Historical Map and Points of Interest." In *The Soul of New Orleans: The Official GNOBTN Visitor's Guide*, 12–13. New Orleans: Greater New Orleans Black Tourism Network, 1993.

"Historically Speaking." New Orleans Metropolitan Convention and Visitors Bureau, June 2000. Accessed March 1, 2003. http://www.neworleanscvb.com/new_site/visitor/vismultimedia.cfm#.

"History." SoulofNewOrleans.com, March 17, 2003. Accessed June 5, 2003. http://www.soulofneworleans.com/naturally%20New%20Orleans.htm#History.

Hodder, Robert. "Savannah's Changing Past: Historic Preservation Planning and the Social Construction of a Historic Landscape, 1955 to 1985." In *Planning the Twentieth-Century American City*, edited by Mary Corbin Sies and Christopher Silver, 361–82. Baltimore, MD: Johns Hopkins University Press, 1996.

Hodge, G. Jeannette. "New Orleans Culture." In *The Soul of New Orleans: Greater New Orleans Black Tourism Network Official Visitors Guide*, 26. New Orleans: Greater New Orleans Black Tourism Network, 1994–95.

Hogan, Nakia. "New Orleans Saints' Monday Night Football Game against Atlanta in the Dome Return Was Memorable for Broadcasters." NOLA.com. Accessed November 26, 2012. http://www.nola.com/saints/index.ssf/2011/09/saints _mnf_win_vs_falcons_a_me.html.

Hollandsworth, James G. *The Louisiana Native Guards: The Black Military Experience during the Civil War*. Baton Rouge: Louisiana State University Press, 1998.

Home page. Africansinlouisiana.com. Accessed March 6, 2003. http://www .Africansinlouisiana.com.

Home page. New Orleans Convention and Visitors Bureau. Accessed July 30, 2006. http://www.neworleanscvb.com.

"Hope, Healing for New Orleans after Super Bowl." PBS, February 8, 2010. Accessed July 12, 2012. http://www.pbs.org/newshour/bb/sports/jan-june10/nola2_02-08 .html.

Hopkins, Karin Grant. "Essence Music Festival: A Party with a Purpose." In *The Soul of New Orleans: Greater New Orleans Black Tourism Network Official Visitors Guide*, 28. New Orleans: Greater New Orleans Black Tourism Network, 1997.

Horton, Carol A. *Race and the Making of American Liberalism*. Oxford: Oxford University Press, 2005.

Horton, James Oliver, and Lois E. Horton, eds. *Slavery and Public History: The Tough Stuff of American Memory*. Chapel Hill: University of North Carolina Press, 2008.

"Hotard Gray Line Tours." In *The Soul of New Orleans: Greater New Orleans Black Tourism Network Official Visitors Guide*, 57. New Orleans: Greater New Orleans Black Tourism Network, 1994–95.

"Houmas House Plantation and Garden." In *New Orleans Official Visitors Guide*, 116. New Orleans: New Orleans Metropolitan Convention and Visitors Bureau,, 2000.

"Houmas House Plantation and Gardens." In *Official Louisiana Tour Guide*, 196. Baton Rouge: Louisiana Travel Promotion Association, 2003.

Howell, Susan E., and John B. Vinturella. "Forgotten in New Orleans." *New York Times*, April 20, 2006.

"Hurricane Katrina Disaster Tours Still Popular." *Sydney Morning Herald*, June 13, 2007.

Hutchison, Phillip A. "The Political Economy of Colorblindness: Neoliberalism and the Reproduction of Racial Inequality in the United States." PhD diss., George Mason University, 2010.

Huus, Kari. "Panel Challenges Gulf Seafood Safety All-Clear." MSNBC. Accessed August 18, 2011. http://www.msnbc.msn.com/id/40494122/ns/us_news -environment/t/panel-challenges-gulf-seafood-safety-all-clear/#.Tk2R9GHEZn8.

"Iberville Development Neighborhood Snapshot." Greater New Orleans Community

Data Center, November 4, 2002. Accessed June 29, 2009. http://gnocdc.org /orleans/4/41/snapshot.html.

Ingersoll, Thomas N. "Free Blacks in a Slave Society: New Orleans, 1718–1812." *William and Mary Quarterly* 48, no. 2 (1991): 173–200.

Ingersoll, Thomas N. *Mammon and Manon in Early New Orleans: The First Slave Society in the Deep South, 1718–1819*. Knoxville: University of Tennessee Press, 1998.

Ingham, John N. "Building Businesses, Creating Communities: Residential Segregation and the Growth of African American Business in Southern Cities, 1880–1915." *Business History Review* 77, no. 4 (2003): 639–65.

"Introduction to New Orleans." In *New Orleans Official Visitors Guide*, 8+. New Orleans: New Orleans Metropolitan Convention and Visitors Bureau, winter–spring 1999.

Ishiwata, Eric. "'We Are Seeing People We Didn't Know Exist': Katrina and the Neoliberal Erasure of Race." In *The Neoliberal Deluge: Hurricane Katrina, Late Capitalism, and the Remaking of New Orleans*, edited by Cedric Johnson, 32–59. Minneapolis: University of Minnesota Press, 2011.

Izenberg, Jerry. "New Orleans Saints Brought Salvation to Their City; Now They'll Try to Bring a Super Bowl Championship." [Newark] *Star-Ledger*, January 31, 2010.

Jacobson, Matthew Frye. *Whiteness of a Different Color: European Immigrants and the Alchemy of Race*. Cambridge, MA: Harvard University Press, 1999.

"The Jazz Funeral." New Orleans Online. Accessed March 6, 2003. http://www .neworleansonline.com/neworleans/history/jazzfuneral.html.

"The Jazz Funeral, a New Orleans Cultural Tradition Steeped in African Roots." In *The Soul of New Orleans: Greater New Orleans Black Tourism Network Official Visitors Guide*, 43. New Orleans: Greater New Orleans Black Tourism Network, 1994–95.

Johnson, Allen, Jr. "Black Historical Sites." *New Orleans Tribune*, November 1987.

Johnson, Cedric. "Introduction: The Neoliberal Deluge." In *The Neoliberal Deluge: Hurricane Katrina, Late Capitalism, and the Remaking of New Orleans*, edited by Cedric Johnson, xvii–1. Minneapolis: University of Minnesota Press, 2011.

Johnson, Cedric. "Preface: 'Obama's Katrina.'" In *The Neoliberal Deluge: Hurricane Katrina, Late Capitalism, and the Remaking of New Orleans*, edited by Cedric Johnson, vii–xv. Minneapolis: University of Minnesota Press, 2011.

Johnson, Jerah. "Colonial New Orleans: A Fragment of the Eighteenth-Century French Ethos." In *Creole New Orleans: Race and Americanization*, edited by Arnold R. Hirsch and Joseph Logsdon, 12–57. Baton Rouge: Louisiana State University Press, 1992.

Johnson, Phil. "Thank God the French Got Here First." GumboPages.com. Accessed June 5, 2003. http://www.gumbopages.com/neworleans.html.

Johnson, Walter. *Soul by Soul: Life inside the Antebellum Slave Market*. Cambridge, MA: Harvard University Press, 2001.

Judice, Mary. "Group Polishes N.O. Image." *Times-Picayune*, February 17, 1996.

Juhasz, Antonia. "Investigation: Two Years after the BP Spill, a Hidden Health Crisis Festers." *Nation*, May 7, 2012. Accessed July 13, 2012. http://www.thenation.com

/article/167461/investigation-two-years-after-bp-spill-hidden-health-crisis
-festers.

Kammen, Michael G. *Mystic Chords of Memory: The Transformation of Tradition in American Culture*. New York: Knopf, 1991.

Kao, Grace. "Where Are the Asian and Hispanic Victims of Katrina? A Metaphor for Invisible Minorities in Contemporary Racial Discourse." *Du Bois Review* 3, no. 1 (2006): 223–31.

Karp, Ivan, Christine Mullen Kreamer, and Steven Levine, eds. *Museums and Communities: The Politics of Public Culture*. Washington: Smithsonian Institution Press, 1992.

Kellner, Douglas. "The Katrina Hurricane Spectacle and the Crisis of the Bush Presidency." *Cultural Studies, Critical Methodologies* 7, no. 2 (2007): 222–34.

Kennedy, Richard S., ed. *Literary New Orleans in the Modern World*. Baton Rouge: Louisiana State University Press, 1998.

Kern-Foxworth, Marilyn. *Aunt Jemima, Uncle Ben, and Rastus: Blacks in Advertising, Yesterday, Today, and Tomorrow*. Westport, CT: Praeger, 1994.

King, Grace Elizabeth. *New Orleans: The Place and the People*. New York: Macmillan, 1895.

King, Ronette. "Blowing Life back into the Birthplace of Jazz." *Newhouse News Service*, 2001. Accessed June 7, 2003. http://www.newhousenews.com/archive/story1b012601.html.

Kinzer, Stephen. "Arts in America: A Struggle to Be Seen." *New York Times*. February 22, 2001.

Kirshenblatt-Gimblett, Barbara. *Destination Culture: Tourism, Museums, and Heritage*. Berkeley: University of California Press, 1998.

Knoettgen, Casey. "We Are the 'Who Dat' Nation: City Identity, Narratives of Renewal, and Football Fandom in New Orleans Public Realm." PhD diss., University of New Orleans, 2012.

Konigsmark, Anne Rochell. "Superdome Reopens to First Post-Katrina NFL Game." *USA Today*, September 26, 2006.

Kristof, Nicholas D. "Racism without Racists." *New York Times*, October 4, 2008.

Krupa, Michelle. "Census Shows Katrina Effects: Racial, Ethnic Shifts Seen since 2005." *Times-Picayune*, June 14, 2010.

Krupa, Michelle. "Fewer Than Half of the Census Questionnaires Sent Out in Orleans and St. Bernard Were Returned." *Times-Picayune*, October 21, 2010.

Krupa, Michelle. "Hurricane Katrina Recovery Assessed Five Years Out." *Times-Picayune*, August 4, 2010.

Krupa, Michelle. "Minority Populations Still Growing in New Orleans Area, but Not as Fast." *Times-Picayune*, June 13, 2010.

Krupa, Michelle. "New Orleans Tourism Breaks Record in 2011." *Times-Picayune*, March 27, 2012.

Krupa, Michelle. "Road Home Isn't Easy Street." *Times-Picayune*, October 7, 2006.

Krupa, Michelle, and Frank Donze. "Mitch Landrieu Claims New Orleans Mayor's Office in a Landslide." *Times-Picayune*, February 10, 2010.

Kytle, Ethan J., and Blain Roberts. "'Is It Okay to Talk about Slaves?': Segregating the Past in Historic Charleston." In *Destination Dixie: Tourism and Southern History*, edited by Karen L. Cox, 137–59. Gainesville: University Press of Florida, 2012.

Lachance, Paul F. "The 1809 Immigration of Saint-Domingue Refugees to New Orleans: Reception, Integration and Impact." *Louisiana History* 29, no. 2 (1988): 109–41.

"Laissez Le Bon Temps Roulet." Gateway New Orleans, 2000. http://www.gateway no.com/culture/culture.html.

"Laissez Les Bon Temps Rouler!" In *New Orleans Official Visitors Guide*, 8–20. New Orleans: New Orleans Metropolitan Convention and Visitors Bureau, 2000.

"Lakeview Neighborhood: People and Household Characteristics." Greater New Orleans Community Data Center, July 25, 2006. Accessed January 8, 2010. http:// gnocdc.org/orleans/5/37/people.html.

"Lakeview Neighborhood Snapshot." Greater New Orleans Community Data Center, October 23, 2002. Accessed January 8, 2010. http://gnocdc.org/orleans/5/37 /snapshot.html.

Land, Monica. "BP Pushes Black Faces to Forefront of Mea Culpa Ad Campaign." Grio, January 10, 2012. Accessed October 13, 2012. http://thegrio.com/2012/01/10 /bp-pushes-black-faces-to-forefront-of-mea-culpa-ad-campaign/.

Landrieu, Mitchell. "State of the City Address: Eyes Wide Open." July 8, 2010. Accessed August 2, 2012. http://www.nola.gov/nola/media/Mayor-s-Office/Files /Landrieu%20Speech%20Texts/MayorMitchellJLandrieu2010StateoftheCity.pdf.

Leavitt, Mel. "Common Blood, Different Cultures." New Orleans Metropolitan Convention and Visitors Bureau, June 2000. Accessed March 1, 2003. http://www .neworleanscvb.com/new_site/visitor/viscajun.cfm.

Leavitt, Mel. "Melting Pot." New Orleans Metropolitan Convention and Visitors Bureau, June 2000. Accessed March 1, 2003. http://www.neworleanscvb.com /new_site/visitor/visneighbor.cfm.

"Le Monde Créole." Advertisement in *This Week in New Orleans*, March 2002, 33.

"Le Monde Creole." In *The Soul of New Orleans: Greater New Orleans Black Tourism Network Official Visitors Guide*, 68. New Orleans: Greater New Orleans Black Tourism Network, 1998.

"Le Monde Creole." In *The Soul of New Orleans: Official Multicultural Visitors Guide*, 56. New Orleans: New Orleans Multicultural Tourism Network, 2002.

"Le Monde Creole French Quarter Courtyards and Cemetery Tour." In *New Orleans Official Visitors Guide*, 142. New Orleans: New Orleans Metropolitan Convention and Visitors Bureau, 2001.

"'Le Monde Creole Tours' Present: The Insider's French Quarter Courtyards and Cemetery Tours." Le Monde Creole Tours. Accessed June 18, 2013. http://www .mondecreole.com.

"LeMonde Creole, French Quarter Courtyards and Cemetery Tour." In *New Orleans Official Visitors Guide*, 142. New Orleans: New Orleans Metropolitan Convention and Visitors Bureau, 2002–3.

"LeMonde Creole, French Quarter Courtyards and Cemetery Tour." In *New Orleans*

Official Visitors Guide, 143. New Orleans: New Orleans Metropolitan Convention and Visitors Bureau, 2003–4.

"Les Grande Dames of the River Road." In *New Orleans Official Visitors Guide*, 127. New Orleans: New Orleans Metropolitan Convention and Visitors Bureau, 2000.

Lewis, Peirce F. *New Orleans: The Making of an Urban Landscape*. 2nd ed. Sante Fe, NM: Center for American Places, 2003.

Lieberman, Robert C. "'The Storm Didn't Discriminate': Katrina and the Politics of Color Blindness." *Du Bois Review* 3, no. 1 (2006): 7–22.

Linenthal, Edward T. "Epilogue: Reflections." In *Slavery and Public History: The Tough Stuff of American Memory*, edited by James Oliver Horton and Lois E. Horton, 213–24. Chapel Hill: University of North Carolina Press, 2008.

Lipsitz, George. "History, Myth, and Counter-Memory: Narrative and Desire in Popular Novels." In *Time Passages: Collective Memory and American Popular Culture*, edited by George Lipsitz, 211–31. Minneapolis: University of Minnesota Press, 1990.

Lipsitz, George. "Learning from New Orleans: The Social Warrant of Hostile Privatism and Competitive Consumer Citizenship." *Cultural Anthropology* 21, no. 3 (2006): 451–68.

Lipsitz, George. "Mardi Gras Indians: Carnival and Counter-Narrative in Black New Orleans." In *Time Passages: Collective Memory and American Popular Culture*, edited by George Lipsitz, 233–53. Minneapolis: University of Minnesota Press, 1990.

Lipsitz, George. *Time Passages: Collective Memory and American Popular Culture*. Minneapolis: University of Minnesota Press, 1990.

Liu, Amy, and Allison Plyer. *New Orleans Index at Five*. Washington: Brookings Institution, August 2010.

Llorens, Terri. "New Orleans' Finest." *New Orleans Tribune*, November 1987.

"Locals' Dictionary." NewOrleans.com, 2003. Accessed April 2, 2003. http://www .neworleans.com/cgi-bin/oracle/hs.cgi?search=CAT&Category=FACTS %3Alocals%20Dictionary.

Logsdon, Dawn, and Lolis Eric Elie. *Faubourg Tremé: The Untold Story of Black New Orleans*. 2008. Arlington, VA: PBS, 2009. DVD.

Logsdon, Joseph. "Americans and Creoles in New Orleans: The Origins of Black Citizenship in the United States." *Amerikastudien/American Studies* 34, no. 2 (1989): 187–202.

Logsdon, Joseph, and Caryn Cossé Bell. "The Americanization of Black New Orleans, 1850–1900." In *Creole New Orleans: Race and Americanization*, edited by Arnold R. Hirsch and Joseph Logsdon, 201–61. Baton Rouge: Louisiana State University Press, 1992.

Lomax, Michael E. "The African American Experience in Professional Football." *Journal of Social History* 33, no. 1 (1999): 163–78.

Long, Alecia P. *The Great Southern Babylon: Sex, Race, and Respectability in New Orleans, 1865–1920*. Baton Rouge: Louisiana State University Press, 2004.

Long, Alecia P. "'A Notorious Attraction': Sex and Tourism in New Orleans, 1897–1917." In *Southern Journeys: Tourism, History, and Culture in the Modern South*, edited by Richard D. Starnes, 15–41. Tuscaloosa: University Alabama Press, 2003.

Lott, Eric. *Love and Theft: Blackface Minstrelsy and the American Working Class*. New York: Oxford University Press, 1995.

Lott, Tommy L. *The Invention of Race: Black Culture and the Politics of Representation*. Malden, MA: Wiley-Blackwell, 1999.

"Louisiana." Gateway New Orleans, 2000. Accessed June 5, 2003. http://www.gateway no.com/history/louisiana.html.

"Louisiana Basics." Baton-Rouge.com. Accessed October 10, 2003. http://www .baton-rouge.com/BatonRouge/labasics.htm.

"The Louisiana Superdome—An Icon Transformed." Superdome.com. August 10, 2011. Accessed November 27, 2012. superdome.com/uploads/SUPERDOME MEDIAKIT81011final.pdf.

Lowenthal, David. *The Past Is a Foreign Country*. Cambridge: Cambridge University Press, 1985.

Lowenthal, David. *Possessed by the Past: The Heritage Crusade and the Spoils of History*. New York: Free Press, 1996.

Luft, Rachel E. "Beyond Disaster Exceptionalism: Social Movement Developments in New Orleans after Hurricane Katrina." *American Quarterly* 61, no. 3 (2009): 499–527.

Lum, Lydia. "The Obama Era: A Post-Racial Society?" *Diverse* 25, no. 26 (2009): 14–16.

MacCannell, Dean. *The Tourist: A New Theory of the Leisure Class*. 3rd ed. Berkeley: University of California Press, 1999.

Manning, Diane T., and Perry Rogers. "Desegregation of the New Orleans Parochial Schools." *Journal of Negro Education* 71, nos. 1–2 (2002): 31–42.

Manring, Maurice M. *Slave in a Box: The Strange Career of Aunt Jemima*. Charlottes-ville: University of Virginia Press, 1998.

"Mardi Gras." Soul of America.com. Accessed June 5, 2003. http://www.soulofamerica .com/cityfldr/orleans11.html.

Marshall, Bob. "New Orleans Saints Have a Special Bond with Their Fans." NOLA .com, February 9, 2010. Accessed September 20, 2012. http://www.nola.com/saints /index.ssf/2010/02/new_orleans_saints_have_a_spec.html.

McClain, Randy. "Black History Tour Proves Tough Sell." *New Orleans CityBusiness*, August 15, 1994.

McConnaughey, Janet. "Demand for Post-Katrina Disaster Tours Remains High." *USA Today*, August 13, 2007.

McConnaughey, Janet. "Katrina Tours Get Mixed Reaction." Seattlepi.com, December 16, 2005. Accessed July 31, 2007. http://www.seattlepi.com/national/article /Katrina-tours-get-mixed-reaction-1190113.php#src=fb.

McElya, Micki. *Clinging to Mammy: The Faithful Slave in Twentieth-Century America*. Cambridge, MA: Harvard University Press, 2007.

McGill, Kevin. "Saints, Parades Overshadow New Orleans Mayor Race." Associated Press, February 6, 2010.

McKible, Adam. "'These Are the Facts of the Darky's History': Thinking History and Reading Names in Four African American Texts." *African American Review* 28, no. 2 (1994): 223–35.

"Media." OakAlleyPlantation.com. Accessed October 6, 2003. http://www.oakalley plantation.com/.

Medley, Keith Weldon. "Dryades Street/Oretha Castle Haley Boulevard: Remembrance and Reclamation." *New Orleans Tribune*, April 2001.

"A Message from GNOBTN." In *The Soul of New Orleans: Greater New Orleans Black Tourism Network Official Visitors Guide*, 4. New Orleans: Greater New Orleans Black Tourism Network, 1994–95.

"Metairie CDP, Louisiana." U.S. Census Bureau. Accessed January 8, 2010. http://factfinder.census.gov/servlet/ADPTable?_bm=y&-geo_id=16000US2250115&-qr_name=ACS_2006_EST_G00_DP5&-ds_name=ACS_2006_EST_G00_&-_lang=en&-_sse=on.

Michna, Catherine. "Theatre, Spiritual Healing, and Democracy in the City: Go Ye Therefore . . . in Katrina+5 New Orleans." *TheatreForum*, no. 39 (2011): 57–65.

Mildenberg, David. "Census Data Show a Far Less Populous New Orleans." *Washington Post*, February 5, 2011.

Mildenberg, David. "Census Finds Hurricane Katrina Left New Orleans Richer, Whiter, Emptier." *Bloomberg*, February 4, 2011. Accessed August 2, 2012. http://www.bloomberg.com/news/2011-02-04/census-finds-post-katrina-new-orleans-richer-whiter-emptier.html.

The Minority Traveler. 2000 Edition. Washington: Travel Industry Association of America, 2000.

"Mitch's Mandate." TheLensNola.org, February 9, 2010. Accessed September 18, 2012. http://thelensnola.org/2010/02/09/mitch%E2%80%99s-mandate/.

Mock, Brentin. "The Problem with New Orleans's Charter Schools." *Newsweek*, October 6, 2010. Accessed October 6, 2010. http://www.thedailybeast.com/newsweek/2010/10/06/new-orleans-accused-of-failing-disabled-students.html.

Moller, Jan. "First Installment of BP Money for Louisiana Tourism to Be Divided among All 64 Parishes." *Times-Picayune*, March 10, 2011.

Moller, Jan. "Gov. Bobby Jindal Proclaims 'Who Dat Nation Week' in Louisiana." *Times-Picayune*, January 25, 2010.

Molyneaux, Brian L. "Introduction: The Represented Past." In *The Presented Past: Heritage, Museums and Education*, edited by Brian L. Molyneaux and Peter G. Stone, 1–13. London: Routledge, 1994.

Molyneaux, Brian L., and Peter G. Stone. *The Presented Past: Heritage, Museums and Education*. London: Routledge, 1994.

Moran, Kate. "Without Charity Hospital, the Poor and Uninsured Struggle to Find Health Care." *Times-Picayune*, August 24, 2007.

"Morial Keeps Heat on Foster." *Times-Picayune*, February 12, 1996.

Morial, Marc H. "Dear Friends." In *New Orleans Official Visitors Guide*, 3. New Orleans: New Orleans Metropolitan Convention and Visitors Bureau, 2000.

Morial, Marc H. "Greetings." In *The Soul of New Orleans: Greater New Orleans Black Tourism Network Official Visitors Guide*, 1. New Orleans: Greater New Orleans Black Tourism Network, 1994–95.

Morrison, Toni. "10 Questions for Toni Morrison." *Time*. May 19, 2008, 4.

Morrison, Toni. *Playing in the Dark*. Cambridge, MA: Harvard University Press, 1992.

Morrison, Toni. "The Talk of the Town: Comment." *New Yorker*, October 5, 1998, 31–32.

Mouawad, Jad, and Clifford Krauss. "Another Torrent BP Works to Stem: Its C.E.O." *New York Times*, June 3, 2010.

Muller, David. "Officials Try to Allay Fears of Oil-Spoiled Seafood." *New Orleans CityBusiness*, April 30, 2010.

"My Name Is 6508799": State of the Gulf, One Year after the Oil Drilling Disaster. Baltimore: NAACP, April 20, 2011.

Nagin, C. Ray. "Welcome to New Orleans." In *The Soul of New Orleans: Official Multicultural Visitor Guide*, 5. New Orleans: New Orleans Multicultural Tourism Network, 2002.

"Naturally New Orleans." SoulofNewOrleans.com, March 17, 2003. Accessed June 5, 2003. http://www.soulofneworleans.com/Naturally%20New%20Orleans.htm.

Nelson, Connie. "Katrina's Lesson: Recreation Leading Re-Creation." Public Strategies Group, 2012. Accessed August 28, 2012. http://www.psg.us/resources/cckatrinaslesson.html.

Nelson, Dana D. *The Word in Black and White: Reading "Race" in American Literature, 1638–1867*. New York: Oxford University Press, 1992.

"Network Profile." In *The Soul of New Orleans: The Official GNOBTN Visitor's Guide*, 18–19. New Orleans: Greater New Orleans Black Tourism Network, 1993.

"New Orleans." Explore-New-Orleans.com, May 14, 2002. Accessed June 5, 2003. http://www.explore-new-orleans.com/nola_uk.html.

"New Orleans—A WorldWeb Review." *WorldWeb Travel Guide*. Accessed October 10, 2003. http://www.usa.worldweb.com/FeaturesReviews/TownCityReviews/8-322.html.

"New Orleans Achieves Major Tourism Milestone: 8.3 Million Visitors in 2010." New Orleans: New Orleans Convention and Visitors Bureau, April 14, 2011.

"New Orleans Area—Women to Watch in 1992." *Times-Picayune*, January 5, 1992.

"New Orleans City and Post Katrina." Louisiana Tour Company. Accessed June 27, 2012. http://www.louisianaswamp.com/html/citykatrinatours.html.

"New Orleans Cuisine." New Orleans Metropolitan Convention and Visitors Bureau, June 2000. Accessed March 1, 2003. http://www.neworleanscvb.com/new_site/visitor/viscuisines.cfm.

"New Orleans CVB Announces Aggressive Rebranding Campaign to Focus on Authentic and Dynamic Culture of New Orleans." Hotel-Online.com, January 25, 2007. Accessed October 6, 2008. http://www.hotel-online.com/News/PR2007_1st/Jan07_NewOrleansCVB.html.

"New Orleans CVB Encourages Locals to Be a Tourist in Your Own Hometown." New Orleans Convention and Visitors Bureau, May 14, 2007. Accessed August 3, 2007. http://www.neworleanscvb.com/articles/index.cfm/action/view/typeID/1/articleID/1058/.

"New Orleans Map and Points of Interest." In *The Soul of New Orleans: Greater New*

Orleans Black Tourism Network Official Visitors Guide, n.p. New Orleans: Greater New Orleans Black Tourism Network, 1994–95.

"New Orleans Mayor Mitch Landrieu's Hurricane Katrina Anniversary Remarks." NOLA.com, August 30, 2010. Accessed September 6, 2012. http://www.nola.com/katrina/index.ssf/2010/08/post_1.html.

New Orleans Multicultural Tourism Network. 2004 Annual Report. New Orleans: New Orleans Multicultural Tourism Network, 2004.

"New Orleans Multicultural Tourism Network." March 17, 2003. Accessed June 5, 2003. http://www.soulofneworleans.com/.

"New Orleans Official Tourism Web Site." New Orleans Online. Accessed June 5, 2003. http://www.neworleansonline.com/.

"New Orleans Ready for EXPO!" Forest Products Machinery and Equipment Exposition. Accessed September 20, 2008. http://sfpaexpo.com/News/071218.htm.

"New Orleans Real Estate: Elegant Victorian Home." Nolarealtor.com, 2000. Accessed October 7, 2003. http://www.mathildenelson.com/vt_3727_coliseum.htm.

"New Orleans Update: Frequently Asked Questions about Safety and Health Concerns." New Orleans Metropolitan Convention and Visitors Bureau, March 24, 2006. Accessed July 15, 2009. http://www.cme.tulane.edu/nofaq-mcvb.pdf.

"New Racist Forms: Jim Crow in the 21st Century." Jim Crow Museum of Racist Memorabilia, September 2000. http://www.ferris.edu/news/jimcrow/newforms/.

Newman, Maria. "Bush Notes Progress in New Orleans Cleanup." New York Times, January 12, 2006.

Nickel, Patti. "New Tourism Philosophy: Eat, Drink, Be Merry,—and Learn." New Orleans CityBusiness, July 16, 1987.

Nielsen, Aldon Lynn. Writing between the Lines: Race and Intertextuality. Athens: University of Georgia Press, 1994.

"N.O. Tourism Reaches a Milestone." New Orleans CityBusiness, April 15, 2011.

Nolan, Bruce. "Henriette Delille Moves Closer to Sainthood for Work with New Orleans Slaves." Times-Picayune, March 29, 2010.

"NOPD Blues." 60 Minutes. CBS, October 30, 1994.

"NORD: New Orleans Recreation Department." In The Soul of New Orleans: Greater New Orleans Black Tourism Network Official Visitors Guide, 24. New Orleans: Greater New Orleans Black Tourism Network, 1994–95.

Northrup, Solomon. Twelve Years a Slave. Auburn, NY: Derby and Miller, 1853.

Nossiter, Adam. "After Fanfare, Hurricane Grants Leave Little Mark." New York Times, August 30, 2008.

Nossiter, Adam. "Largely Alone, Pioneers Reclaim New Orleans." New York Times, July 2, 2007.

Nossiter, Adam. "With Regrets, New Orleans Is Left Behind." New York Times, December 18, 2007.

"Nottoway Plantation Restaurant and Inn." In New Orleans Official Visitors Guide, 42. New Orleans: New Orleans Metropolitan Convention and Visitors Bureau, 2002–3.

"Oak Alley Plantation." GrayLineNewOrleans.com, 2002. Accessed October 2, 2003. http://www.graylineneworleans.com/plantation.shtml.

Obama, Barack. "Remarks by the President on the Fifth Anniversary of Hurricane Katrina in New Orleans, Louisiana." White House, August 29, 2010. Accessed July 10, 2012. http://www.whitehouse.gov/the-press-office/2010/08/29/remarks-president-fifth-anniversary-hurricane-katrina-new-orleans-louisi.

"Official: Astrodome Can't Take More Refugees." FoxNews.com, September 2, 2005. Accessed July 10, 2006. http://www.foxnews.com/story/0,2933,168112,00.html.

Omi, Michael, and Howard Winant. *Racial Formation in the United States: From the 1960s to the 1990s.* 2nd ed. New York: Routledge, 1994.

"One of the French Quarter's 'Best Kept Secrets' . . . Le Monde Creole: Unique Courtyards, Cemetery, Voodoo Tours, and Heritage Store." *This Week in New Orleans,* March 2002, 5.

Onion, Rebecca. "A Midcentury Travel Guide for African-American Drivers Navigating Jim Crow." Vault, February 11, 2013. Accessed June 17, 2013. http://www.slate.com/blogs/the_vault/2013/02/11/the_negro_motorist_green_book_the_mid_century_guide_for_african_american.html.

Oriard, Michael. *Brand NFL: Making and Selling America's Favorite Sport.* Chapel Hill: University of North Carolina Press, 2007.

Ortega, Mariana. "Othering the Other: The Spectacle of Katrina for Our Racial Entertainment Pleasure." *Contemporary Aesthetics* special volume, no. 2 (2009). http://hdl.handle.net/2027/spo.7523862.spec.204.

Osbey, Brenda Marie. "Tourism in New Orleans: The Black Side." *New Orleans Tribune,* November 1987.

Osborn, Gregory. "Free People of Color and Creoles." In *The Soul of New Orleans: Greater New Orleans Black Tourism Network Official Visitors Guide,* 63. New Orleans: Greater New Orleans Black Tourism Network, 1994–95.

Ott, Kenneth. "The Closure of New Orleans' Charity Hospital after Hurricane Katrina: A Case of Disaster Capitalism." MA thesis, University of New Orleans, 2012.

"Our Culture Abounds: A Pictorial Directory of Louisiana's African-American Attractions." Baton Rouge: Louisiana Office of Tourism, 1995.

Owens, Reginald. "Black Tourism Gained Respect via Essence." *Times-Picayune,* July 16, 1995.

Ownby, Ted. "Thoughtful Souvenirs." In *Dixie Emporium: Tourism, Foodways, and Consumer Culture in the American South,* edited by Anthony J. Stanonis, 19–23. Athens: University of Georgia Press, 2008.

Parent, Tawn. "Hit on Tourism Only a Flesh Wound, So Far." *New Orleans CityBusiness,* April 3, 1995.

Passavant, Paul A. "Mega-Events, the Superdome, and the Return of the Repressed in New Orleans." In *The Neoliberal Deluge: Hurricane Katrina, Late Capitalism, and the Remaking of New Orleans,* edited by Cedric Johnson, 87–129. Minneapolis: University of Minnesota Press, 2011.

"Past Perfect Reservations." Ppreservations.com. Accessed October 7, 2003. http://www.ppreservations.com/index.html.

Pecot-Hebert, Lisa. "Le'Ob's Tours: A Louisiana Treasure." *New Orleans Tribune,* July 1998.

Pecot-Hebert, Lisa. "UNO Metropolitan College Leads Effort to Diversify Tourism Industry." *New Orleans Tribune*, July 1998.

Penner, D'Ann R., and Keith C. Ferdinand. *Overcoming Katrina: African American Voices from the Crescent City and Beyond.* New York: Palgrave Macmillan, 2009.

Pennington, Richard. "Welcome to New Orleans." In *The Soul of New Orleans: New Orleans Official Multicultural Visitors Guide*, 5. [1999.]

Perlman, Allison. "Rush Limbaugh and the Problem of the Color Line." *Cinema Journal* 51, no. 4 (2012): 198–204.

Perry, James. "New Orleans Residents Still Struggling to Get Back Home." Interview by Tony Cox. National Public Radio, August 31, 2010. Accessed September 22, 2010. http://www.npr.org/templates/story/story.php?storyId=129555680&sc=emaf.

Pezzullo, Phaedra C. "'This Is the Only Tour That Sells': Tourism, Disaster, and National Identity in New Orleans." *Journal of Tourism and Cultural Change* 7, no. 2 (2009): 99–114.

Pezzullo, Phaedra C. "Tourists and/as Disasters: Rebuilding, Remembering, and Responsibility in New Orleans." *Tourist Studies* 9, no. 1 (2009): 23–41.

"Phil Johnson at the Table." *New Orleans Magazine*, May 2010. Accessed May 22, 2013. http://www.myneworleans.com/New-Orleans-Magazine/May-2010/PHIL-Johnson-at-the-table/.

"Pines Village Neighborhood Snapshot." Greater New Orleans Community Data Center, October 5, 2002. http://www.gnocdc.org/orleans/9/50/snapshot.html.

Pipes, Pamela. "Events and Festivals." New Orleans a La Net, 1995. Accessed June 5, 2003. http://www.alanet.com/events.html.

Pipes, Pamela. "History." New Orleans a La Net, 1995. Accessed June 5, 2003. http://www.alanet.com/history.html.

Pipes, Pamela. "Spirit." New Orleans a La Net, 1995. Accessed June 5, 2003. http://www.alanet.com/spirit.html.

Pittman, Philip. "New Orleans in the 1760s." In *Louisiana Sojourns: Travelers' Tales and Literary Journeys*, edited by Frank A. De Caro and Rosan A. Jordan, 73–75. Baton Rouge: Louisiana State University Press, 1998.

Plaisance, Stacey. "Demand High for Bus Tour of Katrina Devastation." DeseretNews.com, January 5, 2006. Accessed July 31, 2007. http://www.deseretnews.com/article/635173982/Demand-high-for-bus-tour-of-Katrina-devastation.html?pg=all.

"Plum Orchard Neighborhood Snapshot." Greater New Orleans Community Data Center, October 5, 2002. Accessed November 16, 2010. http://www.gnocdc.org/orleans/9/51/snapshot.html.

Pope, John. "Evoking King, Nagin Calls N.O. 'Chocolate' City." *Times-Picayune*. January 17, 2006.

Powell, Caletha. "Visitor's Welcome." In *The Soul of New Orleans: The Official GNOBTN Visitors Guide*, 4. New Orleans: Greater New Orleans Black Tourism Network, 1993.

"President George W. Bush and Laura Bush Stop in at Stewart's Diner in the Ninth Ward of New Orleans." White House, March 2006. Accessed October 4, 2008.

http://www.whitehouse.gov/news/releases/2006/03/images/20060308-1_otr
-515h.html.

"President Participates in Roundtable with Small Business Owners and Community
Leaders in New Orleans." White House, January 12, 2006. Accessed July 31, 2006.
http://georgewbush-whitehouse.archives.gov/news/releases/2006/01/20060112-1
.html.

Price, Tom, et al. "Zulu Social Aid and Pleasure Club." NewOrleansOnline.com.
Accessed April 15, 2003. http://www.neworleansonline.com/tours-attractions
/multicultural/zulu.html.

[Price, Tom, et al.] "Zulu Social Aid and Pleasure Club," In *The Soul of New Orleans:
Greater New Orleans Black Tourism Network Official Visitors Guide*, 37–38. New
Orleans: Greater New Orleans Black Tourism Network, 1994–95.

"Promoting Tourism." *Gambit*, July 13, 1985.

*Public School Performance in New Orleans: A Supplement to the 2008 State of Public
Education in New Orleans*. New Orleans: Scott S. Cowen Institute for Public Education Initiatives at Tulane University, January 2009. Accessed March 23, 2010. http://
www.coweninstitute.com/our-work/applied-research/education-archive
/education-transformation-archive/public-school-performance-in-new-orleans/.

Quigley, Bill. "The Right to Return to New Orleans." Counterpunch, February 26,
2007. Accessed March 20, 2007. http://www.counterpunch.org/2007/02/26
/the-right-to-return-to-new-orleans/.

Quigley, Bill, Davida Finger, and Lance Hill. "Five Years Later: Katrina Pain Index
2010 New Orleans." *San Francisco Bay View*, August 6, 2010.

Rankin, David C. "The Forgotten People: Free People of Color in New Orleans,
1850–1870." PhD diss., Johns Hopkins University, 1976.

Rankin, David C. "The Impact of the Civil War on the Free Colored Community
of New Orleans." *Perspectives in American History* 11 (1977–78): 379–416.

Rankin, David C. "The Politics of Caste: Free Colored Leadership in New Orleans
during the Civil War." In *Louisiana's Black Heritage*, edited by Robert R. MacDonald, John R. Kemp, and Edward F. Haas, 107–46. New Orleans: Louisiana State
Museum, 1979.

Rasmussen, Daniel. *American Uprising: The Untold Story of America's Largest Slave
Revolt*. New York: Harper, 2011.

"Read Blvd West Neighborhood Snapshot." Greater New Orleans Community Data
Center, October 8, 2002. Accessed November 16, 2010. http://www.gnocdc.org
/orleans/9/53/snapshot.html.

"Read the Text of Mayor Mitch Landrieu's Inauguration Speech." *Times-Picayune*,
May 3, 2010.

Reckdahl, Katy. "Armstrong Park Sculpture Garden Already Crumbling." *Times-
Picayune*, June 6, 2010.

Reckdahl, Katy. "City May Move Homeless from Underpass to Shelter." *Times-
Picayune*, February 9, 2008.

Reckdahl, Katy. "HANO Gets $30.5 Million to Re-Do Iberville Public-Housing Com-
plex." *Times-Picayune*, August 31, 2011.

Reckdahl, Katy. "Homeless Camp Springs Up on Claiborne Avenue." *Times-Picayune*, January 1, 2008.

Reckdahl, Katy. "Mayor Mitch Landrieu: Armstrong Park Contractor A.M.E. Has Been Taken Off Job." *Times-Picayune*, November 20, 2012.

Reckdahl, Katy. "On the Streets." *Times-Picayune*, August 6, 2007.

Reckdahl, Katy. "Spruced-Up Armstrong Park Reopens Friday with New Sculptures." *Times-Picayune*, November 18, 2011.

Reckdahl, Katy. "Staying at the Plaza." *Times-Picayune*, November 8, 2007.

Regis, Helen A. "Blackness and the Politics of Memory in the New Orleans Second Line." *American Ethnologist* 28, no. 4 (2001): 752–77.

Regis, Helen A. "'Keeping Jazz Funerals Alive': Blackness and the Politics of Memory in New Orleans." In *Southern Heritage on Display: Public Ritual and Ethnic Diversity within Southern Regionalism*, edited by Celeste Ray, 38–56. Tuscaloosa: University of Alabama Press, 2003.

Regis, Helen A. "Second Lines, Minstrelsy, and the Contested Landscapes of New Orleans Afro-Creole Festivals." *Cultural Anthropology* 14, no. 4 (1999): 472–504.

Reno, Dawn E. *Collecting Black Americana*. New York: Crown, 1986.

Restrepo, Alex. "Five Years Later: Reopening of the Superdome." NewOrleansSaints.com, September 23, 2011. Accessed October 28, 2012. http://www.neworleanssaints.com/news-and-events/article-1/Five-Years-Later-Reopening-of-the-Superdome/12623af3-df25-43d1-8aa0-5a68fdc55c04.

Ridenhour, Ron. "Can Tourism Halt Boom, Bust Cycle?" *New Orleans CityBusiness*, December 7, 1987.

"The River Road." National Park Service. Accessed October 6, 2003. http://www.cr.nps.gov/nr/travel/louisiana/riverroad.htm.

Roach, Joseph. *Cities of the Dead: Circum-Atlantic Performance*. New York: Columbia University Press, 1996.

Robertson, Campbell. "New Orleanians Gather to Watch as the City Takes the Spotlight on HBO." *New York Times*, April 12, 2010.

Robertson, Campbell. "Smaller New Orleans after Katrina, Census Shows." *New York Times*, February 3, 2011.

Roddewig, Richard J. "What *Is* Cultural Tourism?" *New Orleans Preservation in Print* 15, no. 6 (1988): 5–11.

Roediger, David R. *The Wages of Whiteness: Race and the Making of the American Working Class*. New York: Verso, 1991.

"Romance, History and Beauty on the Great River Road." In *New Orleans Official Visitors Guide*, 131. New Orleans: New Orleans Metropolitan Convention and Visitors Bureau, March 2002.

"Roots of New Orleans: A Heritage Tour." In *The Soul of New Orleans: Greater New Orleans Black Tourism Network Official Visitors Guide*, 48. New Orleans: Greater New Orleans Black Touism Network, 1994–95.

Rothman, Hal. *The Culture of Tourism, The Tourism of Culture: Selling the Past to the Present in the American Southwest*. Albuquerque: University of New Mexico Press, 2003.

Rudawsky, Gil. "Five Years after Hurricane Katrina, New Orleans Tourism Rebounds." DailyFinance.com, August 27, 2010. Accessed July 3, 2012, http://www.dailyfinance.com/2010/08/27/five-years-after-hurricane-katrina-new-orleans-tourism-rebounds/.

Ruffins, Fath. "Mythos, Memory, and History: African American Preservation Efforts, 1820–1990." In *History and Memory in African-American Culture*, edited by Genevieve Fabre and Robert O'Meally, 506–611. New York: Oxford University Press, 1994.

"Safety Tips." *Dave & Susie's Guide to New Orleans*. Accessed June 7, 2003. http://www.angelfire.com/jazz/davensusie/safety.htm.

Sakakeeny, Matt. "'Under the Bridge': An Orientation to Soundscapes in New Orleans." *Ethnomusicology* 54, no. 1 (2010): 1–27.

Salvail, André. "Efforts to Lure More Minority Events to City Are Paying Off." *New Orleans City Business*, July 10, 1998.

Samuel, Raphael. *Theatres of Memory: Past and Present in Contemporary Culture*. Vol. 1. London: Verso, 1994.

Sando, Mike. "Dungy's Prediction No Match for Destiny." ESPN.com, February 8, 2010. Accessed September 20, 2012. http://espn.go.com/blog/nfcwest/post/_/id/14090/dungys-prediction-no-match-for-destiny.

"San Francisco Plantation." In *New Orleans Official Visitors Guide*, 107. New Orleans: New Orleans Metropolitan Convention and Visitors Bureau, winter–spring 1999.

Sasser, Bill. "Our Town: Bush Visits Local Diner, Promises Help Is Coming." TheBeehive.org, March 16, 2006. Accessed October 4, 2008. http://www.thebeehive.org/Templates/HurricaneKatrina/Level3NoFrills.aspx?PageId=1.5369.6532.7343.

Saulny, Susan. "5,000 Public Housing Units in New Orleans Are to Be Razed." *New York Times*, June 15, 2006.

Schafer, Judith Kelleher. *Becoming Free, Remaining Free: Manumission and Enslavement in New Orleans, 1846–1862*. Baton Rouge: Louisiana State University Press, 2003.

Scott, Rebecca J. "The Atlantic World and the Road to Plessy v. Ferguson." *Journal of American History* 94, no. 3 (2007): 726–33.

"Second Linin': A New Orleans Soulful Experience." In *The Soul of New Orleans: Greater New Orleans Black Tourism Network Official Visitors Guide*, 27. New Orleans: Greater New Orleans Black Tourism Network, 1994–95.

"Second Linin': A New Orleans Soulful Experience." New Orleans Online. Accessed April 15, 2003. http://www.neworleansonline.com/tours-attractions/multicultural/secondline.html.

"Second Linin': A New Orleans Soulful Experience." SoulofNewOrleans.com. Accessed June 5, 2003. http://www.soulofneworleans.com/Naturally%20New%20Orleans.htm#Music%20&%20Entertainment.

Seiler, Cotten. "'So That We as a Race Might Have Something Authentic to Travel By': African American Automobility and Cold-War Liberalism." *American Quarterly* 58, no. 4 (2006): 1091–117.

Shaban, Bigad. "In Address, Nagin Announces Several Big Plans." WWLTV.com, May 20, 2009. http://www.wwltv.com/topstories/stories/wwl052009cbnagin.22c93cbc.html.

Shaffer, Marguerite S. *See America First: Tourism and National Identity, 1880–1940*. Washington: Smithsonian Institution Press, 2001.

Silber, Nina. *The Romance of Reunion: Northerners and the South, 1865–1900*. Chapel Hill: University of North Carolina Press, 1993.

Simmons, Lakisha Michelle. "Black Girls Coming of Age: Sexuality and Segregation in New Orleans, 1930–1954." PhD diss., University of Michigan, 2009.

Simon, Darran. "Report Critical of Charter Schools." *Times-Picayune*, October 26, 2007.

Slaton, James. "Hoteliers Say Crime Is Partly to Blame for Sluggish Bookings." *New Orleans CityBusiness*, March 10, 1997.

Slaton, James. "New Orleans Seen as a Good Fit with Changing Vacation Trends." *New Orleans CityBusiness*, September 1, 1997.

Slaton, James. "Tourism Holding Up under Weight of Crime—So Far." *New Orleans CityBusiness*, December 16, 1996.

"Slave Tour Itinerary." Africansinlouisiana.com, 2003. http://www.africansinlouisiana.com.

"Social Traditions and Cemeteries." Soul of America. Accessed June 5, 2003. http://www.soulofamerica.com/cityfldr/orleans19.html.

Sollors, Werner. *Neither Black nor White yet Both: Thematic Explorations of Interracial Literature*. Cambridge, MA: Harvard University Press, 1999.

"Some Grassroots Racial Justice Organizations." A Katrina Reader. Accessed April 16, 2013. http://katrinareader.org/some-grassroots-racial-justice-organizations.

Sothern, Billy. *Down in New Orleans: Reflections from a Drowned City*. Berkeley: University of California Press, 2007.

"'Soul of New Orleans': African American Heritage Map." New Orleans: Greater New Orleans Black Tourism Network, n.d.

Souther, J. Mark. "The Disneyfication of New Orleans: The French Quarter as Facade in a Divided City." *Journal of American History* 94, no. 3 (2007): 804–11.

Souther, J. Mark. "Making 'America's Most Interesting City': Tourism and the Construction of Cultural Image in New Orleans, 1940–1984." In *Southern Journeys: Tourism, History, and Culture in the Modern South*, edited by Richard D. Starnes, 114–37. Tuscaloosa: University of Alabama Press, 2003.

Souther, J. Mark. *New Orleans on Parade: Tourism and the Transformation of the Crescent City*. Baton Rouge: Louisiana State University Press, 2006.

Souther, J. Mark. "Suburban Swamp: The Rise and Fall of Planned New-Town Communities in New Orleans East." *Planning Perspectives* 23, no. 2 (2008): 197–219.

Spain, Daphne. "Race Relations and Residential Segregation in New Orleans: Two Centuries of Paradox." *Annals of the American Academy of Political and Social Science* 441, no. 1 (1979): 82–96.

Spear, Jennifer M. *Race, Sex, and Social Order in Early New Orleans*. Baltimore, MD: Johns Hopkins University Press, 2009.

Spirou, Costas. *Urban Tourism and Urban Change: Cities in a Global Economy*. New York: Routledge, 2010.

"St. Mike's Hardware." Katrina New Orleans, October 26, 2005. Accessed February 6,

2006. http://katrinola.typepad.com/katrina_new_orleans/2005/week43/index
.html.

Stabile, Carol A. *White Victims, Black Villains: Gender, Race, and Crime News in US Culture*. New York: Routledge, 2006.

Stanonis, Anthony J. *Creating the Big Easy: New Orleans and the Emergence of Modern Tourism, 1918–1945*. Athens: University of Georgia Press, 2006.

Stanonis, Anthony J. "Dead but Delightful: Tourism and Memory in New Orleans Cemeteries." In *Destination Dixie: Tourism and Southern History*, edited by Karen L. Cox, 247–66. Gainesville: University Press of Florida, 2012.

Stanonis, Anthony J. "Just Like Mammy Used to Make: Foodways in the Jim Crow South." In *Dixie Emporium: Tourism, Foodways, and Consumer Culture in the American South*, edited by Anthony J. Stanonis, 208–33. Athens: University of Georgia Press, 2008.

Stanton, Cathy. *The Lowell Experiment: Public History in a Postindustrial City*. Amherst: University of Massachusetts Press, 2006.

Starnes, Richard D. Introduction to *Southern Journeys: Tourism, History, and Culture in the Modern South*, edited by Richard D. Starnes, 1–14. Tuscaloosa: University of Alabama Press, 2003.

Starnes, Richard D., ed. *Southern Journeys: Tourism, History, and Culture in the Modern South*. Tuscaloosa: University of Alabama Press, 2003.

Starr, S. Frederick. "Introduction: The Man Who Invented New Orleans." *Inventing New Orleans: Writings of Lafcadio Hearn*, edited by S. Frederick Starr, xi–xxvii. Jackson: University Press of Mississippi, 2001.

Stodghill, Ron. "Driving Back into Louisiana's History." *New York Times*, May 25, 2008.

Sturken, Marita. *Tourists of History: Memory, Kitsch, and Consumerism from Oklahoma City to Ground Zero*. Durham, NC: Duke University Press, 2007.

Sublette, Ned. *The World That Made New Orleans: From Spanish Silver to Congo Square*. Chicago: Lawrence Hill, 2008.

Sugrue, Thomas J. *The Origins of the Urban Crisis: Race and Inequality in Postwar Detroit*. Princeton, NJ: Princeton University Press, 2005.

Sumpter, Amy R. "Segregation of the Free People of Color and the Construction of Race in Antebellum New Orleans." *Southeastern Geographer* 48, no. 1 (2008): 19–37.

Taggart, Chuck. "A Lexicon of New Orleans Terminology and Speech." GumboPages. com. Accessed June 10, 2003. http://www.gumbopages.com/yatspeak.html.

Taggart, Chuck. "The Music, Culture and Food of New Orleans." GumboPages.com, July 10, 2002. Accessed June 5, 2003. http://www.gumbopages.com/neworleans .html.

Tan, Cheryl Lu-Lien. "In Treme, Where Jazz Was Born, You Feel the Heartbeat of New Orleans." *Washington Post*, June 10, 2010.

Tannenbaum, Frank. *Slave and Citizen: The Negro in the Americas*. New York: Vintage, 1946.

"Tezcuco Plantation." In *New Orleans Official Visitors Guide*, 107. New Orleans: New Orleans Metropolitan Convention and Visitors Bureau, winter–spring 1999.

Thevenot, Brian, and Gordon Russell. "Rumors of Deaths Greatly Exaggerated." *Times-Picayune*, September 26, 2005.

"Things to Do in New Orleans: River Road Ramble." Thingstodo-NewOrleans.com. Accessed October 6, 2003. http://www.thingstodo-neworleans.com/brochure/content.jsp?FIELD=Out_Of_Town#4.

Thomas, Lynnell L. "'The City I Used to . . . Visit': Tourist New Orleans and the Racialized Response to Hurricane Katrina." In *Seeking Higher Ground: The Hurricane Katrina Crisis, Race, and Public Policy Reader,* edited by Manning Marable and Kristen Clarke, 255–70. New York: Palgrave Macmillan, 2007.

Thomas, Lynnell L. "Kissing Ass and Other Performative Acts of Resistance: Austin, Fanon and New Orleans Tourism." *Performance Research* 12, no. 3 (2007): 137–45.

Thomas, Lynnell L. "'People Want to See What Happened': Treme, Televisual Tourism, and the Racial Remapping of Post-Katrina New Orleans." *Television and New Media* 13, no. 3 (2012): 213–24.

Thomas, Lynnell L. "Race and Erasure in New Orleans Tourism." PhD diss., Emory University, 2005.

Thomas, Lynnell L. "'Roots Run Deep Here': The Construction of Black New Orleans in Post-Katrina Tourism Narratives." *American Quarterly* 61, no. 3 (2009): 749–68.

Thompson, Richard. "Hurricane Katrina Recovery Highlighted in Bus Tour." NOLA .com, August 24, 2010. Accessed June 27, 2012. http://www.nola.com/katrina/index.ssf/2010/08/hurricane_katrina_recovery_highlighted_in_bus_tour.html.

Thrasher, Albert. *On to New Orleans! Louisiana's Heroic 1811 Slave Revolt.* New Orleans: Cypress, 1996.

Tilove, Jonathan. "Five Years after Hurricane Katrina, 100,000 New Orleanians Have Yet to Return." *Times-Picayune*, August 24, 2010.

"Tourism in Louisiana Could Suffer from a Violent Image." *Executive Digest*, July 1993.

"Tourism with Culture." *Gambit*, March 29, 1988.

"Tours by Isabelle" brochure. New Orleans: Tours by Isabelle, May 2007.

"Tours by Isabelle" brochure. New Orleans: Tours by Isabelle, March 2008.

"Tours: Swamp, Ghost, Mardi Gras and More." NewOrleans.com, 2003. Accessed April 2, 2003. http://www.neworleans.com/cgi-bin/oracle/hs.cgi?search=CAT&Category=HISTORY.

Toussaint, Allen, Wynton Marsalis, Patricia Clarkson, and Emeril Lagasse. "Welcome to New Orleans." In *New Orleans Official Visitors Guide,* 3. New Orleans: New Orleans Metropolitan Convention and Visitors Bureau, 2007.

"Travelers' Desire to Experience History and Culture Stronger Than Ever." Travel Industry Association of America, June 30, 2003. Accessed June 30, 2003. http://www.tia.org/Press/pressrec.asp?Item=284.

Treadway, Joan. "Essence Music Festival to Return to N.O. in 1998." *Times-Picayune*, October 14, 1997.

"Tremé/Lafitte Neighborhood Snapshot." Greater New Orleans Community Data Center, April 27, 2005. Accessed December 1, 2010. http://www.gnocdc.org/orleans/4/42/snapshot.html.

Turner, Patricia A. *Ceramic Uncles and Celluloid Mammies: Black Images and Their Influence on Culture*. New York: Anchor, 1994.

"Update #3, Sept 1, about Looting." Acid Test, September 1, 2005. Accessed June 22, 2010. http://www.molvray.com/acid-test/2005/09/.

Usner, Daniel H. *Indians, Settlers and Slaves in a Frontier Exchange Economy*. Chapel Hill: University of North Carolina Press, 1992.

Uzzell, David L., ed. *Heritage Interpretation*. 2 vols. London: Belhaven, 1989 and 1992.

Varney, James. "Superdome Reopening Is Something New Orleans Saints Still Marvel at Performance vs. Atlanta Falcons." NOLA.com, September 22, 2011. Accessed October 28, 2012. http://www.nola.com/saints/index.ssf/2011/09/new_orleans _saints_still_marve.html.

Verney, Kevern. *African Americans and US Popular Culture*. New York: Routledge, 2003.

"Village de l'Est Neighborhood Snapshot." Greater New Orleans Community Data Center, October 4, 2002. Accessed November 16, 2010. http://www.gnocdc.org /orleans/10/56/snapshot.html.

Vincent, Charles. *The African American Experience in Louisiana: From the Civil War to Jim Crow*. Lafayette: Center for Louisiana Studies, University of Southwestern Louisiana, 2000.

Vogel, Scott. "Hurricane Katrina: This Bus for You?" *Washington Post*, September 19, 2007. Accessed November 9, 2007. http://voices.washingtonpost.com /travellog/2007/09/hurricane_katrina_this_bus_for_1.html.

Vogt, Justin. "A Time against Race." *Washington Monthly*, February 2011. Accessed September 6, 2012. http://www.washingtonmonthly.com/features/2011/1101.vogt.html.

Vrasti, Wanda. *Volunteer Tourism in the Global South: Giving back in Neoliberal Times*. New York: Routledge, 2012.

Wade, Sharon Ann. "Black Heritage City Tour." *New Orleans Tribune*, November 1987.

Walker, Daniel E. *No More, No More: Slavery and Cultural Resistance in Havana and New Orleans*. Minneapolis: University of Minnesota Press, 2004.

Walker, Dave. "HBO Sets Drama Series in Treme with Focus on City's Musicians." NOLA.com, last modified July 11, 2008. Accessed January 19, 2011. http://blog .nola.com/davewalker/2008/07/hbo_sets_drama_series_in_treme.html #TheWireHBO.

Walker, Dave. "HBO's 'Treme' Finally Gets New Orleans Right." NOLA.com, last modified February 14, 2011. Accessed July 16, 2011. http://www.nola.com/treme-hbo /index.ssf/2010/04/treme_is_probably_as_good_as_i.html.

Walker, Susannah. "Black Dollar Power: Assessing African American Consumerism since 1945." In *African American Urban History since World War II*, edited by Kenneth L. Kusmer and Joe William Trotter, 376–403. Chicago: University of Chicago Press, 2009.

Wallace, Michael. *Mickey Mouse History and Other Essays on American Memory*. Philadelphia: Temple University Press, 1996.

Wallace-Sanders, Kimberly Gisele. *Mammy: A Century of Race, Gender, and Southern Memory*. Ann Arbor: University of Michigan Press, 2009.

Walsh, Kevin. *The Representation of the Past: Museums and Heritage in the Post-Modern World*. London: Routledge, 1992.

Walton, Shana. "Sabor Latino: Central American Folk Traditions in New Orleans." LouisianaFolklife.org. Accessed January 27, 2010. http://www.louisianafolklife.org /LT/Articles_Essays/latinos.html.

Webster, Richard A. "Demolition of Iberville Housing Development Begins." NOLA .com, September 10, 2013. Accessed November 18, 2013. http://www.nola.com /politics/index.ssf/2013/09/demolition_of_iberville_housin.html.

Webster, Richard A. "New Orleans Tourism Industry Still Plagued with Same Problems It Had in Late 2005." *New Orleans CityBusiness*, December 25, 2006. Accessed April 15, 2013. http://www.highbeam.com/doc/1P2-8985579.html.

Weeks, Jim. *Gettysburg: Memory, Market, and an American Shrine*. Princeton, NJ: Princeton University Press, 2003.

Weeks, Linton. "A Bus Tour of Hurricane Hell." *Washington Post*, February 18, 2006.

Weems, Robert E., Jr. "African American Consumers since World War II." In *African American Urban History since World War II*, edited by Kenneth L. Kusmer and Joe William Trotter, 359–75. Chicago: University of Chicago Press, 2009.

"Welcome." In *The Soul of New Orleans: Official Multicultural Visitors Guide*, 1. New Orleans: New Orleans Multicultural Tourism Network, 2002.

"Welcome, Essence Fest." *Times-Picayune*, July 1, 1995.

"Welcome to New Orleans!" Virtually New Orleans, February 18, 1997. Accessed April 2, 2003. http://www.yatcom.com/neworl/vno.html.

"Welcome to New Orleans, Louisiana." SoulofAmerica.com. Accessed June 5, 2003. http://www.soulofamerica.com/cityfldr/orleans.html.

"Welcome to New Orleans—the Past and Present." LeObsTours.com. Accessed November 26, 2003. http://www.leobstours.com/city-tour.html.

"Welcome to the New Orleans French Quarter." New Orleans Online. Accessed March 6, 2003. http://www.neworleansonline.com/tours-attractions/attractions /fqwelcome.html.

Wells-Barnett, Ida B. *Mob Rule in New Orleans: Robert Charles and His Fight to Death, the Story of His Life, Burning Human Beings Alive, Other Lynching Statistics*. Chicago: Ida B. Wells-Barnett, 1900.

"West Lake Forest Neighborhood Snapshot." Greater New Orleans Community Data Center, October 5, 2002. Accessed November 11, 2010. http://www.gnocdc.org /orleans/9/55/snapshot.html.

"What's a Creole?" New Orleans Online. Accessed April 2, 2003. http://www .neworleansonline.com/tours-attractions/multicultural/creole.html.

"What's Creole? What's Cajun?" In *The Soul of New Orleans: Official Multicultural Visitors Guide*, 9. New Orleans: Multicultural Tourism Network, 2002.

White, Jaquetta. "Ad Campaign Fights Katrina Myths." *Times-Picayune*, January 26, 2007.

White, Jaquetta. "If You Sell It, Will They Come?" *Times-Picayune*, August 30, 2006.

White, Jaquetta. "Multicultural Tourism Network Hit Hard by Storm." *Times-Picayune*, May 11, 2008.

White, Jaquetta. "Multicultural Welcome: Touting Its History, Music and Heritage, New Orleans Is Staking Out a Place in the Fast-Growing African-American Travel Market." *Times-Picayune*, July 7, 2002.

White, Jaquetta. "New Orleans Tourism Officials Expect One of the Strongest Springs Ever." *Times-Picayune*, April 3, 2011.

White, John Valery. "The Persistence of Race Politics and the Restraint of Recovery in Katrina's Wake." In *After the Storm: Black Intellectuals Explore the Meaning of Hurricane Katrina*, edited by David Dante Troutt, 41–62. New York: New Press, 2006.

Williams, Kim Howard. "A Comparison of Travel Behaviors of African American and White Travelers to an Urban Destination: The Case of New Orleans." PhD diss., University of New Orleans, 2006.

Williams, Linda. *Playing the Race Card: Melodramas of Black and White from Uncle Tom to O. J. Simpson*. Princeton, NJ: Princeton University Press, 2001.

Williams-Myers, A. J. "Slavery, Rebellion, and Revolution in the Americas: A Historiographical Scenario on the Theses of Genovese and Others." *Journal of Black Studies* 26, no. 4 (1996): 381–400.

Wise, Tim. *Colorblind: The Rise of Post-Racial Politics and the Retreat from Racial Equity*. San Francisco: City Lights, 2010.

Wonham, Henry, ed. *Criticism and the Color Line: Desegregating American Literary Studies*. New Brunswick, NJ: Rutgers University Press, 1996.

Woods, Clyde Adrian. "Les Misérables of New Orleans: Trap Economics and the Asset Stripping Blues, Part 1." *American Quarterly* 61, no. 3 (2009): 769–96.

Works Progress Administration. 1938. *New Orleans City Guide*. New Orleans: Garrett County, 2009.

"Yatspeak: A New Orleans Lexicon." Virtually New Orleans, February 18, 1997. Accessed April 2, 2003. http://www.yatcom.com/neworl/lifestyle/language.html.

Yerton, Stewart. "Celebration of Heritage, Music Will Aid Tourism." *Times-Picayune*, June 25, 1995.

Yerton, Stewart. "Essence Festival a Jewel in N.O. Hospitality Crown: Black Travelers a Target Market." *Times-Picayune*, July 3, 1997.

Yerton, Stewart. "Essence Festival Back for Seconds: Event Overcomes Foster Remarks." *Times-Picayune*, June 30, 1996.

Yerton, Stewart. "Essence Trying to Broaden Audience." *Times-Picayune*, July 4, 1996.

Yuhl, Stephanie. *A Golden Haze of Memory: The Making of Historic Charleston*. Chapel Hill: University of North Carolina Press, 2005.

Index

Campanella, Richard, 178n40
Cashmore, Ellis, 176n15
Celebration Tours, 127, 204n35
Central Business District (CBD) (New Orleans), police patrols of, 30–31
Charles, Robert, 200n86
civil rights movement, 6; black heritage tourism, 95–97, 181n19
Civil War: in black heritage literature, 115; history of New Orleans after, 44, 180n4
class structure: middle class collapse and, 19–23; in post-Katrina tourism narratives, 140–43; racial inequalities and, 8–16
Coble, William, 53–54, 57–61, 76–91, 191n54
Code Noir, 37, 84–85, 90
colonialism: dominance in history of New Orleans of, 34–44; plagues and violence in era of, 182n35; racial designations and, 177n19; in tourism narrative, 8–16
Colonial Williamsburg, black history program of, 118–19
colorblind narrative: mythology of, 6, 28, 70, 88–90; race and class and, 141–43; Super Bowl and, 163–65
"Compair Lapin" stories, 188n8
Contract with America, 54–55
Cossart, Isabelle, 151–52, 153
countermemory, black heritage and culture and, 131–36, 194n1
counternarratives of resistance: black heritage tourism and, 92–126; Lower Ninth Ward tourism and, 136–40; race and class in, 140–43
Creole identity: black heritage counternarrative of, 111–17, 122–26; class divisions in, 177n18, 187n96, 187n98; historical evolution of, 48–52; in historical narrative of New Orleans, 37–44; Le Monde Créole and, 53–91; non-Anglo definitions of, 55; in tourism narrative, 11–16
crime in New Orleans, 7, 17, 21–22, 30, 121, 159, 166, 180n10, 193n84
Cross, Iris, 169–70
cultural tourism, New Orleans's adoption of, 44–52

Dahomey culture, 114
Databases for the Study of Afro-Louisiana History and Genealogy, 1699–1860, 122
David, Emmanuel, 139
De Certeau, Michel, 24–25
de Crèvecoeur, J. Hector St. John de, 48
Deepwater Horizon explosion, 168–70. *See also* BP oil spill
Delille, Henriette, 83, 112, 122, 192n69
Delisle (Madam), 81–83
Dent, Tom, 100–101
Department of Housing and Urban Development (HUD), 135
desire: African American cultural depictions of, 144–47; black desire in post-civil rights tourism narrative, 27–52; black heritage tourism dispelling of, 118–26; disaster and, 6–16; in Le Monde Créole narrative, 75–91
Deslondes, Charles, 120
disaster: African American cultural depictions of, 144–47; desire and, 6–16; in Lower Ninth Ward tourism narrative, 136–40
DiscoverNewOrleans, 36
"Disney's America" project, failure of, 60
diversity, in tourism narrative, 25–28
Dixie Tours, 204n35, 207n75
Du Bois, W. E. B., 63, 66, 190n38
Duparc-Locoul family, 55, 71–73, 72; counternarratives of resistance and, 92–94; genealogy of, 73–75, 74; in Le Monde Créole narrative, 75–91

economic development in New Orleans: black heritage tourism and, 97–102, 106–7, 124–26; tourism's dominance in, 12–16
Eichstedt, Jennifer, 201n104
Ernest N. Morial Convention Center, 134–35
Essence Communications, 97–102
Essence magazine, 97–102
Essence Music Festival, 12, 97–102, 99, 125, 155–57
"essence" of black heritage tourism, 97–102
European cultural influences: black heritage counternarrative concerning, 111;

Pitt, Brad, 142–43, 169

plaçage (common-law marriages), 82, 189n31; black heritage counternarrative concerning, 111

place identity, history in New Orleans of, 3–5

plantation culture and tourism: black heritage counternarrative of, 119, 201n104; dominance in New Orleans historical narrative of, 38–44, 183n44, 183n48

Plessy, Homer G., 21, 89, 124, 189n31, 193n86

Plessy v. Ferguson case, 124, 189n31, 193n86

"The Political Economy of Colorblindness: Neoliberalism and the Reproduction of Inequality in the United States" (Hutchison), 165

politics of representation: black heritage tourism and, 12–16, 95–97; post-Katrina racial politics and, 161–62; tourism as racial project and, 23–25

population demographics in post-Katrina era, 161–62, 209n14

post-civil rights public sphere: black desire in context of, 27–52; black heritage tourism and, 95–97; in Le Monde Créole French Quarter Courtyard Tour, 55–61; multicultural New Orleans image and, 45–52; post-Katrina politics and, 161–62; racial contradictions in, 176n14; racial geography and, 17–23; recovery efforts and, 171–73; Super Bowl and, 163–65; tourism industry and, 5–6

"Post-Katrina City Tour," 127, 151–52, 153

poverty levels in New Orleans, racial geography and, 19–23

Powell, Caletha, 101–3

public housing, post-Katrina protests about, 135

public policy, tourism narrative impact on, 15–16

quadroon balls, 7, 30, 82, 111, 122

"quickie weddings" in New Orleans, 157

Quigley, Bill, 158, 160

race and racism: Creole identity and, 49–52; desire and disaster and, 6–16; historical ambivalence concerning, 31–34,

192n72; Le Monde Créole narrative, 55–91; minimization in history of, 41–44; New Orleans caste system and, 84–91; post-civil rights public sphere and, 6; in post-Katrina politics, 161–62; post-Katrina reconstruction of, 127–57; in post-Katrina tourism narratives, 140–43; in Super Bowl, 163–65; tourism narrative and, 1–3, 23–25

racial geography: black heritage tourism and, 29–31, 112–17; post-Katrina racial demographics, 161–62, 209n14; tourism narrative and, 17–23, 180n10

racial projects, 179n46

Reconstruction era, history of New Orleans during, 44

recovery efforts: African American marginalization in, 171–73; Armstrong Park renovation and, 168; black cultural production and, 158–73; BP oil spill and, 168–70; promotion of tourism over, 150–52; tourism narrative concerning, 207n85

redlining of New Orleans black neighborhoods, 15–16

Regis, Helen, 145

rememory, narratives of, 131–36, 194n1, 202n1

Rex Mardi Gras parade, 204n34

Rice, Toni, 127, 152, 154–56, 208n91

Rising Tide: The Great Mississippi Flood of 1927 and How It Changed America, 139–40

River Road plantations, 38–44, *40*, 56, 183n44; black heritage counternarrative of, 120

Roach, Joseph, 130, 204n34

Robinette, Garland, 158, 160

Roddewig, Richard, 45–52

"Roots Run Deep Here" sign, 145–47, *146*

safety stereotypes, black heritage tourism and, 30–31. *See also* crime in New Orleans

St. Bernard Housing Project, 135, 145

St. Joe's Plantation, 119–20

San Francisco Plantation, 183n48

second line procession, 114

Viator's Thingstodo-NewOrleans.com, 38
Visitor Magazine, 35
voodoo: colonialism and, 48; in Le Monde
    Créole narrative, 62, 88–89, 193n82; in
    tourism narrative, 7, 13, 35
Voodoo Spiritual Botanical Temple, 122
Voting Rights Act, 6, 95–97; racial geogra-
    phy of New Orleans and, 17–23

Wagner Bill, 193n84
Wallace, Michael, 60
websites: for black heritage tourism, 102–17,
    119–26; history of New Orleans on,
    34–44; images of multiculturalism on,
    48–52; New Orleans tourism on, 32–34,
    180n10. *See also specific websites*
"We Will Make This Right" (BP public
    relations campaign), 169–70
"What's Creole? What's Cajun?," 112
White, Michael, 114
white supremacist ideology: Creole iden-

tity and, 50–52; tourism narrative and,
    7–16, 38–44
white tourism: dominance over black
    heritage tourism, 121–26; Le Monde
    Créole French Quarter Courtyard Tour
    and, 55–61; mythical narrative of New
    Orleans and, 31–34; race and class and,
    140–43
Who Dat Nation, 163–65
Williams, Linda, 80
Williams Tours and Transportation, 119, 122
Willis, Darryl, 169–70
WLAE television station, 45
Women of the Storm, 139
Woods, Clyde, 142

Yoruba culture, 114
Yuhl, Stephanie, 13

Zulu Social Aid and Pleasure Club, 113,
    204n34

LIBRARY, UNIVERSITY OF CHESTER